Using the Icons That Appear in This Book

For, the *Five Star Tour of the World Wide Web* and the *Dozen Whacky, Fun, and Useless Things* sections, we've included icons to help you determine whether each particular Web site is for you. Here's a quick rundown on the meaning of the icons that you'll see in these sections.

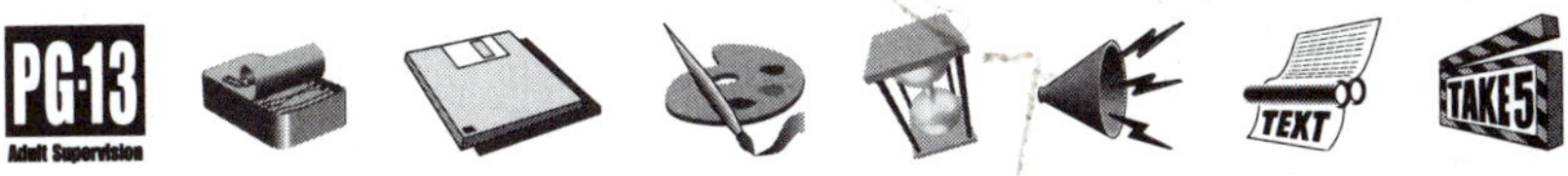

This icon means the site can be crowded at times, which obviously means that the site is quite popular among Webbies. You'll see this icon for a lot of the Web pages that Pat has selected, simply because most of the sites he's found are excellent sources of information. If a page is crowded, your best bet is to try to get in before or after peak traffic hours.

This icon indicates that
load, usually because th
images or because traffi
see this icon, you might
Inline Images option i
the pages will load much faster, although you won't see the brilliant graphics that the author has built into his or her pages.

This icon indicates that the site is rich in graphics. As I mentioned with the previous icon, graphical pages can be slow to load. On the other hand, these pages tend to be interesting, even exciting, to view and have plenty of images to download.

Some sites include sound and/or video (motion pictures). To get the most viewing and listening pleasure from sites that have these icons, you'll need a sound card (many Macs and all MPC-compliant PCs have this built in), at least a 486 CPU (or 040 machine for Mac users), and enough fast memory to display the video at acceptable speeds. Some multimedia-based sites include sound only, and a few others include video only, but many include both.

Some of the sites contain material that is not necessarily suitable for young folk. Pat's a family man and hasn't included any of the strictly adult sites (the hardcore stuff), so you don't have to be concerned that we're directing your kids toward the gutter. This icon just means that the site may contain material that's somewhat violent or sexual in nature—stuff you might not want your younger children to see or hear.

Contents

Introduction

Last night, I was talking to my friend Tom who's now retired, and the subject of computers came up. He recalled that, when he first started programming, his shop was enthusiastic to the point of giddiness because they had just received an IBM 1401 system with a whopping 16K of memory.

That reminded me of some of my first experiences writing about computers 15 years ago. Back then, I was ghost-writing a lot of college textbooks. I made it a point to include, in every book, a chapter discussing the history of computing. I wanted to show students how rapidly the computing field had evolved in a very short time. But I soon learned that students couldn't relate. It was a little like trying to explain the marvels of the modern cellular phone by describing early phone systems that you started with a hand crank and relied on a local operator for assistance. Who cares?

These days, I feel those old urges to dredge up the past, because George Santayana's too-frequently-quoted statement about repeating the past is worth considering yet again. In the early 1980s, I suffered through the comments of far too many computer-illiterate friends who told me—whenever they found the opportunity—that personal computers were an unnecessary luxury, a waste of time, an electronic gimmick, and even a passing fad. Those same folks are now enlisting their kids' help in configuring their Windows INI files.

I think about all this because, these days, I hear similar comments about the Internet. Media hype regarding the Information Superhighway has, frankly, turned as many people off as it has aroused the interest of others. "Do we really need *more* information?" "We're too reliant on computers already!" "This whole superhighway thing is just talk. It'll never get off the ground." I hear comments like these on an almost daily basis. I don't say anything because I know better.

The Internet Is Fun

It's really that simple. If you've already done some Internet surfing, you know exactly what I'm talking about. You've ridden one of the most exciting waves of the future. The total amount of truly useful and downright fun information that's available to anybody with a modem and a SLIP account is mind boggling. My friend Tom can relate. A 16K IBM 1401 is dinosaur bones compared to the Internet. If you want to expand your horizons and blow your mind at the same time, *go Internet.*

If you haven't yet dived into the Internet but you want to, well, you're in for a treat—especially if you've got Mosaic. I've got to admit that, before Mosaic, the Internet was largely the domain of the techno-nerdy crowd. To find your way around the Internet, you had to mess with UNIX, an ugly and unpleasant business for most PC and Mac users. But the advent of Mosaic has changed that in a big way.

I've Seen the Future, and It's Mosaic

Mosaic, if you don't already know, is a graphical browsing tool that works in several different environments, including Windows and the Mac. Its sole purpose is to make the Internet an easy place to travel, and it accomplishes that purpose in spades. Use it once, and you'll be a believer. I honestly have yet to meet anybody who's used Mosaic who doesn't rave about their experiences traveling the Internet and the World Wide Web. It's a helluva lot more fun than an E-ticket ride at Disneyland.

That's what this book is about. Jeff, Pat, and I all believe that cyberspace (a dumb word, yes, but it's caught on) should be both an educational and an enjoyable place to spend a Sunday afternoon or weekday evening. You don't need to be heavily into the technology of the Internet, nor do you need to know diddly about UNIX.

But here we need to issue a caveat: Getting your system set up with Mosaic and the communications software you'll need to get into cyberspace can admittedly be a bit tricky. But we're prepared to help you get there.

Once you're in, though, this stuff is cake. Internet surfing is about as easy as changing channels on your TV, except that cyberspace won't rot your brain.

How to Use This Book

The best way to use this book is simply to read it and enjoy, because much of it is self explanatory. But there *are* a few things worth pointing out, one of which is the way we've organized the book.

Using the Mosaic Centerfold

We start off with a visual tour of Mosaic—called the *Mosaic Centerfold* because we undress Mosaic and take a look at some of its more alluring parts—but it's a tour a bit out of the ordinary. We could have elected to annotate every button, every menu item, and every component of Mosaic, but frankly that would have been—you guessed it—BORING. And boredom is the antithesis of what Mosaic is all about.

Instead, we've chosen to point out and explain the features of Mosaic that are the most useful and that offer some of the best ways to navigate the Internet and the World Wide Web. Read this section before you begin surfing.

Using Forty Questions You Can Ask Us

The next section is Jeff's question-and-answer session, *Forty Questions You Can Ask Us without Getting Flamed.* Here, Jeff takes on some of the more technical questions you might have about installing and configuring Mosaic and the related communications software required to get up and running on the Net. It's humorous, it's irreverant, but most of all it's genuinely informative. If you're having problems getting connected, or if you want to know more about configuring and using Mosaic and your Internet account, this is the place to look.

Using the Five Star Tour of the World Wide Web

The third section is a *tour de force* provided by Pat, which we call *A Five Star Tour of the World Wide Web* because this is really the best of the best of the Web. Pat spent hundreds of hours (honest to God, this is true) navigating cyberspace to find the most informative, most interesting, most fun, and most creative sites available on the Web. Pat's a really picky guy—kind of the Felix Unger of the Internet. If he likes something, chances are you will too.

There are, however, a few things you should know before you read Pat's *Five Star Tour of the World Wide Web.* Pat, being a fussy guy, decided to rate each site based upon its features and quirks. He's used icons to indicate the high spots and potential problems you'll find at each site. For more information, see the "Using the Icons," section at the front of the book.

Pat has also provided his opinionated selection of the best links, his *hot links*, available at each site. It's worth noting that a site might contain many other links. Pat's goal in identifying *hot links* was simply to point you to the links that offer the most possibilities in terms of information and entertainment.

Using the Dozen Whacky, Fun, and Useless Things Section

There's not much I need to say about this section, except "Try it, you'll probably like it." One good (some would say bad) thing about the Web is that nobody censors or restricts the content of what can be placed in cyberspace. This section proves that point to a hilarious degree. This stuff is offbeat and off key. Just enjoy.

Using All the HTML You Really Need

HTML (which stands for Hyper Text Markup Language) is a mystery to a lot of Web users, but it needn't be. As Jeff points out, a few simple HTML commands go a long way toward creating a very attractive home page, something that's getting to be quite popular these days. If you want to try your hand at creating your own Web page, follow along with Jeff's informative, educational, and I dare say entertaining explanation of HTML basics.

Webs of the World

The Web is truly an international affair. We're writing this from the U.S., but we certainly acknowledge that a majority of Internet and Web users are outside of the U.S. So, toward this end, we've included a selected list of Web sites around the world. If you're looking for something local, and if local means something that most people think of as foreign, then you'll want to look here. We've included sites in virtually every "corner" of the globe.

PART 1

Mosaic Centerfold: A Visual Guide to the User Interface

In terms of ease of use, Mosaic is as close to a no-brainer as any other piece of software or utility you'll find on the Internet. That's what makes Mosaic so popular and downright fun to browse with. By the way, that's just what Mosaic is: a *browser* that you can use to check out the sites and sounds on the World Wide Web. To get you started quickly, we offer this simple guide to the menus and other components of the Mosaic interface.

The Starting Line

This is the title bar, of course, just like any other title bar you would expect to see in a Windows application. NCSA stands for the National Center for Supercomputing Applications, creators of Mosaic, which is shareware in this incarnation.

The toolbar provides buttons that replicate frequently used menu functions, such as navigating through the World Wide Web, printing, and getting help. To find out what a particular button does, click and hold on the button, and then read the brief description in the bottom left corner of the Mosaic window.

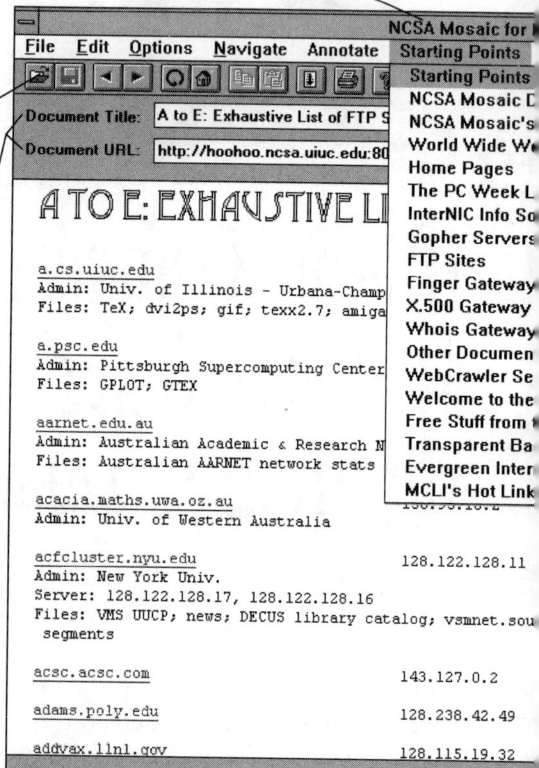

These two text boxes display the name of the Web page or other document currently displayed (the Document Title) and the address that Mosaic followed to get there (the Document URL). It's important to note that you can't actually type a URL address in the Document URL box; it's for display only.

The menu bar works like any other menu bar in a Windows application, with the notable exception that you can customize the Mosaic menu bar and its menus (by using the Menu Editor available from the Navigate menu). In this menu bar, "Evergreen's Menu" was added by our service provider; we added the "Space Crawl" and "Freebies!" menus ourselves.

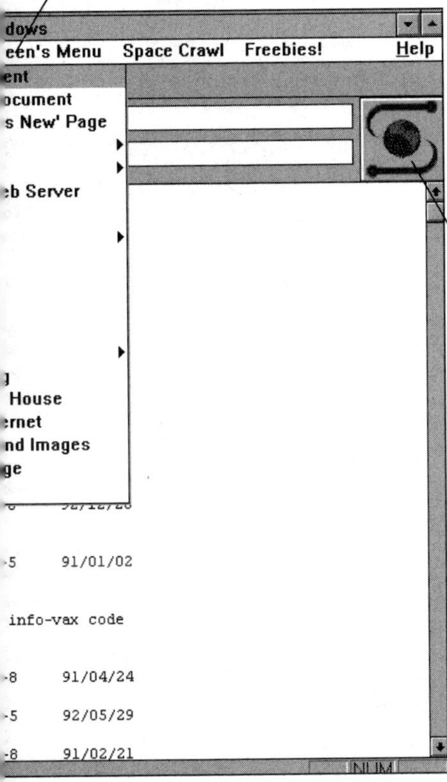

The Mosaic globe lets you know whether Mosaic is still at work trying to load a file or image, or to connect to a server. When the globe is turning, Mosaic is actively looking for whatever you've told it to find. If you want Mosaic to cancel a current search, read, or load operation, click on the turning globe. When the globe is immobile, Mosaic is either idle (not actively looking for anything) or is stalled (which happens from time to time).

There's No Place Like Home

The document title is supplied by the author—in other words, the guy who took the time to design all of the pages and their links.

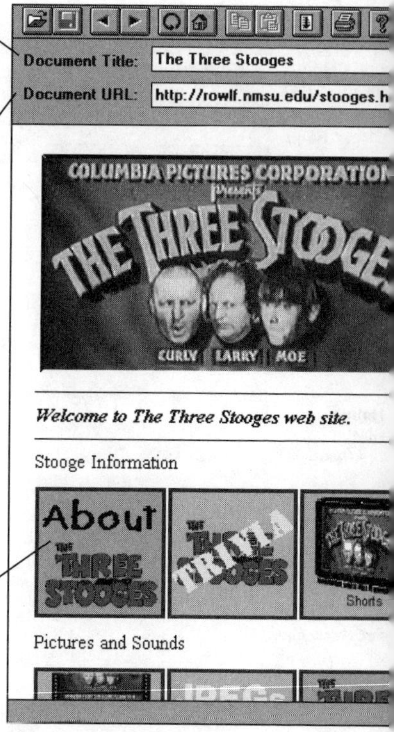

The URL (which stands for Uniform Resource Locator) begins with the *resource type* (in this case, http) followed by a colon and two slashes, followed by the Web site's Internet address. With Mosaic, you often won't need to specify lengthy and error-prone URLs; Mosaic provides several other ways to get to any given location on the Web.

This author chose to use some clever icons to identify the contents of his Web site. When you click on one of the icons, Mosaic automatically displays the related page of information.

There are a lot of demented authors on the Web. This is a typical example of a Web site created by somebody who had perhaps a little too much time on his hands. What you see here is called the *home page*, or the first page for any given Web site. Each Web site is made up of a series of *pages*, or screens.

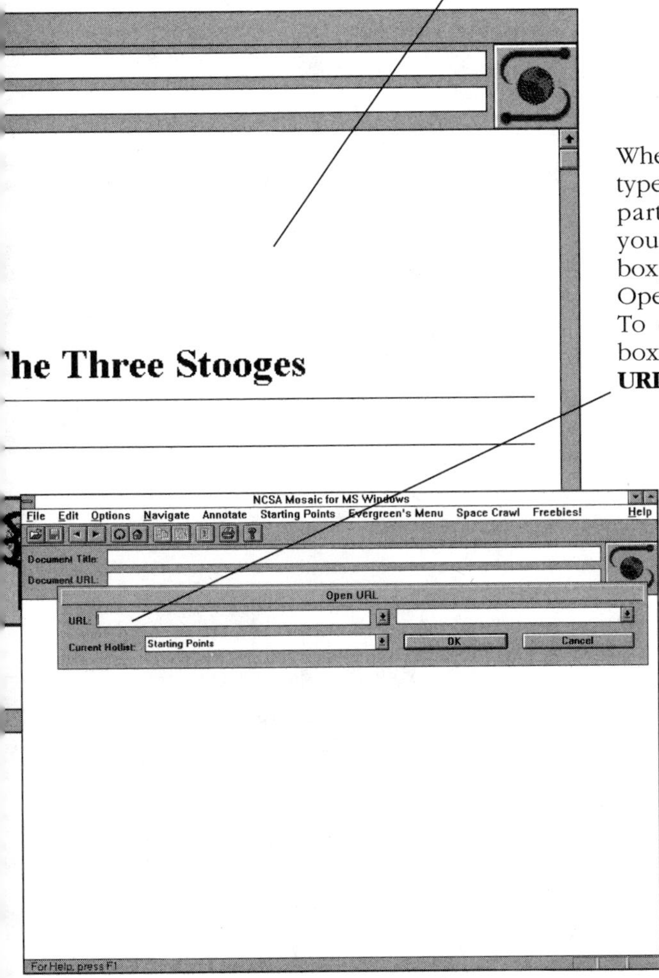

When you do need to type a URL to go to a particular Web page, you do it in this text box, which is part of the Open URL dialog box. To display this dialog box, select **File | Open URL** from the menu bar.

Red Hot Links

You navigate through Web pages by clicking on *hotlinks*, or simply *links*, which the author defines using something called HTML (for Hyper Text Markup Language). All you really need to know about links is where and what to click. In this home page, the author created icons that link you to separate pages that get displayed when you click on the desired icon.

This author used a more sophisticated *button link*, which is just a fancier way to display a hypertext link. In this case, though, the author includes text boxes that you can use to enter search text before you click on a search button.

The most frequently used type of link is called a *hypertext link,* which is simply text that appears underlined and often in a different color than surrounding text. When you click on this text, Mosaic takes you to the corresponding Web page described by the text. A hypertext link can take you to a different page within the same Web site or it can take you to a different Web site on the other side of the globe. Hypertext links can also be the names of text or graphics files that you can view or download.

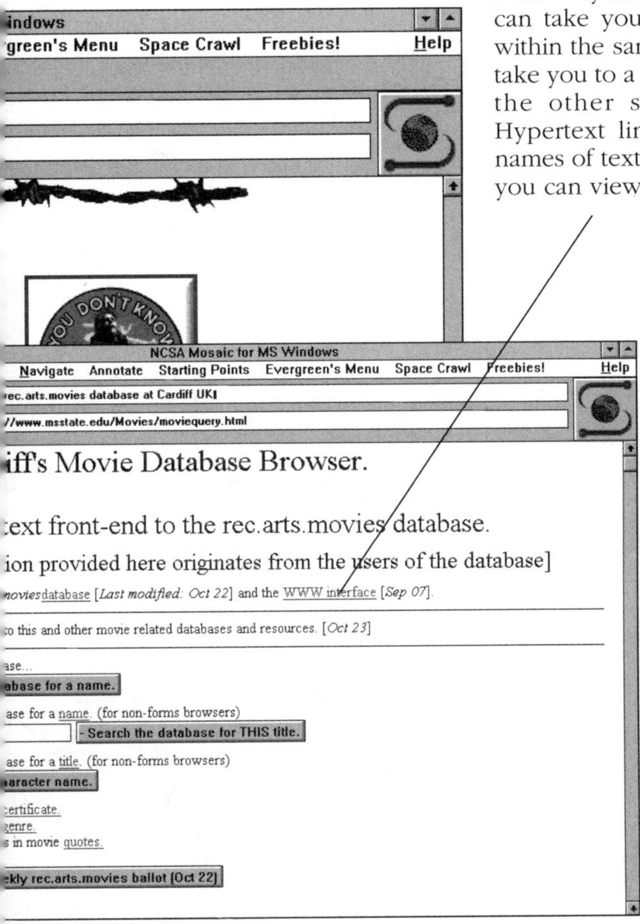

Drawing a GIF

The second type of graphic is called an *inline image*, which you can easily identify by its thick border. An inline image appears within a document when you've set up Mosaic to display inline images automatically (by selecting **Display Inline Images** in the **Options** menu). If you turn this option off, you can still display an inline image by clicking on the inline image icon. This is the preferred approach because some Web page authors load their Web site with graphics to enhance their visual appeal. Unfortunately, inline images can be hundreds of thousands of bytes in size and can require several minutes or more to load. Web pages that are heavy with graphics can bog down your modem. So avoid displaying inline images automatically unless you've got lots of time on your hands.

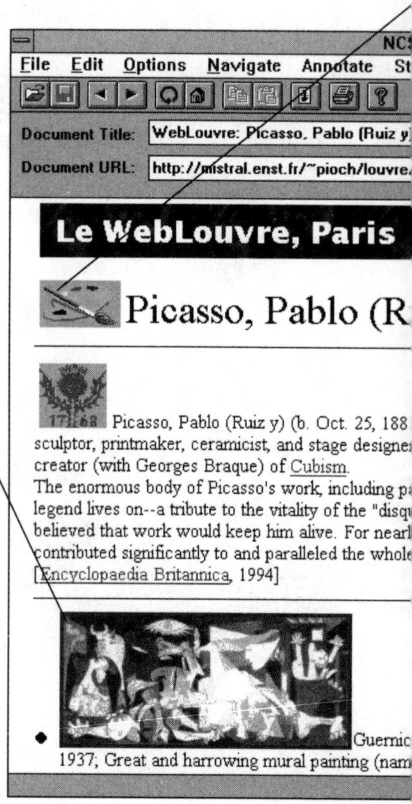

The third type of graphic you can display is a GIF or JPEG image, which requires that a separate GIF/JPEG viewer be installed on your system. Mosaic can usually locate and start your GIF/JPEG viewer automatically whenever you click on an inline image icon or a hypertext link to a GIF or JPEG file. This screen shows the LView 3.1 tool displaying the full-size image indicated in the previous screen. We just clicked on the inline image, and Mosaic invoked LView and opened the JPEG file within the viewer.

There are basically three types of graphics you will see within a Web page. The first is simply a decorative icon, like this one. It's not linked to anything and it's usually small, both visually and in terms of its size in bytes. You can click on a decorative graphic all day long if you really want to, but nothing will happen.

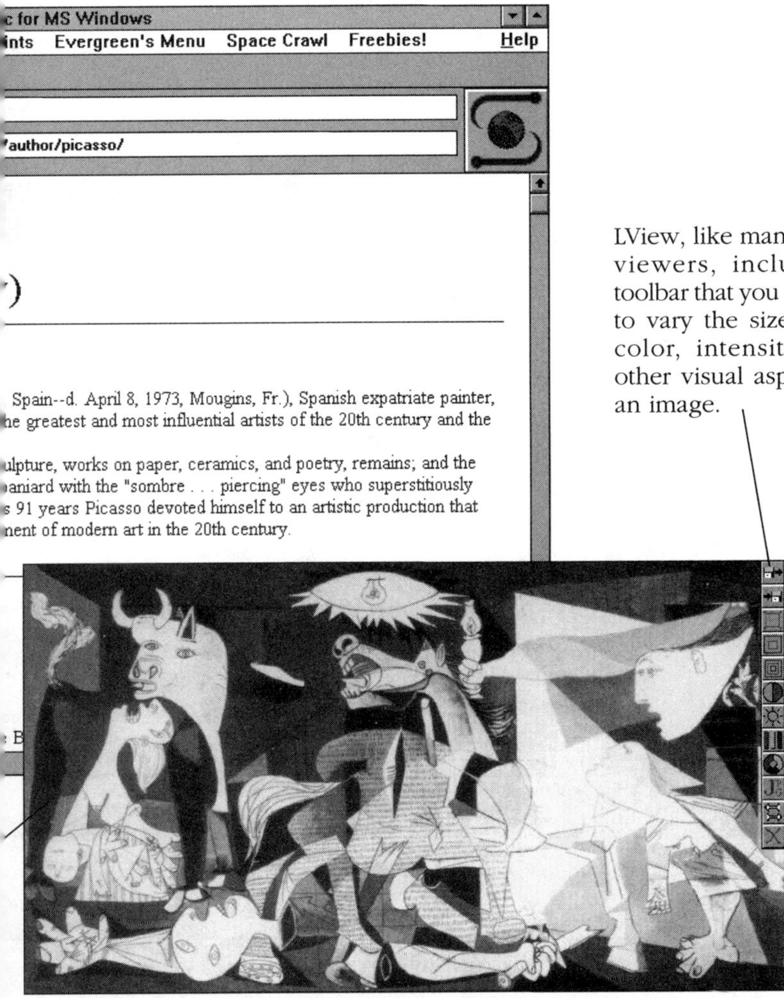

LView, like many other viewers, includes a toolbar that you can use to vary the size, ratio, color, intensity, and other visual aspects of an image.

You've Got Options

In the current version of Mosaic, the Edit menu contains two commands: **Copy** and **Find**. Both are useful. Use the **Copy** command to highlight and copy the contents of the Document URL text box into a different document (say, a document that maintains a list of all URLs you've used). Use the Find command to locate a particular text string within the current Web page.

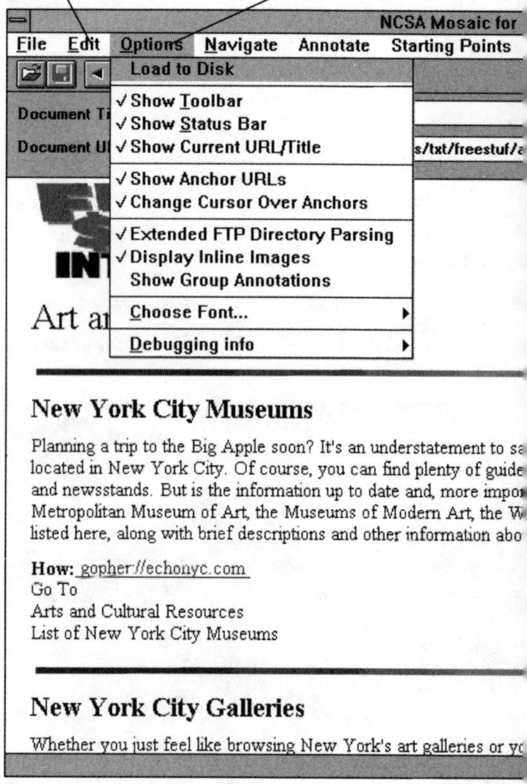

You can use the Options menu to customize the appearance of the Mosaic interface. Most of the options on this menu are toggles that you can turn on or off simply by selecting or deselecting each option. You can elect to display or remove the toolbar, status bar, document title and URL, inline images, and more. You can even change the fonts used for different parts of a Web page.

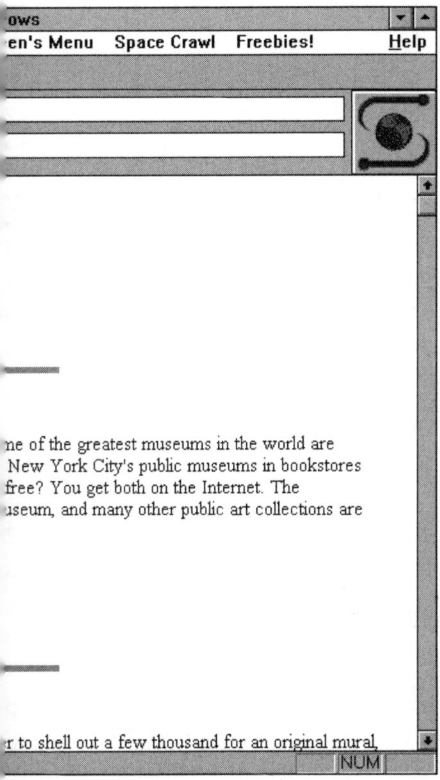

Getting Around and Back

The Navigate menu does just that—provides you with menu commands for moving around the Web.

You'll use **Back** and **Forward** most frequently. Mosaic keeps a history of pages you've viewed in memory (as many as will fit). So, when you select **Back**, Mosaic returns you to the previous Web page stored in memory. When you select **Forward**, Mosaic displays the next Web page in memory.

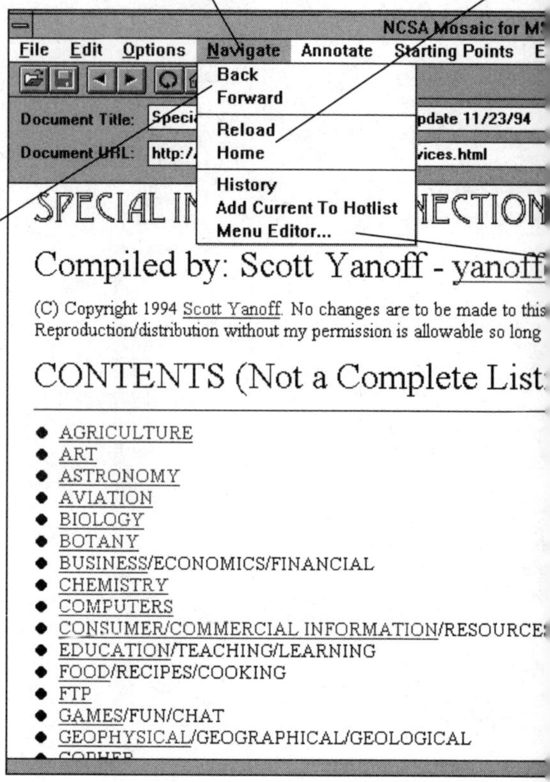

The **Reload** and **Home** commands are occasionally useful, but you'll probably use **Reload** far more often than **Home**. When you select Reload, Mosaic reloads the current Web page. This technique can be useful when the current page is corrupted and you want to try the load operation again. The Home command takes you to the home page setup for your system, which is typically the home page for the service provider or other organization that gave you your copy of Mosaic.

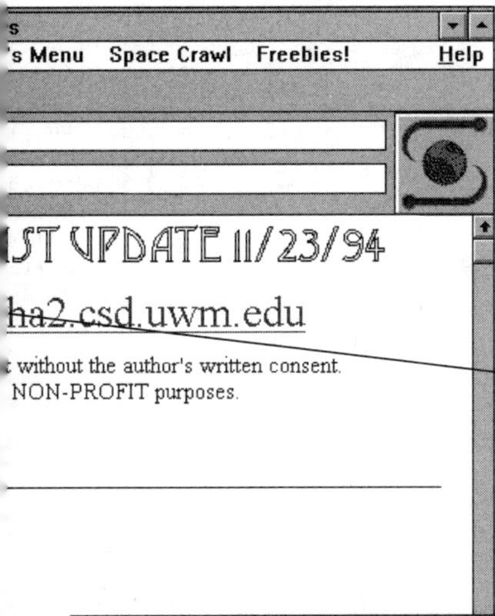

The **History**, **Add Current to Hotlist**, and **Menu Editor** commands are all useful. When you select **History**, Mosaic displays a list of all Web pages you've browsed through during your current session (as shown below). You can then click on one of these pages to return immediately to that site. When you select **Add Current to Hotlist**, Mosaic adds the address of the current Web page to your hotlist, which is by default included in your Starting Points menu. The **Menu Editor** allows you to add or remove menus in the menu bar, and to change which menu to use as your current hotlist.

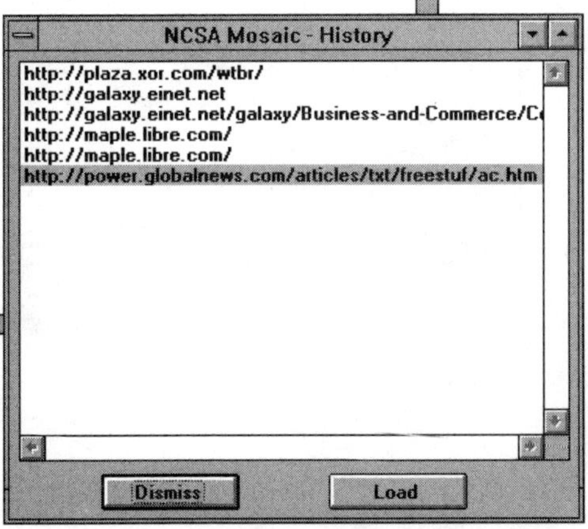

Starting Points

The Starting Points menu is called a "Personal Menu" by Mosaic because you can customize it. To add, remove, or edit items in the Starting Points menu, select **Navigate | Menu Editor**, then double-click on the Starting Points menu name in the Menu Editor. The Personal Menu editor will then be displayed so that you can modify the contents of the menu. You can also select Starting Points as the menu to be used in adding items to your hotlist. The contents of your Starting Points menu may vary from this one, depending on which items your service provider has put there.

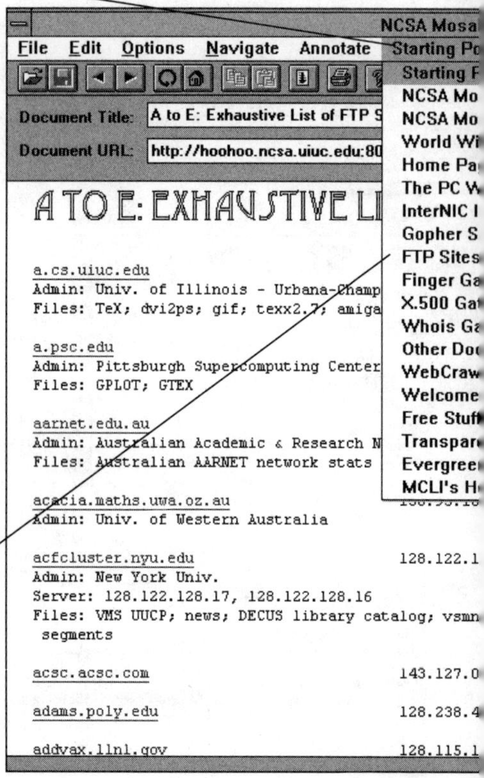

Select **FTP Sites** to display a list of all cataloged FTP sites. Sites are cataloged alphabetically by address, so you need to select an alphabetic-range hypertext link (such as *Sites with names A - E*).

The "Starting Points Document" is a Web site set up by NCSA as a sampling of sites on Mosaic. This is a good place to go to get your Mosaic feet wet.

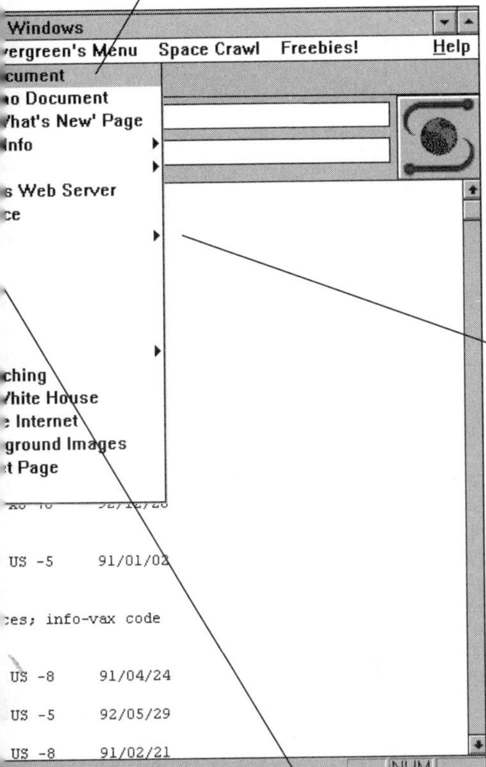

Select **Gopher Servers** to access a list of Gopher sites, then select one from the list so that you can conduct a Gopher search.

Select **Finger Gateway** to access the Finger utility, which allows you to look up information about a specific user.

PART 2

Forty Questions You Can Ask Us Without Getting Flamed

Want to hear a poorly kept secret? The Internet was built by the U.S. Government. Here's another one: Anything the government gets its hands on tends to mushroom in size (welfare, health care, the IRS) until it's totally out of control. And that's your first hint at the vastness and complexity of the Internet and all its various side roads and byways, two of which we'll be exploring in this book: Mosaic and the World Wide Web.

If you're new to the Internet, Mosaic, or the Web, you're probably going to have to get used to a bit of, shall we say, impatient and sarcastic responses to questions that you thought were pretty intelligent. The truth is, there are a lot of oldtimers on the Internet and they can get rather crabby when they're answering the same question for the jillionth time.

So, this section is a slightly wry sendup of some of the characters you can expect to "meet" on the Web. Keep it by your side while you're surfing and it will help keep you out of trouble.

So, What In the World Is Mosaic?

Mosaic is a *viewer*—in other words, a word processor that you can't write with. It allows you to go out on the Internet and look at documents that are stored all over the world, in a format dictated by a set of protocols known as the *World Wide Web*.

What Is the World Wide Web?

Technically, the Web is a *distributed hypertext document*. I'll save you a question by saying that *hypertext* is a system by which *hot links* are defined in a document. Hot links are just words or images underlined or colored a distinctive way so as to make them look different from the bulk of the text in the document. Clicking on a hot link takes you somewhere else in that document. Ordinary Windows help files are hypertext documents.

Now imagine that clicking on a hot link can take you not only to some other place in the document, but to another document entirely. Better still, suppose that the document on the other end of that hot link could be anywhere on the Internet. *That's* the World Wide Web.

What Ties Those Web Documents Together?

Behind every hot link defined in a Web document (which is actually called a Web *page* for reasons that no one remembers but everyone regrets) is a kind of Internet address called a URL, for *Universal Resource Locator*. That's a good name, because with a URL you can pin down any document or file of any kind existing anywhere on the Internet. A URL looks something like this:

```
http://www.biotech.washington.edu/WebCrawler/WebQuery.html
```

Sure, it's messy, but you don't always have to type it. URLs are hidden behind hot links, so you just click on the hot link, and off you go to wherever the URL points.

Now kick back in your chair and imagine each hot link as a thin blue line, starting from a computer in one place and pointing toward a computer in another place. Imagine hundreds of thousands of documents and millions of hot links with their thin blue lines going every which way, from Poughkeepsie to Paris to Adelaide to Cape Town to Tokyo and back to Fish Guts, Idaho. *That's* a web. Big one. World-wide one, in fact. It's a lot of fun, and if your significant other objects, you can always tell them it's *educational.*

Doesn't the "U" in URL Stand For "Uniform"?

Actually, it stands most truthfully for "undecided." Both "universal" and "uniform" are widely used in the literature. But look at it this way: If it's universal that means everybody's using it, and if everybody's using it, it must be uniform, or else we'd all be tripping over each other. So either way you aim the question, one follows from the other. Use whichever U prefer.

What Kind of Data Lives in a Web Document?

Text, mostly—and pretty text, at that, with cool fonts. However, the real magic in Mosaic is that it can accept and display full-color bitmapped graphics images in many formats, like JPEG, GIF, and others. When comet Shoemaker-Levy got sucked into Jupiter's gravitational field and flamed out in July of 1994, NASA put pictures of the glowing comet impact sites on the Web, and so many people tried to get in and download the photos that the NASA sites went down on their knees (and that was before Mosaic got *really* popular).

But there's more. Mosaic is *multimedia-aware.* In addition to images, Mosaic can download and play digital sound—and slow-frame movies stored in MPEG format. You have to have a sound board in your machine, but granted that, well, you're at the head of the table for a feast of Cindy Crawford pictures, Irish folk songs, and jerky animation the likes of which no one has been willing to sit through until now.

What Is "HTML"?

HTML means HyperText Markup Language, and it is the format that all Web documents adhere to. HTML is a little like the Rich Text Format that many word processors support, in that it is all-ASCII and contains no binary data. HTML defines special sequences of charac-

Cindy as seen on the Web

ters called *tags* that define things like fonts and font sizes and hot links to other Web documents.

Mosaic automatically interprets HTML documents into its marvelous screen displays, so unless you're the kind who insists on turning over stones looking for centipedes, there's no serious reason to sit down and try to learn it.

On the other hand, if you intend to become a World Wide Web author (and be somebody who puts things on the Web for other people to read), you had better learn HTML good and proper. But that'll be the least of your problems—and an entirely different book that we haven't written yet.

Can I Read the Web in Text Mode?

Sure. There's a World Wide Web reader called Lynx that operates in text mode using VT100 control sequences. If you're dialing into the Internet using a text-mode shell account, your host machine almost certainly has a copy, and Lynx will function at modem speeds down to even 1200 baud. In a Web context Lynx works well, as long as you don't have any desire for pictures of Mick Jagger or comets hitting Jupiter or for digital recordings of ocarina music or somewhat jerky MPEG movies that take your entire lunch hour to download. But what kind of life is *that?*

Where Do I Get Mosaic?

You can grab Mosaic from an FTP server at the National Center for Supercomputing Applications (NCSA) at the University of Illinois. They have it for three platforms, Windows, Mac, and X for Unix. The full FTP addresses are these:

```
Windows: ftp://ftp.ncsa.uiuc.edu/Mosaic/Windows/wmos20a7.zip
Mac 68K: ftp://ftp.ncsa.uiuc.edu/Mosaic/Mac/NCSAMosaicA6.68k.hqx
Power Mac: ftp://ftp.ncsa.uiuc.edu/Mosaic/Mac/NCSAMosaica6.PPC.hqx
Unix: ftp://ftp.ncsa.uiuc.edu/Mosaic/Unix/binaries/2.4/
```

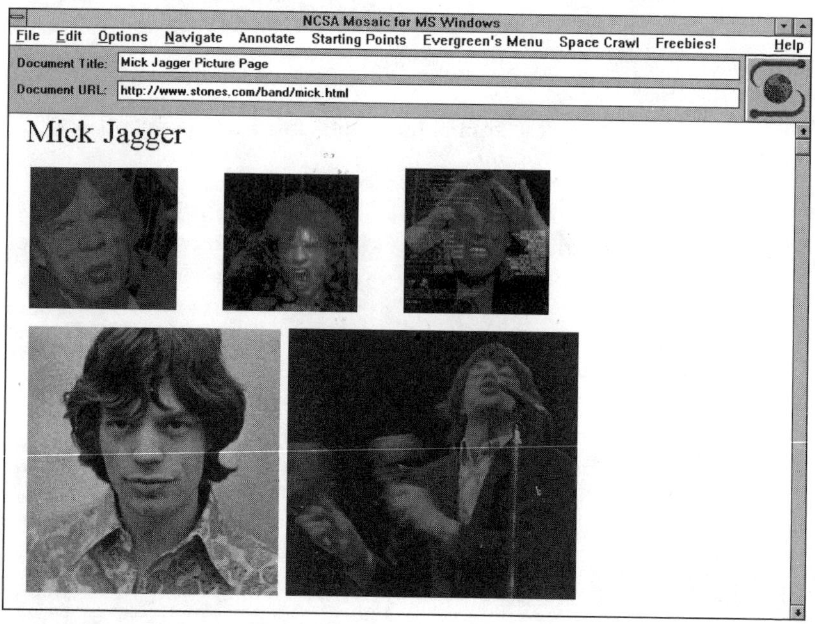

Jam with Mick and the Stones on the Web

You may also be able to get it from your Internet provider. Or you could hit up one of your friends who already uses it. By this time, Mosaic is all over the place. It's freeware, so it won't cost you much but the time it takes to find it.

What Does "Freeware" Mean?

Freeware is software that somebody gives away while reserving copyright. It's not the same as public domain software, in that the copyright owner attempts to maintain some control over how the software is distributed. Nor is it shareware, in which the vendor expects to receive payment for the software on the honor system. Freeware is often "baitware" that demonstrates the concepts of a larger product without providing all its features—in the hope that you'll get aggravated enough to pop for the "commercial" product. Sometimes freeware is prerelease software that's still heavily under development. Mosaic definitely falls into this category.

You can give freeware to your friends and not feel bad about it. You can't *sell* it to your friends, though, or . . . or . . . awful things of an unspecified nature may happen.

What Is an Internet Provider?

Your provider is the organization you buy your Internet connection from. It's usually a small company consisting of four guys in a basement and an overburdened Unix workstation with lots of modems hung off of it. What these small companies do is buy a fast connection to the Internet through a national common carrier like Sprint, or else from a local university or research center that is already on the Internet. They then sell connections into their machine to you.

Internet providing is still a kind of a cowboy boutique business. This may change, but for now it's what you're dealing with. Very commonly small providers fail to upgrade their equipment quite as rapidly as they need to as their number of subscribers grows, and sometimes you'll get a busy signal dialing in. If you do, gripe loudly. The squeaky modem gets the carrier.

In general, connecting to the Internet is about as exact a science as parapsychology. Expect delays, mistakes, and lots of assorted weirdness for the first few weeks. It happened to me. It'll happen to you.

What Kind of Modem Do I Need to Use Mosaic?

A fast one. The faster the better—and by *fast* I'm not talking 4800 baud anymore. Unless you have or can budget for a 14.4 Kbps modem, don't even bother. It'll drive you nuts. If you intend to do any serious surfing on Mosaic, I'd recommend what they call a Vfast modem, which ostensibly runs at 28.8 Kbps. (How fast they actually run depends on how good a phone connection you have to your provider. Where I live that usually means 21 Kbps. Your baudage may vary.) Vfast modems are only a few hundred dollars now, and Mosaic is feeding the demand for them so strongly that they'll probably be only half that expensive in another six months.

I've heard that in some parts of California you can get a service to your house called Home ISDN, which is a 56 Kbps link and makes Mosaic almost pleasant. The ISDN service itself isn't expensive on the surface of it (about $30 a month) but it needs specialized hardware for your computer that could set you back a grand or more. Maybe 1997.

The best way to use Mosaic, of course, is to work for a big company or a university that will give you Mosaic on a workstation through a true dedicated digital connection like T1, which is so fast that the jerky movies almost don't jerk anymore. Almost.

What Kind of Connection Do I Need to Run Mosaic?

Mosaic requires something better than the creaky VT100 text-mode link that 80 percent of all Internetworkers use. That something better is called a SLIP (Serial Line Internet Protocol) or PPP (Point to Point Protocol). The two differ in unimportant ways. See what your provider offers and take it. Either one will do. My experience has been that PPP is maybe a little crankier than SLIP to set up, but people I don't entirely respect claim that PPP gives you a faster connection.

Unlike your canonical VT100 shell connection, PPP and SLIP connections require something called a TCP/IP stack, which is so complex it'll turn your brain inside out if you try to think about it too hard.

What's a TCP/IP Stack?

TCP/IP is a packet-switching protocol; that is, a specification defining a mechanism for dividing data into chunks and getting all the chunks that belong together to the same place at pretty much the same time. A *TCP/IP stack* is a piece of software that implements the TCP/IP protocol. (I don't know why it's called a "stack"—and I suspect I could live out a full and relatively normal life without ever needing to know.)

Your TCP/IP stack breaks files and network commands into packets, slaps an address on each packet, and sends them out onto the Net. The packets are passed from hand to hand by machines connected to the Internet, moving closer to their destination with each handoff. If nothing untoward happens, each packet will find its way to the destination specified in the address it was given. At the packets' destination, the receiving TCP/IP stack reassembles them into the original file or command. OK, sure, it may be a little more involved than that, but this is a thin book and I need to generalize or I'll never finish.

Under Windows, a TCP/IP stack typically handles dialing into your provider's host machine. After dialup is complete, you minimize the stack to an icon in the icon bar. At that point it manages the modem and accepts data from Internet-aware applications like Mosaic. Mosaic talks to the stack, the stack talks to the modem, and the modem talks to the next machine down the line, typically your provider's. When you're dialed in via SLIP or PPP and TCP/IP, your machine is literally a part of the Internet—kind of like being one pine needle on a giant Sequoia. I still get a kick out of that.

What If I Don't Have Access to a Modem Line?

You mean at your office? Then you're stuck—unless you're connected to a LAN. If you work for a big company or a university, it's possible that you can get access to the Internet through the LAN cable. In that case, your TCP/IP stack will be provided and is probably already on your system. The LAN cable connects your machine to a specialized computer (called a *comm server*) somewhere else in the building, and the comm server actually talks to the Internet, passing those packets down the cable to your machine. How quickly this works depends on how good a LAN you have, and (as always) how many other people are using it, how much data they're trying to push through the LAN, and how many people are playing Network Doom.

Where Do I Get a TCP/IP Stack?

Often, you can get one from your provider. Configuring a TCP/IP stack can be a mind-numbing operation if you're not already a Net guru, so if your provider hands you a preconfigured stack and a login script to go with it, snag it. Recently, publishers have been publishing Internet books with TCP/IP stacks on diskettes bound into the back cover. Look around. If a friend has a freeware or shareware stack that works, take a copy and do *exactly* what he or she does.

The two TCP/IP stacks I've used are Trumpet WinSock and Chameleon. Both are available free on the Internet, and Chameleon is also available in a commercial product as well. Both seem bug-free and reliable. I say "seem" because an Internet environment is a crowded room, and when things start to smell, it's often a little hard to tell which piece of the system has the gas problem.

NetManage's Chameleon Sampler product (which is a TCP/IP stack bundled with several useful Internet utilities) has been bound into several books and can be downloaded from various places.

When Microsoft starts its sly "pre-release" marketing program for Windows, rumor holds that it will contain a very good TCP/IP stack that configures itself and requires no significant fooling-with. If I were the Trumpet and Chameleon folks, I'd be diversifying into bath fashions about now.

Near term, if you can FTP from your shell account, here's where to get yourself a TCP/IP stack:

```
Trumpet: ftp://ftp.utas.edu.au/pc/trumpet/winsock/twsk10a.zip
```

NCSA has a Web page with pointers to a number of TCP/IP stacks for Windows (which are collectively known as WinSocks), but of course that won't help you if you don't already have Mosaic and

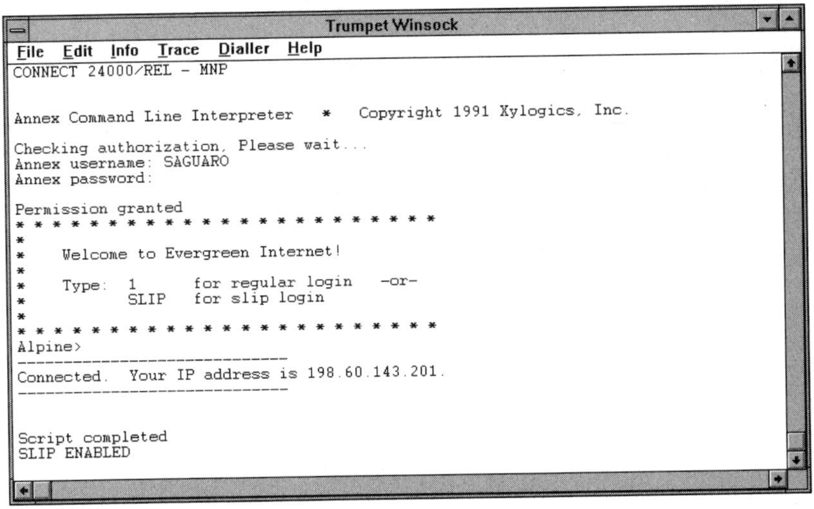

Here's a quick look at Trumpet in action

TCP/IP up and running. Here's the page anyway, in case you decide to try a different stack:

`http://www.ncsa.uiuc.edu/SDG/Software/WinMosaic/winsocks.html`

What Does WinSock Mean?

WinSock is short for Windows Sockets, which is the name for a Windows communications API derived from another, Unix-oriented API called Berkeley Sockets. Berkeley Sockets is a venerable TCP/IP stack that has become a standard in the Unix business. All Windows Internet software that I'm aware of requires the presence of a WinSock-compatible TCP/IP stack. This is usually (but not always) present in a file called WINSOCK.DLL.

How Do I Set Up a TCP/IP Stack?

Egad. The Cowardly Lion you *ain't*. Do it over a long weekend with a lot of beer in the fridge and enough Advil to go around. It is a *very* hairy business unless you're very lucky or have spent your whole adult life studying communications software. If it seems like half the world is now running Mosaic, well, the task of setting up a TCP/IP stack is what's keeping the *other* half from running it, too.

If you have correctly installed a 14.4Kbps internal modem and have already used it to log into some online service like CompuServe, you're a lot of the way there. An external modem running through a typical PC serial port may or may not cut it at the sorts of speeds that allow Mosaic to run faster than your average banana slug. To be sure, your serial port must be a fairly new one, with the 16550 UART in it.

No other UART chip will do here. Don't take your salesperson's word for it until the box is opened and you see the "16550" printed on the chip. Make sure that number is there; the whole chip ID might be something like "NS16550A" but the "16550" is the important part. That's the *only* kind of serial port that'll run an external modem at 14.4Kbps.

Vfast modems can go as fast as 28,800 bps, which is so fast that they get bogged down under Windows if you run them through any type of serial port. The Vfast modem I use is the Microcom DeskPorte FAST, which has a really nifty driver that moves data into and out of your PC through your *parallel* port instead. Parallel ports are inherently faster than any serial port. Data *can* move both ways through a parallel port, and on a typical 386 or 486 PC you can work as fast through the parallel port as the Vfast modem can run. Don't try this trick, however, on any machine that isn't fast enough to run Windows well.

Each TCP/IP stack program will have some kind of configuration screen that will need to know the port your modem is on, what kind of connection you want (SLIP or PPP), your Internet address, your network mask, and other gruesome things like that. Much of this will have to come from your provider, particularly things with the word "address" in them. An Internet address is a group of four numbers separated by periods and looks something like this: 198.60.143.121. Your provider defines this and gives it to you when you set up your Internet account.

Ultimately, your provider has to help you get your TCP/IP stack running. There are some providers who have had to spend so much time and trouble helping people with their stacks that they stopped offering SLIP and PPP accounts!

Before you despair, RTFM (read the flipping manual, as the PG definition goes). If you don't *have* a manual, despair may well be in order. The best practical advice is to find a friend who's already been through it, and look hard at a *working* configuration screen for the TCP/IP stack that you have. Duplicate everything but your friend's Internet addresses and masks, and then plug your own in. Finally, try dialing in manually—that is, don't try to set up a script right away. Sooner or later you'll nail it—or maybe you'll go back to MCI Mail.

What's The Best Way to Set Up Mosaic?

The best way? Deja vu yourself to the previous question and find somebody who's already running it (without having torn all his or her hair out yet) and set it up exactly the same way.

Failing that, I've done pretty well just creating an INTERNET subdirectory on a hard drive partition and then creating a separate subdirectory for each of the major Internet utilities (your TCP/IP stack, Eudora, HGopher, Mosaic, and so on). To keep things from getting cluttered, define a separate subdirectory under INTERNET called DOWNLOAD to collect all that fabulous free stuff that you'll be spending a fortune on phone calls grabbing off the Net. It looks like this on my system:

```
C:\INTERNET\
   WINSOCK\
   HGOPHER\
   EUDORA\
   MOSAIC2\
   UTILS\
   DOWNLOAD\
```

In general, you can place the ZIP file for each program in its subdirectory, and then unzip the ZIP files into that same subdirectory. That's all it takes for Mosaic. Most other utilities that I have used work the same way. The WINSOCK subdirectory shown here holds Trumpet WinSock, which is the TCP/IP stack that I use.

Having set up your subdirectories, create a program group called Internet and an icon for each executable that you install. Create separate icons in the same group for useful non-Internet utilities you

LView lets you look at GIF and JPEG graphics on-screen and online

use in Internet work, like LView 3.1 (an image viewer for GIF/JPEG files) and WinZip, a Windows shell for PKZIP.

How Do I Load a Web Document?

You won't always have a hot link to a Web document. You'll pick up a lot of interesting URLs from friends and in messages and newsgroups. Cut and paste what you can, but be prepared to do some odd typing. Mosaic has a dialog box you bring up by either selecting **File | Open URL** or clicking on the open file icon on the toolbar. You type the URL, hit the OK button, and off you go.

What Does the Turning Globe Mean?

Mosaic's world turns when it's either moving data through your TCP/IP connection or waiting for data to show up from the other end—far more of the latter, I'm afraid. The whole idea behind the globe is to

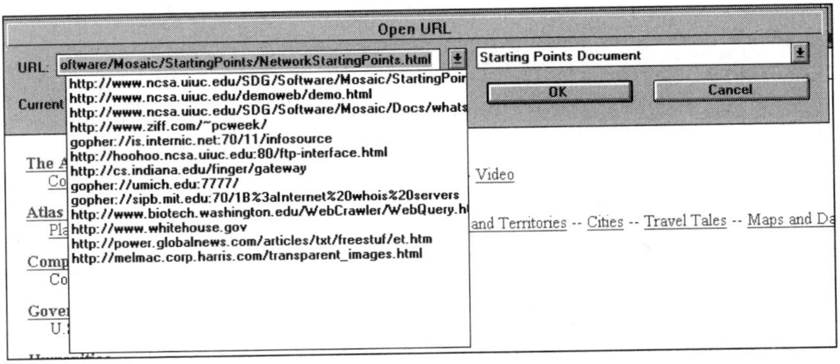

Type a URL in this dialog box, or select one from the list, and away you'll go

let you know that something is underway (I won't go so far as to say "happening") and that the system isn't just sitting there ignoring you.

When Mosaic is idle and truly waiting for you to tell it to go fetch something, the globe will be still and the two fish hooks above and below it are dark. If the yellow highlights are visible in the fish hooks but not moving, it might mean Mosaic or your system has crashed.

Mosaic's globe has another, less-well-known function: If you click on the globe while the globe is turning, Mosaic will cancel whatever it's trying to do and the globe will stop.

You Stole My Next Question!

Hey, okay, I'm an impatient kind of a guy. I realize that my previous answer has to be amended to state that not *all* versions of Mosaic can be stopped by clicking on the globe. Once you get Mosaic installed, go fetch something and while it's coming in, click on the globe. You'll then know whether you need to go find yourself a better version of Mosaic.

What's the Difference Between Mosaic 1 and Mosaic 2?

Mosaic 1 has bugs. Mosaic 2 has more bugs. Actually, Mosaic 2 is still "alpha" software at this writing, so I can't complain about the bugs without sounding ungrateful. They could have just sat on it until they decided it was ready.

Mosaic 1 is still available from NCSA. It's reasonably reliable and runs comfortably in 8 MB. You can get it via FTP from NCSA:

```
ftp://ftp.ncsa.uiuc.edu/Mosaic/Windows/old/WMOS1_0.ZIP
```

If you're not a total wimp, go get Mosaic 2 instead. Mosaic 2 is a more ambitious piece of work, and the current release requires Win32, the 32-bit extender module for Windows 3.1. If you're running Windows 95 (which technically isn't out yet, but that hasn't stopped everybody in the observable universe from running it) you don't need Win32, because Windows 95 *is* Win32.

The biggest functional difference between the two major releases of Mosaic is that Mosaic 2 supports "fill-out forms" and control buttons in HTML documents. Many HTML documents now allow you to enter data and then push a button to send that data somewhere, typically back to the owner of the page containing the forms. WebCrawler (see page 109) works this way; it's a snazzy search utility that periodically builds an index of all the Web documents it can find. You can search the index it creates if you're running Mosaic 2. If you're still using Mosaic 1, you can only stare at it with your nose pressed up against the screen.

I Have Only 4MB and Mosaic Won't Run. What Do I Do?

Mosaic needs 8 megs and really likes 16. If you only have four and simply can't pop for the SIMMs, there is a way out: Get a copy of EINet's WinWeb program, which is a Mosaic clone that runs reasonably well in 4MB. It won't complain if you have more, but it'll work well. It lacks a little of Mosaic's flash and dash and a few unimportant features, but in general it's a nice piece of work, and essential for the memorially challenged. You can FTP it from EINet at:

```
ftp://einet/pc/winweb/winweb.zip
```

WinWeb is freeware. That being the case, why not take some of the money you won't be spending on it and buy another 4 MB?

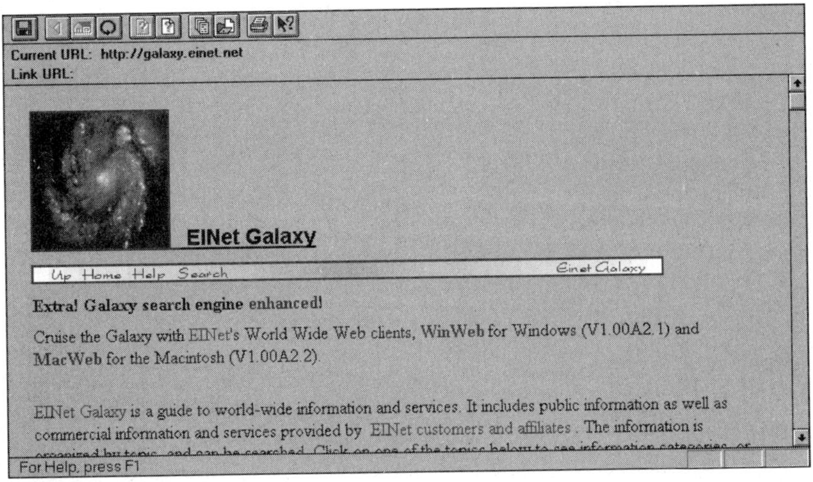

Screen shot of WinWeb

What Is a Mosaic Clone?

Some people have gotten so tired of using the umpteenth alpha version of NCSA Mosaic 2 that they've just gone and written their own Web viewer that does the same things and then some. WinWeb, which I talked about in the previous question, is an early Mosaic clone designed for people too cheap to feed Mosaic all the RAM it wants. Others are appearing all the time. Some are freeware and others actually cost money.

My personal favorite Mosaic clone is NetScape, which is freeware, has more features than Mosaic 2, and doesn't require you to install Win32. It also appears to be less of a memory hog. NetScape will display a Web page's HTML source code for the centipede crowd, and it also has built-in support for reading those great newsgroups you've heard of like alt.sex.bondage and alt.barney.die.die.die. Somebody has been circulating the fiction that NetScape is faster than NCSA Mosaic, but that hasn't been my experience—and besides, virtually any Mosaic version or Mosaic clone is faster than your connection into the Internet. Does it matter if you beat your little sister to the pasture fence if all you want to do is watch the grass grow?

Here's where you can get your own copy of NetScape:

```
ftp://ftp.mcom.com/netscape/
```

A company called Spry sells an entire suite of Internet tools called the Air Series that includes a very good Mosaic clone called AirMosaic. Apart from being fully functional and ostensibly bug-free, AirMosaic has a cool radar-screen logo in place of Mosaic's spinning globe, and the green line revolves and makes you feel like you're in an old *Voyage to the Bottom of the Sea* episode, minus flying sparks.

What's a Home Page?

When you first execute Mosaic, it will go onto the Web and fetch a page to display, even before you give it any commands. The page it goes out and gets is your *home page*. Any Web page can be your home page; there's nothing special about a page to make it a home page. If you got your copy of Mosaic from its originators, NCSA, the home page it gets will be the NCSA home page. If you got a copy of

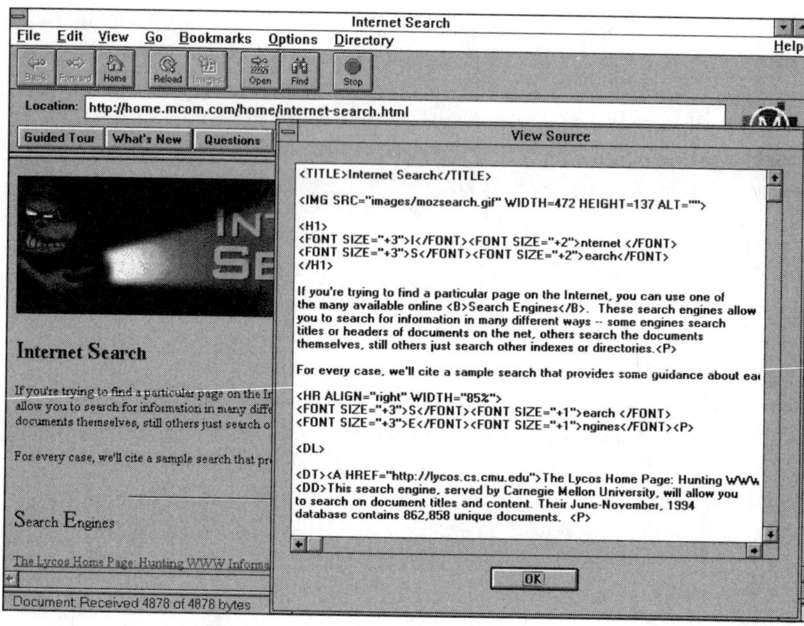

You can use NetScape to take a quick behind-the-scenes look at a home page's HTML

Mosaic from your provider, your provider may have configured it to fetch your provider's own home page, which might contain timely information on local dialup numbers, system crashes, rate boosts, and things like that.

For my money, fetching a home page automatically on startup is a serious waste of time. I've configured my copy of Mosaic to present me with a blank screen when I run it, and then I choose a destination from one of my menus. To disable automatic home page fetch, you have to edit the MOSAIC.INI file that Mosaic copies into your Windows/System directory. The first few lines in that file look like this:

```
[Main]
E-mail="someone@libre.com"
Autoload Home Page=no
Home Page=http://maple.libre.com/evergreen.html
Display Inline Images=yes
Grey Background=yes
Fancy Rules=yes
Round List Bullets=yes
Current Hotlist=Personal
```

Change the "Autoload Home Page" item in line three from "yes" to "no," as I've done here. While you're at it, you might also edit in the URL of a reasonable home page. I haven't done that yet. When I come across a home page I like better than a blank screen, I will.

I Didn't Ask About INI Files in My Last Question.

Maybe you should have. Or do you want to waste half your life waiting to see the NCSA Home Page for the 954th time?

Is It Possible to Write My Own Home Page?

More and more people *are* doing this. You have to learn HTML (a relatively simple task), but given that, you can write your very own private home page that lives on your hard disk. (See the chapter "All the HTML You Really Need . . .") Mosaic can read such a home page, even though it isn't stored on the Internet. Mosaic really won't help you *write* it, however. For that you must either create HTML files full of tags, or use one of a growing mob of HTML editing tools that allow you to place and size text on the screen in a WYSIWYG manner before converting your display to HTML.

The Home Page lines in MOSAIC.INI should look something like this if you want to automatically load an HTML document on startup as your personal home page:

```
Autoload Home Page=yes
Home Page=file:///C|/INTERNET/MOSAIC2/MYFILE.HTM
```

This assumes that your HTML file is in a subdirectory whose path is C:\INTERNET\MOSAIC2\; obviously, edit the path to suit your own directory situation. Once you edit your INI file to point Mosaic to the HTML file defining your home page, you can let Mosaic load your private home page every time you run it. The vertical bar character takes the place of the colon, which is not allowed in URLs. And the slashes are Unix-style forward slashes, not DOS-style backslashes.

One caution here: Yet again, not all versions of Mosaic support loading local HTML files. I haven't tested every version (like vampires, they are legion), but with some copies of Mosaic 2 Alpha 2, this pointedly does *not* work—and on others it does.

The current leader among the Mosaic clones, NetScape (which I spoke of earlier) can act as a very effective HTML learning tool. Once you have received and are looking at a Web page with NetScape, selecting the **View | Source** menu item will show you the actual naked HTML source for the page you are reading, tags and all.

That's Not the Same as Having Your Own Home Page on the Web, Is It?

Confusion still reigns, doesn't it? Defining an HTML home page on your hard disk is *not* the same as having a home page on the World Wide Web where people other than you can tune in and read it. Although when your SLIP or PPP connection is dialed up and in place making your machine technically part of the Internet, no one

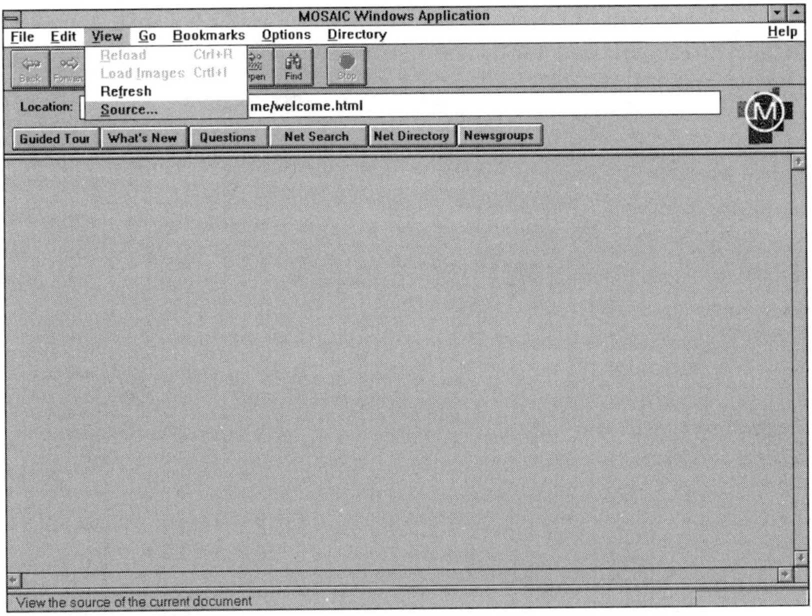

Use View/Source to view the HTML in a home page

can climb down the connection to read pages on your hard disk without an additional piece of fairly ambitious software called a *web server.*

There are web server programs for Windows, and they're even freeware, but they come with so many cautions and warnings that I still consider them another flavor of nuclear waste. Besides, if you want to serve material on the Web, you'll want to be connected to the Internet 24 hours a day, or the guys in Europe and Japan will never get a shot at what you create. And there's that little matter of paying for all that connect time . . . .

Still, some providers (but by no means all or even most) will give you a little bit of Web space on their host machines, and if you put a home-grown HTML home page in that little bit of Web space, the world at large can dial in and read it. Ask your provider about it. There may be an extra monthly charge, but it's a lot of fun and if you don't mind fooling with HTML, you'll find it's relatively easy. That's about all I'll say about the topic in this chapter. If you want to know more about creating a home page and setting up Web servers, read the following page and some of the pages it points to:

```
http://www.pcweek.ziff.com/~pcweek/WebTools.html
```

Also be sure to check out the *All the HTML You Really Need . . .* section.

Does It Matter When I Use Mosaic?

Not if you can spend the bulk of your day watching the world turn. In recent months, and especially during the school year when every college kid in America is playing Internet Relay Chat when they ought to be studying calculus, the Internet has been *mighty* slow during business hours and into the early evening.

For the briskest performance, wait until after 8 PM, when all of Europe is asleep and the college kids are out partying. The best place to be in this regard is on the West Coast, where it's 9 PM when it's midnight in New York. Weekends are good too, though once you get late enough on Sunday night it starts to be Monday morning in Europe and traffic heats up.

I'm beginning to get nervous about how useful the Internet will be if new users keep signing on as quickly as they are.

What's a Hotlist?

A hotlist is a list of URLs that Mosaic keeps somewhere, and appends to when you select the **Navigate | Add Current to Hotlist** item from the Mosaic menu. Mosaic can keep more than one list of URLs, but your hotlist is the specific list that Mosaic adds to at any given time.

Say you're looking at a Web page and you feel like you'll want to return to it quickly in the future. If you select **Navigate | Add Current to Hotlist**, Mosaic will add the URL of the page you're looking at to whatever list is currently your hotlist.

Hotlists take two forms in Mosaic: Custom menus and the Quicklist, which is cleverly named QUICKLIST. You choose your hotlist from the **Navigate | Menu Editor** dialog. Both QUICKLIST and your

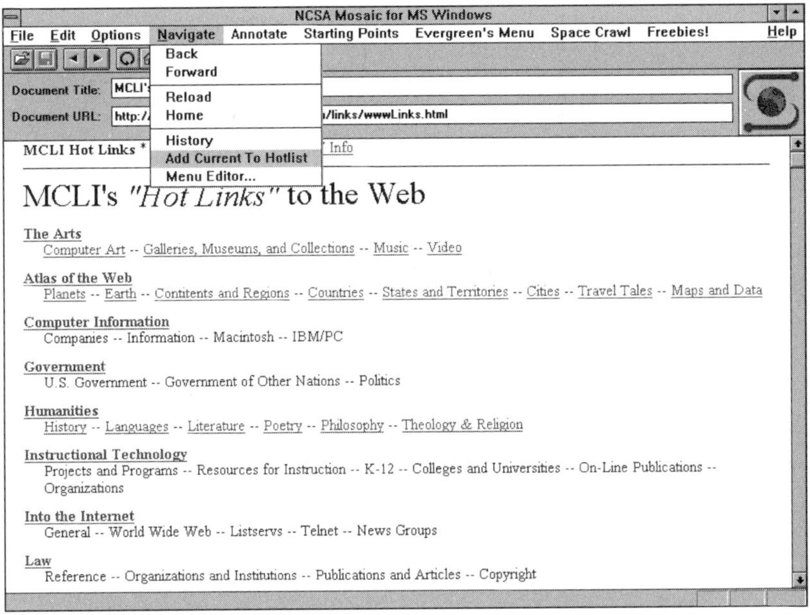

Select Navigate|Add Current to Hotlist to add a hot site to your hotlist

custom menus are just places in your MOSAIC.INI file where URLs and their descriptions are stored. The difference lies in how the two types of hotlists are used.

Custom menus are just that: Windows-style menus that you create and add URLs to. Once a URL is stored in a menu, you can pull down the menu and select the URL for Mosaic to go out and chase down. You can even define menus within menus; it's a very versatile system. Bring up the menu editor dialog and poke around. There's more to it than I have space to go into, but it's also fairly easy to dope out by beating on it.

QUICKLIST (not my fault; Mosaic always presents it in upper case) is a list of URLs that can be examined and picked from while you're in the **File|Open URL** dialog. If QUICKLIST is your current hotlist, it will be the drop-down portion of the URL: combo box.

In its inimitable way, not all releases of Mosaic handle QUICKLIST correctly. You might have to experiment with your copy to see what works and what croaks. I've had much better luck just defining a bunch of menus. If you completely fill Mosaic's menu bar, remember that Windows will add a second menu bar beneath the first as the list of menus grows. This cuts into your screen space a little but will allow you to put a *lot* of hotlist menus up.

NetScape does a much better job of managing its hotlists. However, to add further to the confusion, the Mosaic clones like NetScape generally call hotlists lists of *bookmarks.* They're the same thing: A list of Web page titles that Mosaic will display and allow you to pick from. Pick one, and wham! You're there. Or you will be. Sooner or later. Unless the site is busy. Or something else goes wrong. Or you give up.

Can I FTP from Inside Mosaic?

In style. Of course, you can't use Mosaic to FTP Mosaic down from the Internet if you don't already have Mosaic. But although there's nothing crisp in Mosaic's menus about "going into" FTP, you can use FTP nonetheless.

The trick is in those URLs I mentioned at the start of this little chautauqua. The address of a file on an FTP server is in fact a URL—and theoretically, Mosaic can decode and act on almost any kind of URL. Certainly, I've fetched plenty of material back from FTP sites doing nothing more than typing the URL of the FTP directory or file in question.

You can type the URL of an FTP site you want to visit, or you can select it from lists of hot links. There's a fairly good Web page of that sort called "All the FTP Servers in the World," which is neat even if it has a slightly exaggerated opinion of itself:

```
http://hoohoo.ncsa.uiuc.edu:80/ftp-interface.html
```

This Web page basically takes its huge list of FTP sites and divides them into several more manageable sublists, and you pick the site you want from the sublist by clicking on it. Poof! You're there. It saves a lot of typing, though I've found that about one out of four FTP sites I want isn't listed. (Who'd bother with a page entitled "75% of All the FTP Sites in the World"?)

If you'd just as soon type, then type the URL—but keep in mind that mistakes are easy to make. URLs for FTP sites begin with *ftp*, as in:

```
ftp://oak.oakland.edu/SimTel
```

which has all kinds of good stuff to grab. Go look.

Mosaic treats FTP directories the same way it treats Gopher menus: A list of hot links presented in hierarchical fashion. Click on one of those hot links and something will happen. If it's a subdirectory hot link, you'll move into and see the subdirectory. If you click on a filename, Mosaic will begin bringing back the file.

There's a catch on bringing back files: You must tell Mosaic to save the file to disk, or it will retrieve the file into thin air and do nothing with it. This is true for programs, but text files and GIFs can be retrieved without saving to disk. Before you click on a filename in an FTP directory, select **Options | Load to Disk**, and then enter a filename into the dialog that jumps up at that point. *Then* click on the file you want, and Mosaic will dutifully store it to disk.

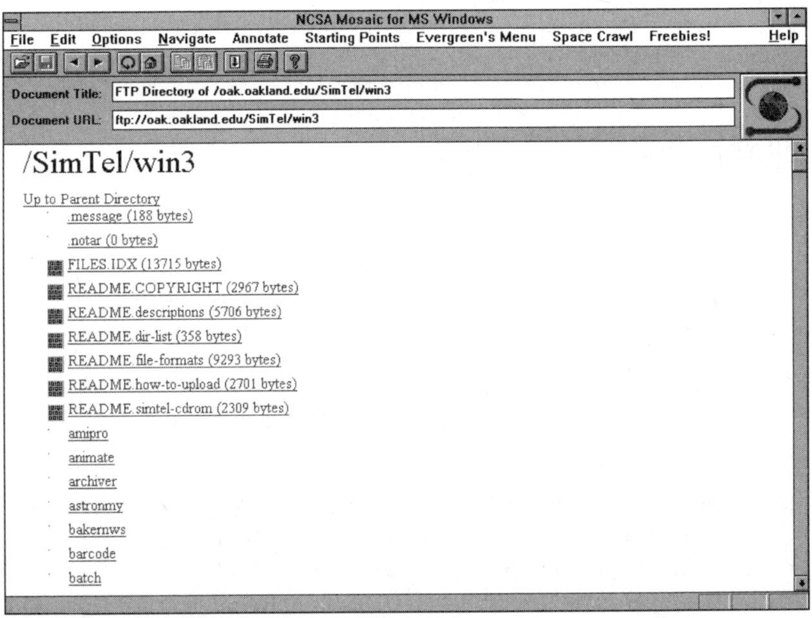

Here's a shot of the Oakland SimTel site, where you'll find literally thousands of different shareware, freeware, and public domain programs

After the file comes in (and this is where most people mess up) go back and turn **Options | Load to Disk** off—or Mosaic will try to store everything you want to read as disk files, without showing you anything on the screen! A window will display asking you to verify that you want to store to disk so it's not likely that you'll store something accidentally.

How About Gopher?

Once you've wrestled FTP to the mat, Gopher will seem almost toothless, which is true for the most part. Mosaic displays Gopher menus exactly the same way it displays FTP menus. Click on one of the hot links, and you go to the next level or select the file. Only the URLs are different; Gopher URLs begin with gopher:// instead of ftp://. The same SimTel site I mentioned in the previous question can be had through a Gopher URL:

```
gopher://gopher.oakland.edu
```

Again, as with FTP, to bring a file back from a Gopher menu, you have to select **Options | Load to Disk** before you click on the filename or nothing useful will happen.

What About Newsgroups?

Mosaic has nothing built in to handle newsgroups. For that you need to go get NetScape, (mentioned on page 38) which has very nice newsgroup support, with a simple E-mail editor and the ability to post to either the newsgroup or directly to someone's E-mail. NetScape has the additional major advantage that it allows you to read and even select from hot links at the top or middle of a Web page while it's still busy bringing over the bottom. And the same goes for WinWeb.

Mosaic, on the other hand, makes you wait until the *entire* page has been brought over before it will show you anything at all. This is an extraordinary disadvantage when you bring in the full list of newsgroups, which, depending on the appetite and prudishness of your provider's server, can top 5 *megabytes*. (In the spirit of conserving system resources, some servers selfishly omit newsgroups like alt.sex.bondage and alt.life.afterlife, but somehow, life goes on.)

And E-Mail?

Here, you lose. Mosaic might as well not even know E-mail exists. NetScape only supports it in connection with newsgroups. Sooner or later the Mosaic cloners will wise up. We're not there yet, so don't trash your Eudora disks.

What's the Best Way to Find Something on the Web?

Ask somebody who's already found it. That's the only way to be sure. Searching the Web is still something of an inexact science, because there's no master index of Web sites and thus no way to know where every Web page is stored. But there have been some good tries. My personal favorite is the WebCrawler (see page 109) but there are others, including the World Wide Web Worm and Lycos Search, which all depend on "Web robots" (in a sense, automated Mosaic users) to go out and read Web pages and then index titles or titles and contents.

Lots of research is currently going on in this area, and in another couple of years (if the whole thing hasn't collapsed of its own weight by then) searching the whole world's Web contents should be an achievable dream.

What's a Viewer?

Mosaic by itself can only do so much. There are a lot of different kinds of data floating around on the Web, and Mosaic's designers knew they couldn't hope to deal with it all in the body of their little monster on its slab. So they included an extendible interface to "helper" programs called *viewers*, which display (or play) data for the user.

MOSAIC.INI includes a list of associations between data types and viewer programs. If a data type comes down the line and Mosaic finds an association for it in MOSAIC.INI, it will invoke the viewer cited in the association and pass the incoming data to it. It sounds clunky but it works amazingly well.

The associations are in two parts: One assigns a name to a set of file extensions for a given data type, and the other assigns a viewer program to handle a data type name. The two associations for JPEG and MPEG data on my system look like this:

```
image/jpeg=.jpeg,.jpe,.jpg
video/mpeg=.mpeg,.mpe,.mpg

image/jpeg="C:\INTERNET\lview\lview31 %ls"
video/mpeg="C:\INTERNET\wmpeg\mpegplay %ls"
```

The first group shows the names given to sets of file extensions for data types. The second group assigns a viewer pathname to those data type names. I show you these because there's no wimp interface for letting Mosaic know about viewers. You have to do it the man's way, and edit MOSAIC.INI. To plug in a new viewer, find the section where this stuff is stored, and fool with things until something works. You can test things by loading data files from your local hard disk, so that you don't have to blow a lunch hour bringing in a 2MB MPEG movie across the Net. I touched on this back on page 40.

Most viewers are freeware. NCSA has put together a Web page with pointers to a number of such viewers along with instructions on how to install them with Mosaic. This one is well worth having on one of your hotlists:

```
http://www.ncsa.uiuc.edu/SDG/Software/WinMosaic/viewers.html
```

Can I Telnet with Mosaic?

In a sense. Mosaic will pass control to what amounts to a "viewer" for Telnet work. In your MOSAIC.INI file in the Viewers section is a line something like this:

```
telnet="C:\INTERNET\winsock\trmptel.exe"
```

What this means is that when Mosaic detects that it has a Telnet session by the tail, it will execute the program whose path is presented in quotes. A Telnet window will open, allowing you to communicate with the remote system as though you were logged in through a typical text-mode terminal.

In the example above, the Telnet "viewer" is TRMPTEL.EXE, created by Peter R. Tattam, who also created Trumpet WinSock. TRMPTEL is actually the program by which you communicate through Telnet, but it appears as a window over Mosaic and seems like just another part of the Mosaic application.

Programs like TRMPTEL are beginning to be called *helper programs* in Web jargon, though this hasn't percolated into the Mosaic documentation just yet. People are finding that the viewers concept, originally designed for looking at graphics images, is a whole lot more versatile than originally thought. In fact, it's a general-purpose system for extending Mosaic features.

Mosaic will invoke its Telnet helper whenever it decodes a URL that begins with the Telnet prefix:

```
telnet://enter help@callsign.cs.buffalo.edu:2000/
```

This one will get you a Telnet session that allows you to query a "big system" database of ham radio callsign information.

Are Dirty Pictures Passed Around On the Web and, If So, Where Are They Stored?

Of course they are, and forget it. This is a *family* book. I gave you a peek at Cindy Crawford, but that's as far as I'm willing to go.

PART 3

A Five Star Tour of the World Wide Web

Seems like everybody and their kid brother Emil are checking out the Web these days. Actually, a good number of Web pages probably really *were* created by some post-pubescent kid with way too much time on his hands.

So we sent our crack(ed) staff of Web surfers off into space, with these marching orders: Travel the World Wide Web and bring back the best—and only the best—of what the Web has to offer. And we did it all for *you*—are we a couple of nice guys or what? As you'll see when you look through this section, there's some amazingly good stuff out there—if you take the time to browse for weeks.

Of course, you don't need to since we've already been there and done that. So here's the best of the best, the pick of the litter, the true five star standout Web sites available to Mosaic users. Have a nice stay.

Art

Vive Le WebLouvre!

Arguably the most famous art trove in the world, Le Louvre is now being honored in cyberspace by this virtual museum of the same (almost) name. Currently, two virtual exhibits are here for your visual feast: art of medieval France and more modern paintings by such household names as Van Gogh, Cezanne, and Dali.

After a day browsing the Louvre, you'll be ready for something a bit less cerebral—say, a little wild and crazy French night life. Try out the virtual tour of Gay Paris, complete with a trip to the Eiffel Tower.

Getting There

`http://mistral.enst.fr/~pioch/louvre/`

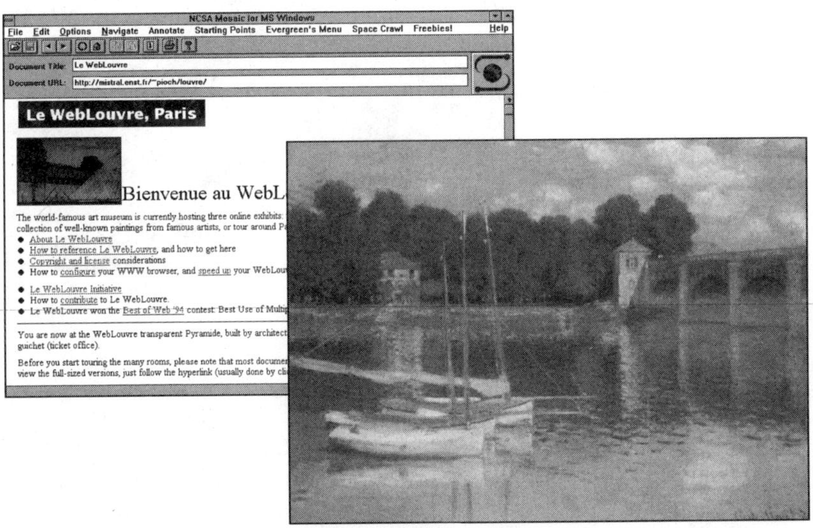

Monet's The Bridge at Argenteuil

Strange But True Web Art

Physics, computers, and art can make strange bedfellows, and Strange Interactions provides the proof. This online art exhibit by physicist/programmer/artist John Jacobsen is a self-described attempt to merge his two lives.

While I don't know if he's succeeded, I *can* say that bizarre, haunting images are the norm here. While some of the images might disturb you, you'll certainly be impressed by the artist's versatility. Jacobsen's online arsenal includes sketches, paintings, lithographs, and woodcuts, as well as other media.

Getting There

`http://amanda.physics.wisc.edu/show.html`

Hot Links

- OTIS
- FineArt Online
- Syracuse University Computer Graphics for the Arts

Here are a few examples of the dark and haunting images you'll find at Strange Interactions

Art Is Thriving on the Web

Art junkies will have no trouble getting their fix on the Internet. Through the Web, you'll find hundreds of sites, with every kind of art imaginable (and some that is, frankly, unimaginable). ArtMap, a multimedia cultural information service, is a collection of links throughout the Internet to art-related sites for all media and genre: visual, mass media, literature, video, performance, and design, with hundreds of links to individual sites scattered around the globe. In fact, *collection* is too tame a word. This site is voluminous in its cognitive scope, globally discombobulated, electronically cornucopial—it's a veritable *plethoral pallet* of all things art. (Artists actually talk this way—scary, isn't it?)

Getting There

`http://wimsey.com/anima/ARTWORLDonline.html`

Hot Links

About a billion.
I can't list 'em all.

Not being particularly well versed in Russian, I wasn't sure what to call this painting, but settled on Guys Taking Their Fish for a Walk; downloaded from the Russian Fine Arts Gallery, one of ArtMap's many links

Art Gallery, Internet Style

How many graphic arts majors does it take to make a digital painting? Find out at this Web site. Explore the digital art gallery from Syracuse University's Computer Graphics for the Arts Department. Students collaborated on these computer-generated images, combining text, audio, and animation into strange and bizarre works of digital art, here for you to browse. Visually stunning, this artwork offers you a glimpse into the future of computer graphics and design.

Getting There

http://ziris.syr.edu/home.html

Hot Links

- OTIS
- Carnegie Mellon Genetic Movies
- Web Playground Gallery
- M.C. Escher Images

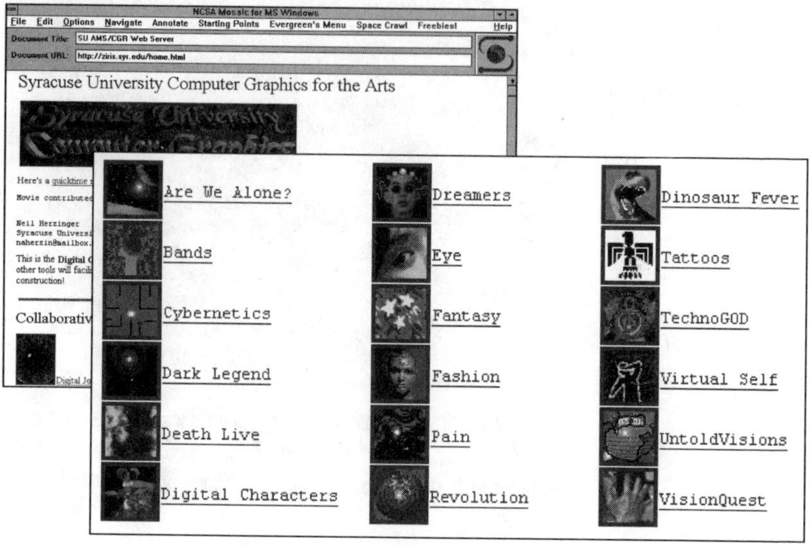

Pick a theme, yank your brain into high gear, and take a digital journey through cyberspace, or upload your own images in this collaborative Internet art project

Ansel Adams

No photographer has better captured the tranquil beauty and rugged power of the West's natural wonders than Ansel Adams. And that's not just my opinion. Even my color-blind mutt stares at his stuff.

Arguably the greatest photographer of the 20th century, Adams captured the breathtaking beauty of America's mountains, rivers, and landscapes without benefit of even a hint of cyan, magenta, or yellow. A staunch environmentalist, Adams helped preserve much of America's wilderness through his photographs.

Now Adams' photographs are available to you on the Web. You can download copies of his famous photos of Yosemite, Mount McKinley, the Snake River, and many more.

Getting There

`http://bookweb.cwis.uci.edu:8042/MuseumGraphics/LandsMount.html`

Hot Links

- Ansel Adams Home Page
- An Ansel Adams Chronology
- Ansel Adams: Fiat Lux

This 1948 picture of Mount McKinley National Park in Alaska is just one of the many Ansel Adams' photographs you can download, or just simply gawk at in awe

It's Your ArtServe

Are you looking for art on the Web? Careful what you ask for because you're liable to get it. When it comes to compiling art in cyberspace, Michael Greenhalgh, professor of Art History at the Australian National University, has outdone any other site I've visited. You'll find over 8,000 images of prints in his database, from the 15th through 19th centuries, Classical architecture and architectural sculpture, and Classical European sculpture. What does this guy do in his *spare* time?

If that's not enough art for you, there are links to many other sources. By the time you're done here, you'll have culture coming out your ears.

Getting There

`http://nearnet.gnn.com/gnn/GNNhome.html`

Hot Links

- Vatican Exhibit
- Soviet Archive Exhibit
- 1492 Exhibit
- Dead Sea Scrolls Exhibit
- Paleontology Exhibit
- Spalato Exhibit

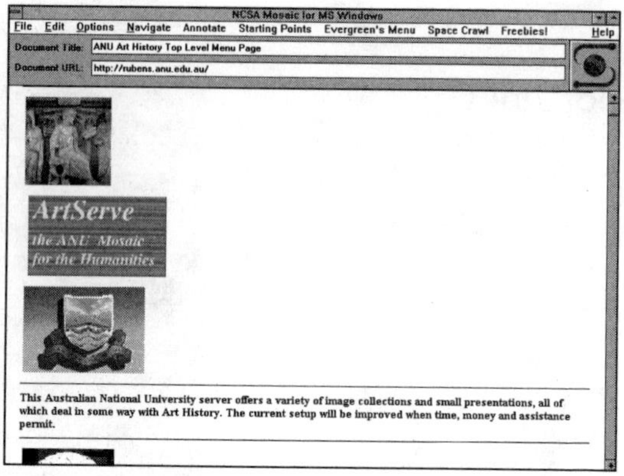

The ArtServe home page

Books

List of 'Lectric Publications

Extra! Extra! All the news that's fit to print is yours to read from these online news sources.

Electronic publications have been popping up on the Web faster than they can be read, and commercial newspapers especially have been experimenting with onlining their issues (yes, I can make up words if I want), often for free.

To keep up with which newspapers are currently online, check out the University of Florida's College of Journalism and Communications list of publications, which is actually a hotlist that you can use to select and go to your publications of choice. The list includes online campus newspapers as well as a list of journalism, media, and communications colleges that maintain Web servers of their own. *Everbody's* trying to get into the act!

Getting There

`http://www.jou.ufl.edu/commres/webjou.htm`

Hot Links

- Detroit Free Press
- GNN News
- The Electronic Newsstand

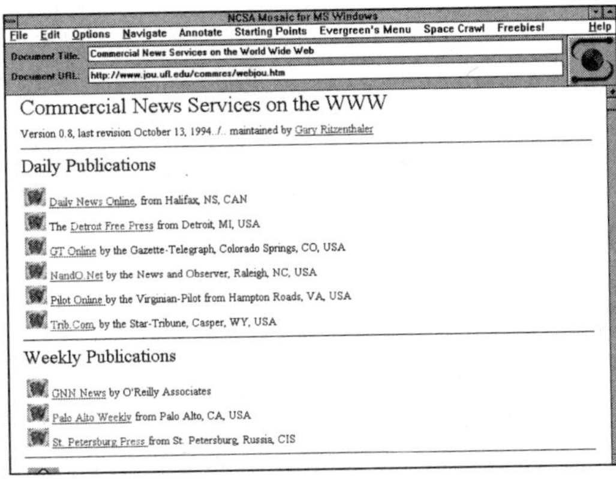

Get the latest news at this Web site

Time for the Latest News

Time magazine online? You bet! But get this one while it's complimentary because it won't be free forever. With *Time* online, not only do you have access to the latest issue on the newsstands, you also get back issues and daily updates to breaking stories.

You'll get more than news, though. There's also an Internet gateway that provides you with links to lots of great places on the Net, including FAQ archives and places to find great shareware. You can even send a letter to the editors. Hey, it's about time!

Getting There

`http://www.timeinc.com/time/universe.html`

Hot Links

- This Week's Time
- Today's News
- Internet Gateway
- Library

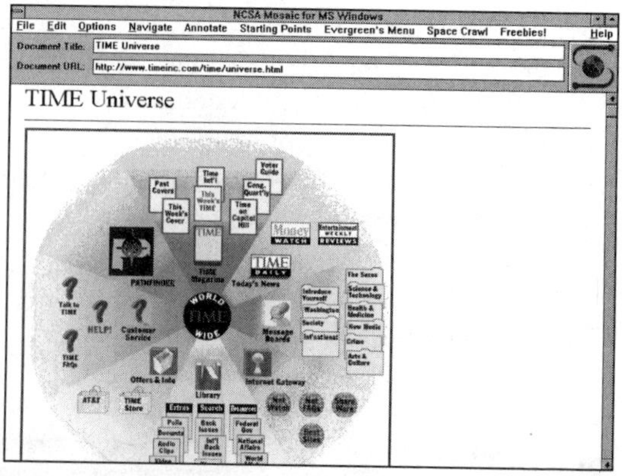

Read Time *magazine online on the Web*

Teletimes Means Electric Eclectic

Here's a theme-oriented online magazine that's as eclectic as it is interesting. Each issue focuses on a specific topic, such as favorite authors or travel, which is then explored in a lively, interesting way by a collection of exceptional writers.

Winner of a Best of the Net award from the Global Network Navigator, *Teletimes* originates from Vancouver, Canada. Though that doesn't mean a lot in cyberspace, it does explain a leaning toward Canadian topics. Still, there are plenty of articles to please the international crowd. Browse some of the back issues. If you like what you see, it's easy to subscribe.

Getting There

`http://www.wimsey.com/teletimes/teletimes_home_page.html`

Hot Links

Links to back issues are a mouse-click away

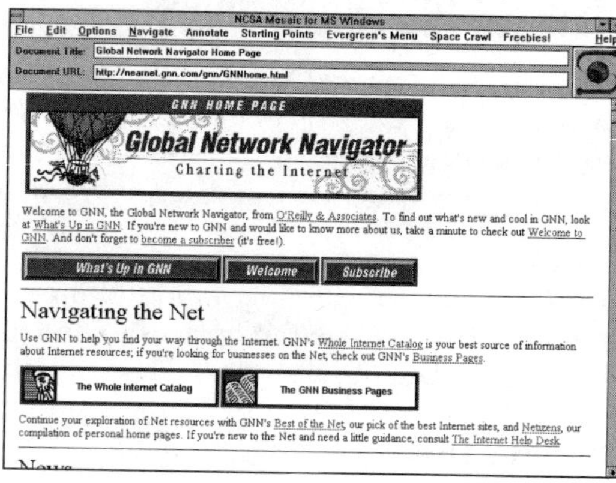

The Teletimes *home page for November '94*

Get Wired

The hottest magazine about cyberspace is now *in* cyberspace—so go get *Wired* on the Web. You'll find online access to back issues, direct connections to their slightly psycho-subversive editorial staff, job information, and even writers' guidelines.

Getting There

`http://www.wired.com/`

Hot Links

- Back Issues
- Promo Video
- Wired/Roadside America Hypertour '94

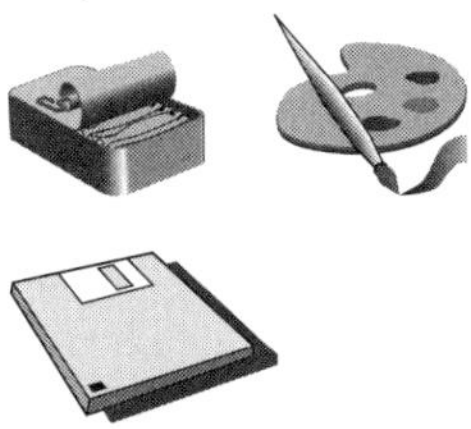

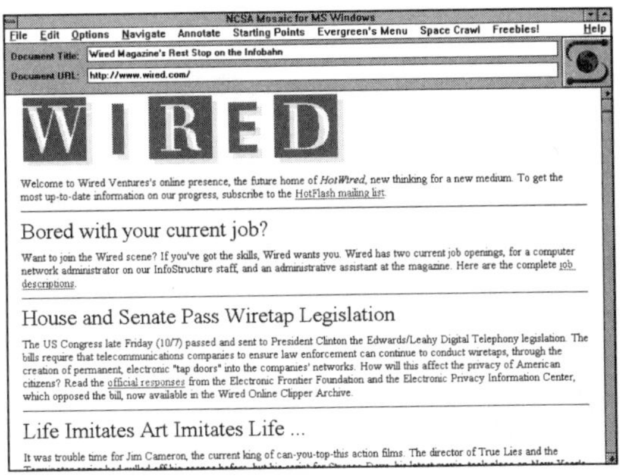

Wired *magazine goes online*

To Log On or Not to Log On?

William Shakespeare, unrivaled in the 17th century, is still surviving the test of time—except now it's realtime. Recently, I read about one of Shakespeare's plays being "acted out" in realtime on the Internet through the magic of Internet relay chat (IRC). No word on how it went or the audience it drew, but it's an interesting choice of media.

In any event, here are the complete plays of William Shakespeare, including *Hamlet*, *Othello*, *Henry IV*, *Henry IV Part 2* (Henry's Back), *Henry IV Part 3* (Henry Won't Leave), *Twelfth Night*, and more, with the promise that his sonnets will soon follow. What makes this site especially interesting are the helpful hyperlinks to the glossary scattered throughout the plays, which act as a sort of Cliffs Notes to the manuscript.

Getting There

http://the-tech.mit.edu/Shakespeare.html

Hot Links

All the plays of Shakespeare (stay tuned for the sonnets)

TEXT

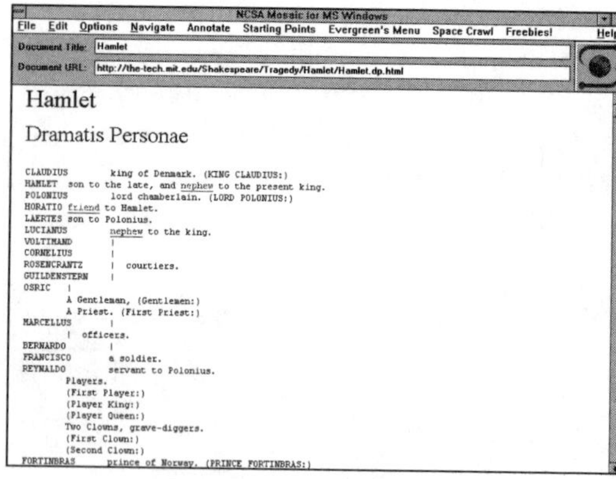

Hamlet, one of the many Shakespearean plays on the Web

Business

Where Greed Is Good

Buy! Buy! Buy! No, wait—sell! Maybe you should decide for yourself. But if you want up-to-the-minute news of the ups and downs of Wall Street, you're not going to get it from your afternoon newspaper. Hop on the Web for free electronic quotes and graphs of the Dow Jones Industrial Average and the S&P 500.

All information is delayed five minutes to satisfy the SEC, but it's definitely more current than you'll find anywhere else. You can even get historical data and graphs of stock performances over the past 25 years.

Getting There

http://www.secapl.com/cgi-bin/qs

Hot Links

- Ticker Search
- Dow Jones Industrial Average
- S&P 500 Index

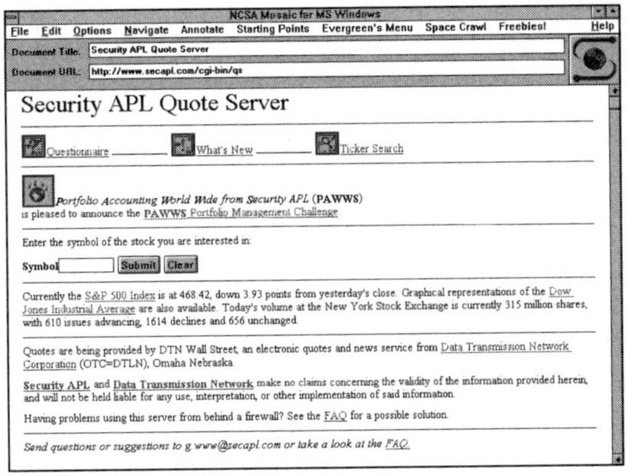

Security APL Quote Server

Questionnaire What's New Ticker Search

Portfolio Accounting World Wide from Security APL (PAWWS) is pleased to announce the PAWWS Portfolio Management Challenge

Enter the symbol of the stock you are interested in:

Symbol Submit Clear

Currently the S&P 500 Index is at 468.42, down 3.93 points from yesterday's close. Graphical representations of the Dow Jones Industrial Average are also available. Today's volume at the New York Stock Exchange is currently 315 million shares, with 610 issues advancing, 1614 declines and 656 unchanged.

Quotes are being provided by DTN Wall Street, an electronic quotes and news service from Data Transmission Network Corporation (OTC=DTLN), Omaha Nebraska.

Security APL and Data Transmission Network make no claims concerning the validity of the information provided herein, and will not be held liable for any use, interpretation, or other implementation of said information.

Having problems using this server from behind a firewall? See the FAQ for a possible solution.

Send questions or suggestions to g.www@secapl.com or take a look at the FAQ.

The APL Quote Server

Now You've Dun It

If you're in business for yourself, then you know how important it is to have an edge against your competition. Get that edge with information from Dun & Bradstreet right off the Web. In addition to valuable data on economic trends, you can get lots of great business how-to's, including:

- Predicting slow payers
- Finding a job
- Managing vendors

In addition, you'll get the latest data on regional growth worldwide, industry profitability, market segment growth, and business failure statistics. Take advantage of this free educational business information and gain an advantage before your competitors do.

Getting There

`http://www.dbisna.com`

Hot Links

- Market Your Business Globally
- Finding a Job
- Predicting Slow Payers

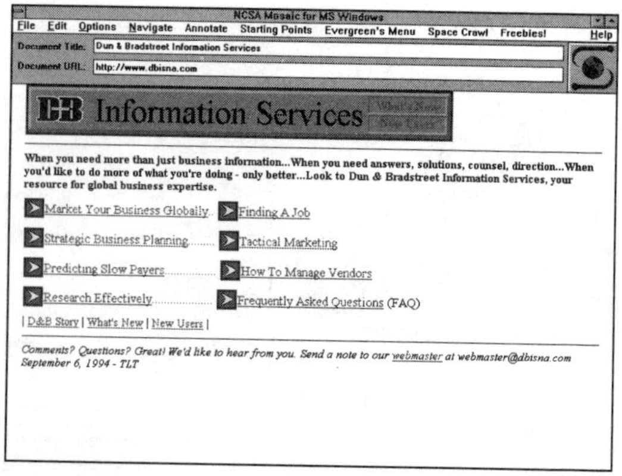

The D&B home page

That's a Quote

You're only as rich as your latest portfolio balance. And it's too late to sell if there's nowhere to go but up. So stay on top of the markets, via QuoteCom. With QuoteCom, Web users get the most up-to-the-minute financial market data available, including:

- End-of-day portfolio updates detailing the performance of your portfolio during the day
- Portfolio alarm monitoring to help monitor your stocks
- Notification of news items concerning your stocks
- Profiles of over 1,200 of the largest, most influential, fastest-growing companies around the world
- Canadian, London, and European market data

Trying the service is free. If it's critical that you have the most up-to-date financial data, you'll be rib-tickled that you checked out QuoteCom.

Getting There

`http://www.quote.com/`

Hot Links

- Free Stock Quotes
- BusinessWire

- Hoover Company Profiles
- Other Links for Investors

The QuoteCom home page

CareerMosaic

Are you thinking about changing jobs? Or is it just about time you *got* a job? Maybe you're ready for a whole new career. Maybe your *boss* thinks you're ready for a whole new career. In any event, make CareerMosaic your first stop. Named "Best Commercial Site on the Web" by PC Week Labs, CareerMosaic gives you the latest information about the best companies to work for. It's like having a buddy on the inside feeding you the pros and cons on working for some of the hottest companies, which FYI currently include:

- US West
- National Semiconductor
- Hewlett-Packard
- Sybase
- Union Bank

You'll get the latest scoop on benefits and employee programs, opportunities for college students, company profiles, career opportunities, and more. Arm yourself with the information you need to make those can't-turn-back-now career decisions.

Getting There

`http://www.service.com/cm/cm1.html`

Hot Links

- Fifth Annual Los Angeles Daily News Women's Career Conference
- Strictly Personnel Seminar Series
- Employment Directory Guide to North American Markets

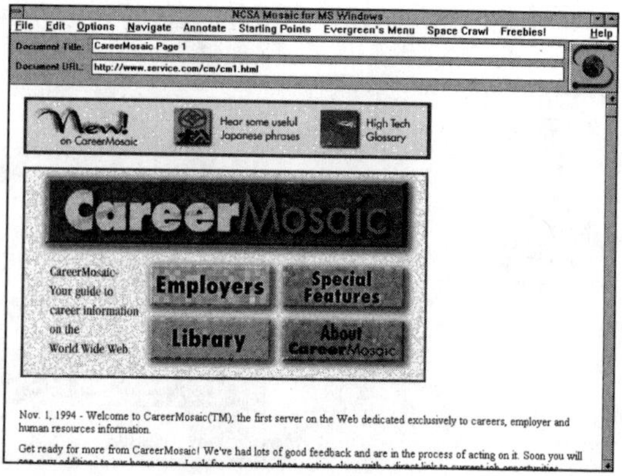

The CareerMosaic home page

E-SPAN's Interactive Employment Network

IEN (Interactive Employment Network) will help you land that job you and everybody else would kill their grandmothers for. Great for job seekers as well as recruiters and human resource managers who want to learn more about current trends in job searching and hiring.

IEN provides the latest resources for job seekers and employers. Post your resume and get invaluable tips on landing the job—or applicant—of a lifetime. You'll get employment listings, salary guides, career fair calendars, and more.

Plus, if you need to polish your interviewing skills (and who doesn't?), there's an interview simulator to help you practice your answers to the tough interview questions. Now let the other guy sweat.

Getting There

`http://www.espan.com/ienhome.html`

Hot Links

- Career Manager
- Job Library
- HR Manager

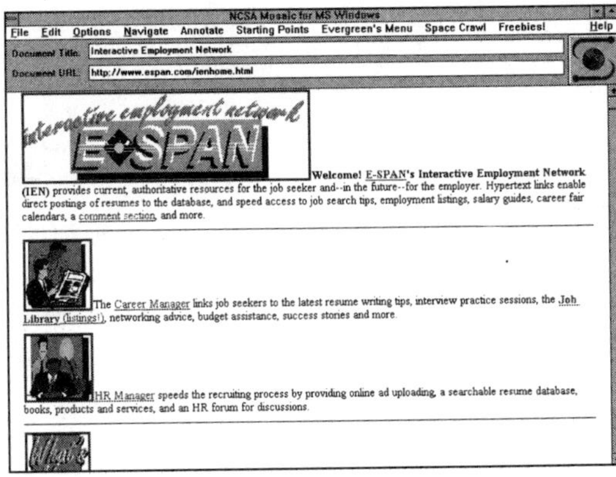

The E-SPAN Interactive Employment Network home page

Business Sources on the Net

Starting your own business is a big step—sometimes off a high cliff. There are a thousand hazards and pitfalls when you're starting out, and no single person is business-savvy enough to identify them all. And no one needs to tell *you* about your chances of "making it." But you can with the right product—and the right information. Arm yourself with information that'll strengthen the odds *your* business will be the one to succeed where others haven't.

If you're looking for information about starting, running, marketing, advertising, or expanding your business, Business Sources on the Net is the place to start. This hot list has links to some serious business resources so scattered across the Net you couldn't find 'em even if you *had* a net. You'll get information on business accounting, finance, management, marketing, and more.

Getting There

`http://kiwiclub.bus`
`.utexas.edu/wwwlecture/businesshotlist.html`

Hot Links

Too many to list. You'll have to check this page out for yourself.

These are just two of the many business resource-related sites linked to Business Sources on the Net

Be Your Own Boss

The entrepreneurial spirit is alive and thrashing on the Web. If you're one of the little fish, you'll want to check out the tons of resources available to help you succeed and make a splash in the big pond.

You can find lots of useful business information here on the Net, gathered specifically with entrepreneurs in mind:

- Your business listed in national directories for free
- Free publicity for your newsletter or magazine
- Laws concerning unsolicited telephoning faxing

Plus, you'll get the latest *entreprenews* with *A-ha! Monthly*, the newsletter for and about entrepreneurs from The IDEA Association, a support group for people starting their own businesses.

Getting There

http://sashimi.wwa.com/~notime/eotw/EOTW.html

Hot Links

- The Internet Business Center
- Advertising on the Internet
- IDEAbase

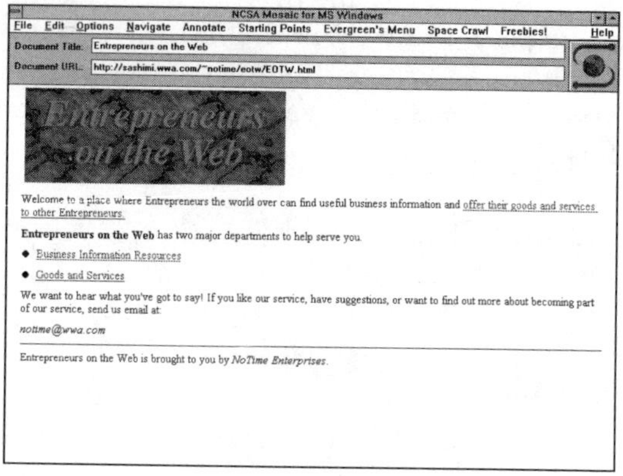

The Entrepreneurs on the Web home page

Computers and Computing

Cruising through SimTel City

Unless you bought your computer with the intention of using it as the world's most overly priced door stop (in place of this book), you've probably got an insatiable appetite for software. Let's face it, go past the word processor and spreadsheet programs—you know, *work stuff*—and what have you got? A couple of hundred megabytes of unused disk space with nothing to eat and no place to go. What better way to use it than by gorging its cylinders with this veritable all-you-can-eat buffet of free software?

The SimTel Software Repository is a software junkie's paradise. You'll find hundreds—no, *thousands*—of programs and utilities for astronomy, business, cooking, all the way to zoology and beyond. You'll notice a gaping hole where games should be, but look under "education" and you'll find some great ones hidden away. Education! C'mon, who are they trying to kid?

Getting There

`http://www.acs.oakland.edu/`

Hot Links

- PC/Blue Disk Library
- SIMTEL-20 Macintosh Archives
- SIMTEL-20 Unix&C Archives

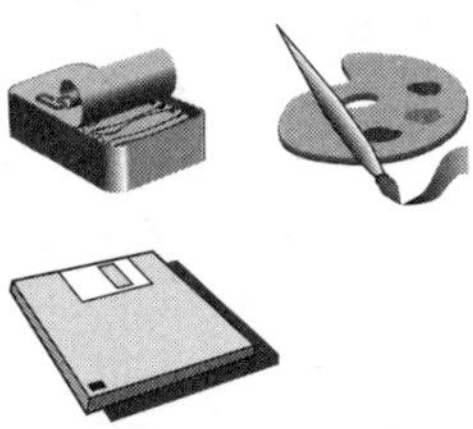

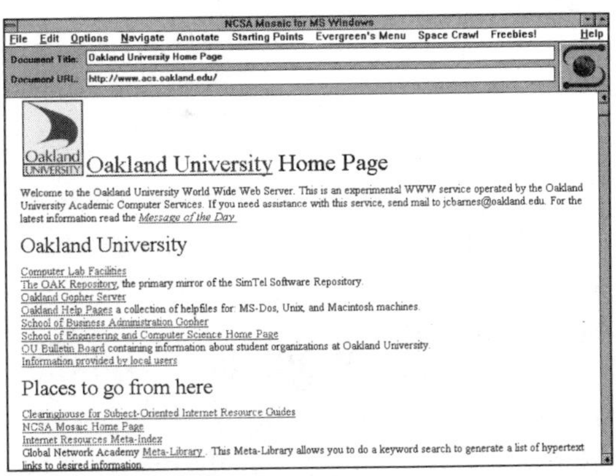

The Oakland University home page

National Center for Supercomputing Applications

Home to some of the country's most talented scientists, engineers, artists, educators, and all-around propellor heads, the National Center for Supercomputing Applications (NCSA) is a high-tech research facility that uses computational science on a high-performance computer to simulate natural phenomena that can't be investigated outside of the laboratory (did you get all of that?).

And don't let the pretty graphics fool you—this site is loaded with great Web info and links to other sites. Picked as the 1994 Best Overall Site on the Web, NCSA is most famous for being the spawning ground for Mosaic. You'll also find great information on what's new in Netdom and many documents helpful in using and contributing to the Web.

Getting There

`http://www.ncsa.uiuc.edu/`

Hot Links

- Multimedia Exhibits
- Software Tools
- Publications

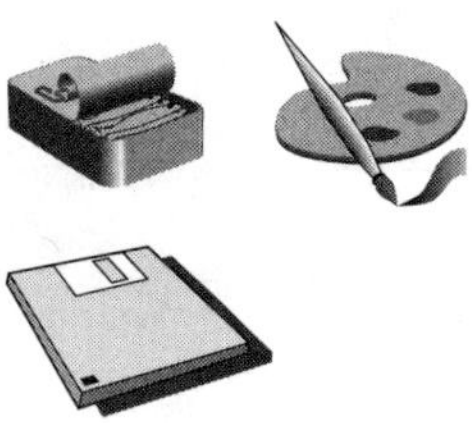

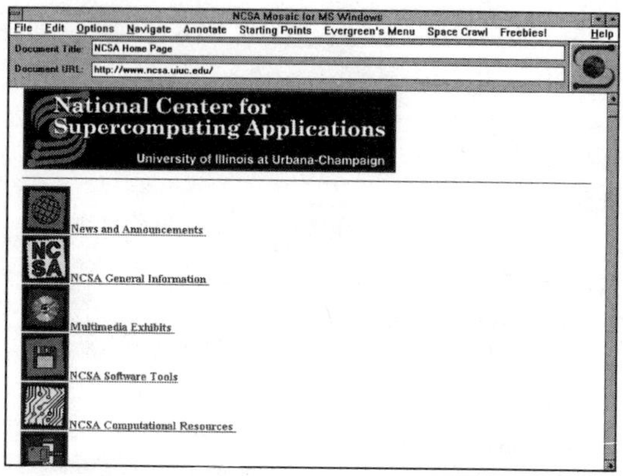

The National Center for Supercomputing Application's home page

The Surf's Up at Silicon Graphics, Inc.

Silicon Graphics, Inc. is a leading developer of applications to create three-dimensional graphics, and is a major corporate booster of and participant on the Internet. Now you can download *Silicon Surf*, SGI's online industry newsletter. Read the latest SGI news, learn about training courses, see videos, and get free software and graphics.

Getting There

`http://www.sgi.com/ss.home.page.html`

Hot Links

- HotWired
- Scott Adams Revealed

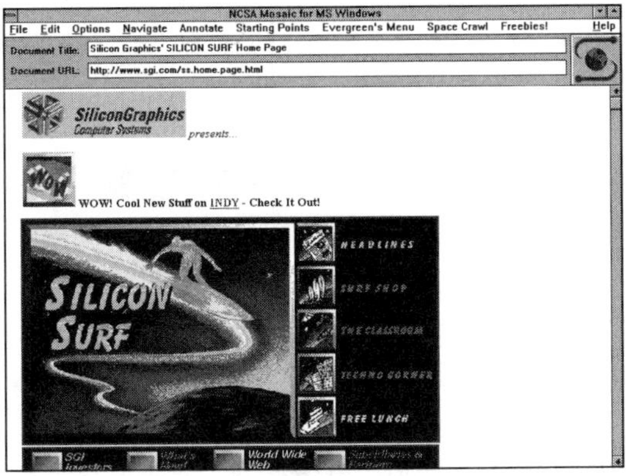

Silicon Graphics, Inc.'s home page

Not Just for Newtons

It's not just the auto industry that comes out with the occasional Edsel. Computer manufacturers have had their share, too (can *you* say PC Junior? And how about that Lisa?) The Newton was no exception. Before its time? Perhaps. Buggy as all get out? Without question. But just as you can still get parts for a '74 Pinto, so it goes with the Newton. If you're among the small band of semigullible users who bought the Newton (and you know who you are), here's the place to go for a one-stop Newton software shopping experience.

Even better, there are hundreds of Mac and PC programs available here as well, including online books, games, and programs for business or pleasure. Click on Mac or PC depending on your computer, then browse the directories.

Getting There

`http://newton.uiowa.edu/`

Hot Links

- Applications
- Books

- Code
- Games
- Utilities

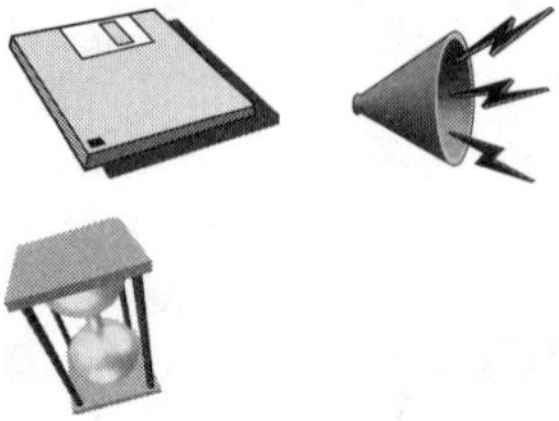

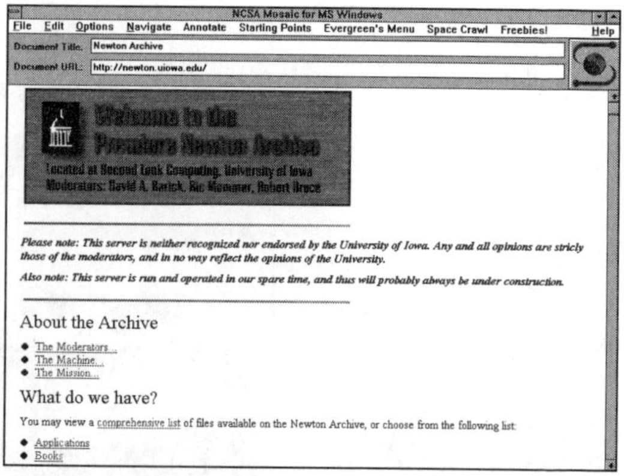

An archive of Newton software and information

Share and Share Alike

You grabbed Mosaic for free and now you're probably using the company telephone to tap into the Web. So none of this Internet stuff's costing you a penny, but you're still not satisfied. What else do you *want*? Well, how about some *more* free software?

If you're running Windows, here's the place to go for hot software available for the right price: *free* (at least on a trial basis). Shareware is the best approach for deciding what kind of software you need. You'll find hundreds of programs here to satisfy your software appetite.

Getting There

`http://coyote.csusm.edu/cwis/winworld/winworld.html`

Hot Links

- Newloads
- Favorite SLIP Clients

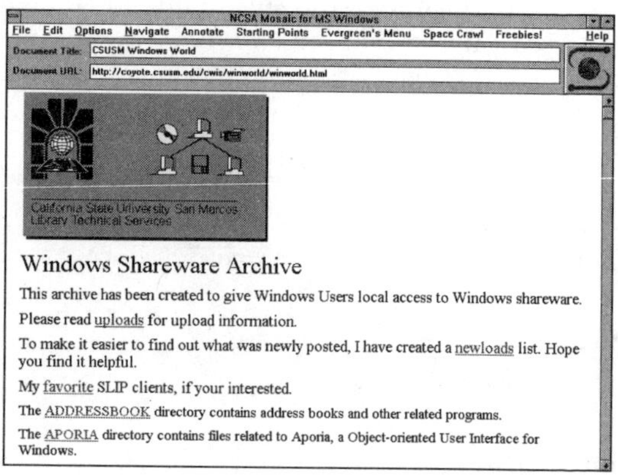

Windows shareware archive with software you can download

Microsoft Web

Want Bill Gates' paycheck? Want his job? Access Microsoft Corporation's World Wide Web server to get the latest information about the company's products and services. You'll find the latest news for developers, product announcements, fixes for bugs, employment opportunities at Microsoft, and more.

Getting There

`http://www.microsoft.com/`

Hot Links

- Windows News
- Employment Opportunities at Microsoft
- Microsoft Sales Information
- Microsoft TechNet

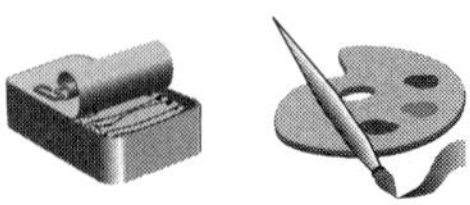

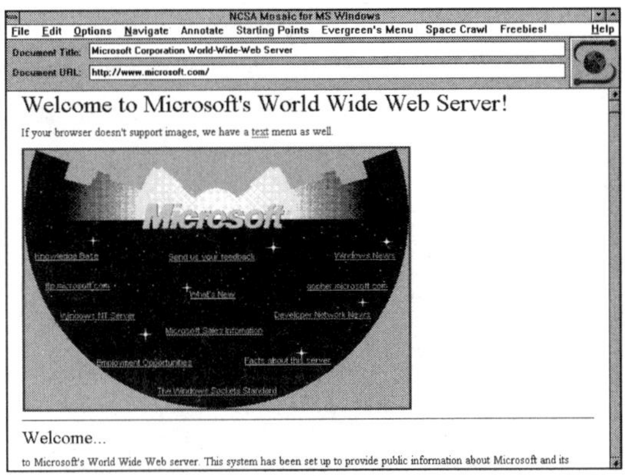

Microsoft Inc.'s home page

Information Highway Roadside Assistance

When you pull off the Information Highway for a quick pit stop and look under the hood, take a few minutes to check out this Web site. PC Tune and Lube is an online information service station that provides help and answers to all your PC-related woes and questions.

So maybe they won't wash your windows and there aren't any free balloons for the kids, but PC Tune and Lube does have valuable information about how your PC works and how to troubleshoot it when it won't. You'll learn more than you ever wanted to know about ethernets, partitioning your hard drive, com ports, what's next in operating systems, and lots more. Now back on the highway.

Getting There

`http://pclt.cis.yale.edu/pclt/default.htm`

Hot Links

- Windows on the World
- Surviving the Next OS
- Introduction to TCP/IP

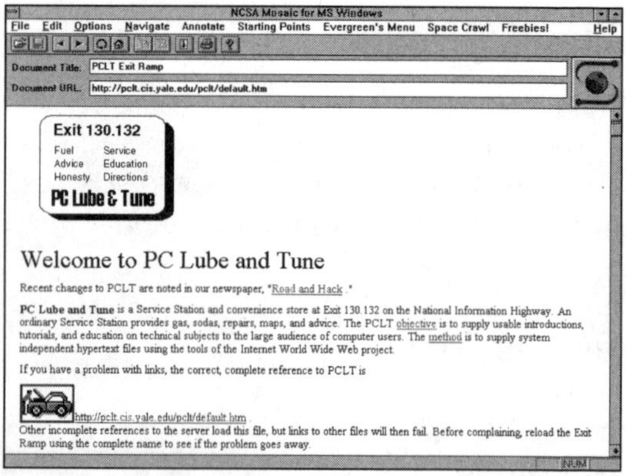

PC Lube and Tune's home page

Cooking

Now You're Cookin'

Tired of cheeseburgers, pizza, and Cheetos? Of course you're not. These are staples of every red-blooded artery-clogged American's diet. Giving up the junk would be like telling Mom and her apple pie to take a hike. Still, an occasional adventure into exotic dishes never hurts (permanently), if for no other reason than to help you garner new-found respect for anything that comes in a Styrofoam box.

And if you're going to get exotic, what better place to start than Africa? Here's the place to find recipes and online cookbooks from all over the African continent: appetizers from Algeria, salads from Senegal, and zesty desserts from Zimbabwe. You get the picture.

You may not want to load the images when you view this site unless you've got a lot of time on your hands (there are 65 images on the home page alone), but if you're interested in experimenting with some exotic culinary creations, these African cookbooks are *the* place to begin.

Getting There

`http://www.african.upenn.edu/African_Studies/Cookbook/`

Hot Links

Dozens of links to online recipes and cookbooks with an African flair

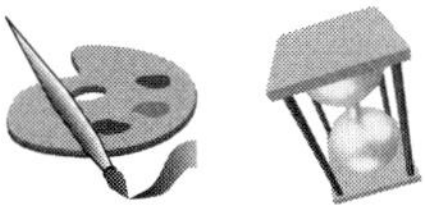

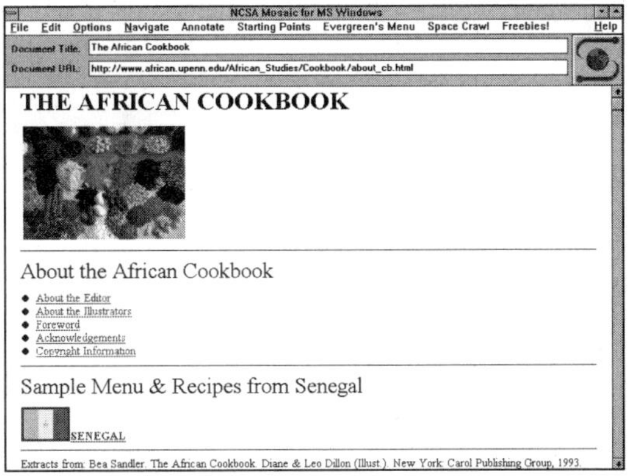

One of the numerous cookbooks with an African flair that you can view and download off the Web

Food Safety

Tucked in the corner of my publisher's lunch room hums the company refrigerator. Deep within, behind a half-eaten Subway sandwich and a forgotten pint of take-out Chinese something-or-other are the remains of a food now dark and furry. Nobody is sure exactly what it is or exactly where it came from, but who knows, with a little ketchup I think it just might be palatable.

Good thing I've got access to the Florida Agricultural Information Retrieval System's guide to food safety and handling. In addition to some great tips on food safety for babies and young children, home canning, and information on pesticides, maybe it'll help me decide the best way to prepare and serve my little culinary treat cum lab experiment.

Getting There

`http://hammock.ifas.ufl.edu/text/he/foodsf.html`

Hot Links

- Recreational Seafood Safety
- Egg Handling Handbook
- Botulism: It Only Takes a Taste!

Cyberbread and Butter

Surfers need sustenance! Here's a great site to help the culinarily challenged learn the difference between a sieve and a salad fork, a garlic press and a vegetable grater, a . . . well, you get the idea.

Actually this Web page includes information on three of the most important components for writers—food, coffee, and beer—so you can see why this is one of my more favorite sites.

Getting There

`http://pubweb.ucdavis.edu/Documents/Quotations/web/drivethru.html`

Hot Links

- Vegetarian
- Coffee
- Homebrew

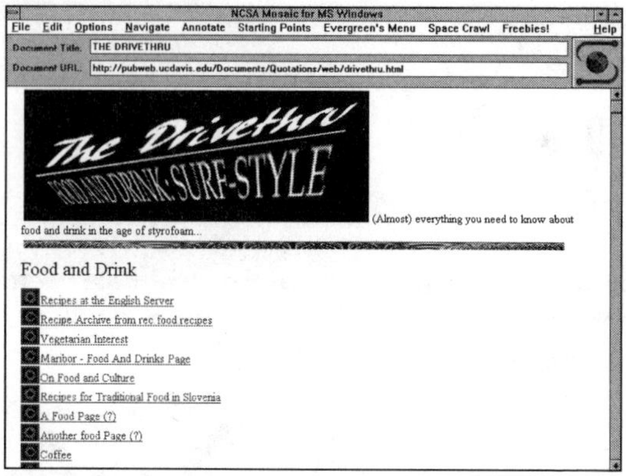

The Drivethru's home page

Tasty Treats for Web Crawlers

Looking for some high protein, low fat dessert ideas your family will love? Here are some treats you won't be able to keep in the cookie jar. It's not that everyone will want to eat them, it's just that they may get up and walk away on their own. The Iowa State entomology department has made available their list of culinary creepy crawlies on the Web for all to enjoy (your tuition dollars at work). Each recipe contains some variety of insect or invertebrate. And what a variety! I hear the Banana Worm Bread is to die for, though I know how hard it can be to find good army worms out of season. And the Rootworm Beetle Dip is right for any occasion.

I never really got the chance to test any of these recipes, busy as I am, but they sure sounded yummy. Now when your kids complain that there's nothing to eat, you can show them some of these recipes. Maybe *then* they'll stop complaining about the lime Jell-O.

Getting There

http://www.public.iastate.edu/~entomology/InsectsAsFood.html

Hot Links

- Iowa State's Entomology Image Gallery
- The Smithsonian Institution
- Biology Image Archive

While this isn't exactly the type of beetle used in Rootworm Beetle Dip, resourceful Web Surfers know they can use whatever's on hand

An A-Maize-ing Web Site

Tired of the same old popcorn? Myers' Gourmet Popcorn is trying to make sure you never again get the blahs when you pop. Their online catalog contains some exotic flavors you've probably never considered on popcorn: Cajun, Italian Blend, Mesquite BBQ, and more. Looking for something that will appeal to your sweet tooth? Try Butter Rum, Chocolate, Tutti Frutti, and, of course, Caramel.

There are over 20 popcorns that you can order online. Can't decide which one is best? Order up to three kinds in a specially divided container. And Myers will even remember to send gifts when you forget. Just send them a list of people to send gifts to for the year and they'll take care of the rest. Finally, popcorn worth sneaking into the theater (if the aroma doesn't give you away).

Getting There

http://www.aus.xanadu.com/GlassWings/arcade/myers/mgp.html

Hot Links

- Popcorn Flavors
- Decorator Tins
- Purchasing Details

Myers' Gourmet Popcorn home page

Education

AskERIC Virtual Library

The Web isn't all fun and games (though it is mostly). Remember, the Internet's original purpose was as a tool to share research information among universities. The only thing that's changed is the number of players. Now millions of users can access educational resources.

ERIC (Educational Resource Information Center) is a federally funded national information system that provides access to many education-related resources on the Internet, like:

- An online dictionary
- Electronic books through Project Gutenberg
- An acronym dictionary
- The *CIA World Fact Book*

Getting There

http://eryx.syr.edu/COWSHome.html

Hot Links

- Sunsite at the University of North Carolina
- NCSA Mosaic Home Page

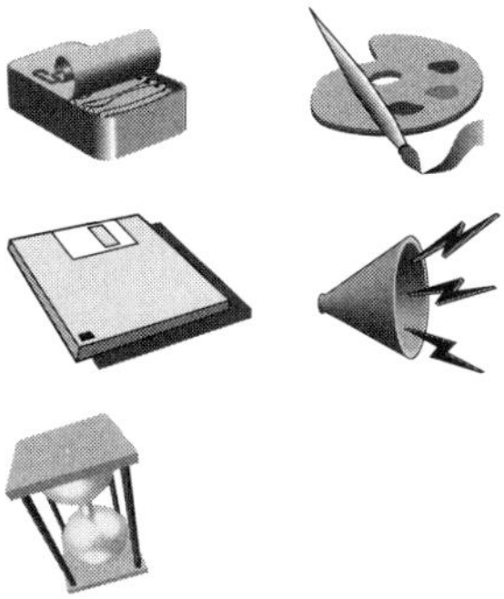

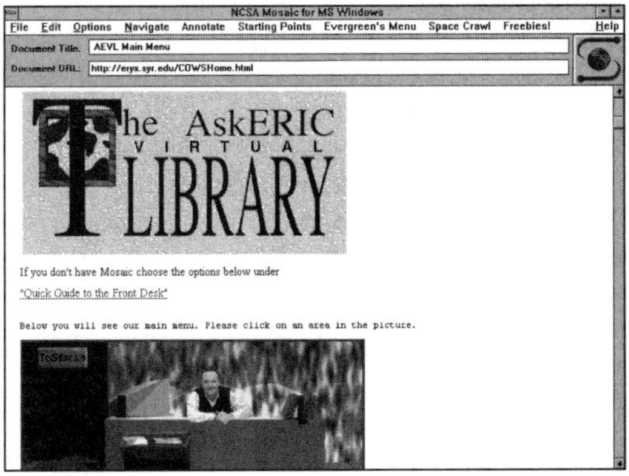

AskERIC's home page

Project GeoSim

Project GeoSim, a joint research project of the Departments of Computer Science and Geography at Virginia Tech (try saying *that* five times fast), is creating educational software for introductory geography courses. You'll find tutorials and simulation programs to help you test your knowledge of topography, landforms, and climate—in short, geography.

Getting There

`http://geosim.cs.vt.edu/index.html`

Hot Links

- Virginia Tech
- Blacksburg Electronic Village

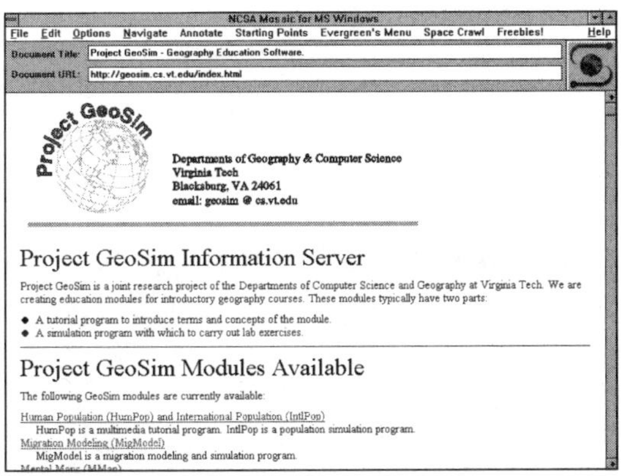

Project GeoSim's home page

Explore the Exploratorium

The Exploratorium, one of San Francisco's most famous museums, is really much more than a museum. It also functions as an "educational center." With a collection of over 650 interactive, hands-on exhibits covering science, art, nature, and technology, it provides maximum exposure to the sciences.

Now you don't have to walk through its front doors to enjoy what the Exploratorium has to offer. You can access many of the exhibits through the World Wide Web, including an extensive collection of images and software.

Getting There

`http://www.exploratorium.edu/`

Hot Links

- The Palace of Fine Arts
- How to Become a Member

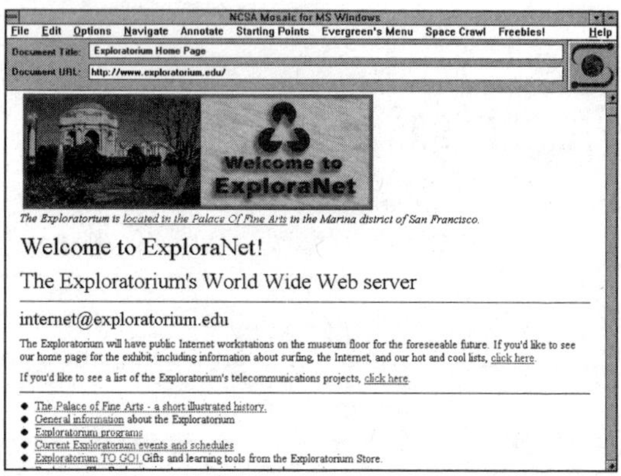

San Francisco's Exploratorium home page

Education Online Sources

School's in session on the Internet and virtual classrooms are thriving. This site lists scores of education-related sights for teachers and students, with everything from course information on language, science, math, adventure (though I don't remember that being a course), and many more.

You can also get information about departments of education around the country, policy and reform movements, special projects for education on the Internet, museums, planetariums, zoos, lists of schools plugged into the Net, and tons of other helpful links for anyone interested in improving education.

Getting There

`http://archive.phish.net/eos1/webs_image.html`

Hot Links

- Free-Nets
- Mars Missions
- JASON Project Voyage 5
- Early Instruments Museum

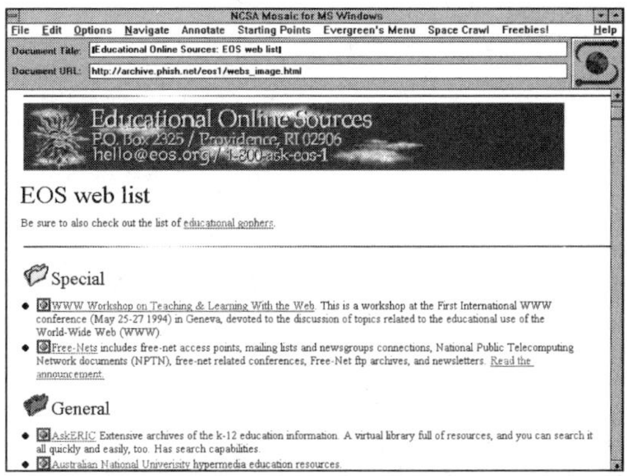

The Educational Online Sources' home page

Learn Globally

The Global SchoolHouse, funded in part by the National Science Foundation, connects 17 K through 12 schools nationally and internationally so they can share and exchange information in this collaborative learning project. Students and teachers communicate with each other by using the tools available on the Internet (E-mail, video-conferencing, the Web, and more).

Besides helping to shape the way kids learn, the Global SchoolHouse Project is demonstrating how the Internet can be used as a classroom tool for research and collaborative learning. Definitely an exciting experiment in education; let's hope we see more projects like this in cyberspace.

Getting There

http://k12.cnidr.org/gshwelcome.html

Hot Links

- GSH Objectives
- GSH Site Reports
- GSH Projects

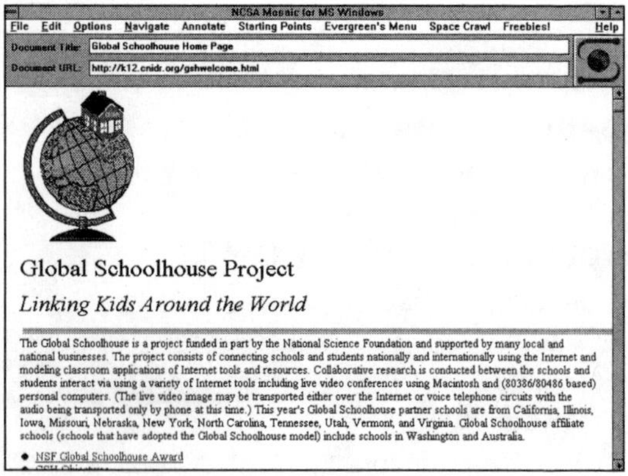

The Global SchoolHouse home page

Entertainment

Roulette, Internet Style

Spin the wheel at URouLette, "the world's first random URL generator." This program sends you to a randomly chosen Web site somewhere in cyberspace. Where you'll end up is anybody's guess, but write me when you get there.

One word of advice: Experienced netters know that offensive material exists on the Web, and random shots in the dark are bound to eventually turn up something less than tasteful (though odds are highly against it). Keep this in mind as you throw caution to the wind and bet the farm on double zero.

Getting There

http://kuhttp.cc.ukans.edu/cwis/organizations/kucia/uroulette/uroulette.html

Hot Links

Your guess is as good as anybody's

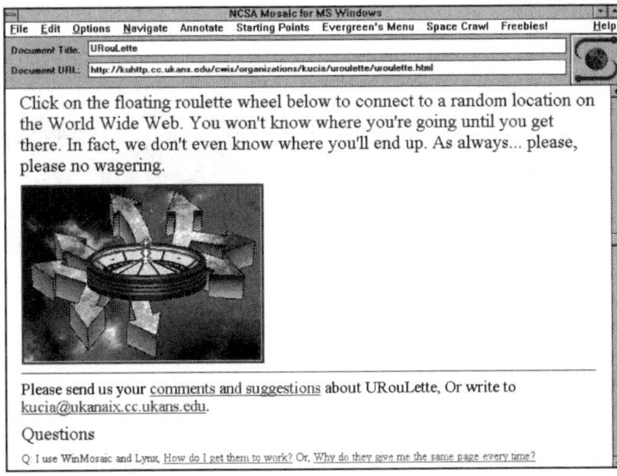

URouLette's home page

Underground Net

Promising entertainment that doesn't fit into the mainstream, Underground Net delivers. Besides being a great source for music samples from many hot and soon-to-be-hot bands, there's concert info, video clips, and the Internet's first weekly comedy show. Promising "anarchy at its worst," this site is still growing, but it's getting more bizarre with each addition.

Download a free Beastie Boys screen saver (I didn't have the guts), sample some sound files from up-and-coming bands, or check out *Un-Cabaret*, the Internet's first weekly alternative comedy show, complete with video and audio clips. For a real taste of the bizarre, try the digital art gallery for art "definitely not commissioned by the NEA." I'd like to show you a sample, but current laws being what they are . . . .

Getting There

`http://bazaar.com/underground.html`

Hot Links

- Space Calendar
- Coffee Pot
- Digital Art Gallery

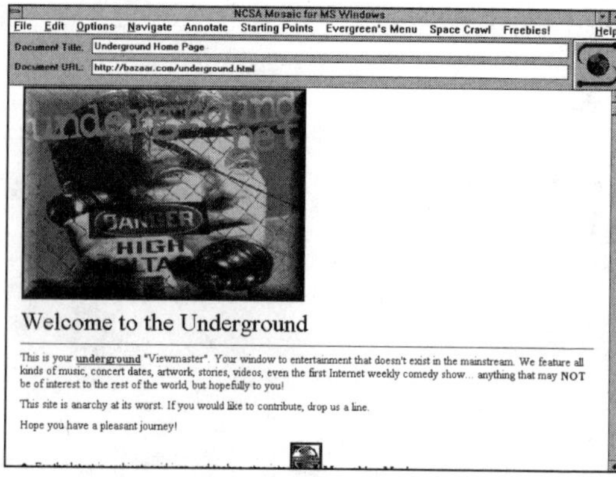

Underground Net's home page

Oh Give Me a Home . . .

Where the Buffalo Roam, a ragged-edge, black and white, hand-drawn cartoon, is definitely for the more subversive among us. Far more gonzo than Dr. Fun and lots more edge than Doonesbury, the strip is drawn weekly by Hans Bjordahl for the Colorado Daily, where it has appeared since 1987.

If you want, you can view previous cartoons going back several weeks, as well as offer your opinions on the cartoons (or anything else, apparently) over the Net.

Getting There

`http://xor.com:80/wtbr/`

Hot Links

- The Archives
- The Catalog
- Plaza Outlets

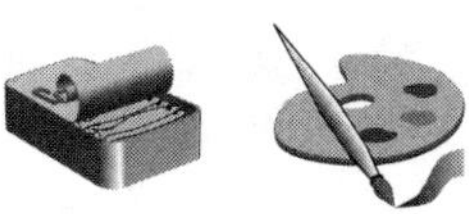

The Where the Buffalo Roam home page

Johnny Nemo

With the promise that the very act of visiting this Web site would instantly make me more attractive to the opposite sex, how could I refuse? Alas, according to my wife, no changes were immediately detectable, but it was still worth the time.

Johnny Nemo is sort of a space-age Sam Spade, a private eye from futuristic New London. Follow the adventures of this comic book hero on the Web as he sleuths and sleazes.

Getting There

`http://underground.net/Nemo/nemo.html`

Hot Links

- New London
- Underground.net

PG-13
Adult Supervision

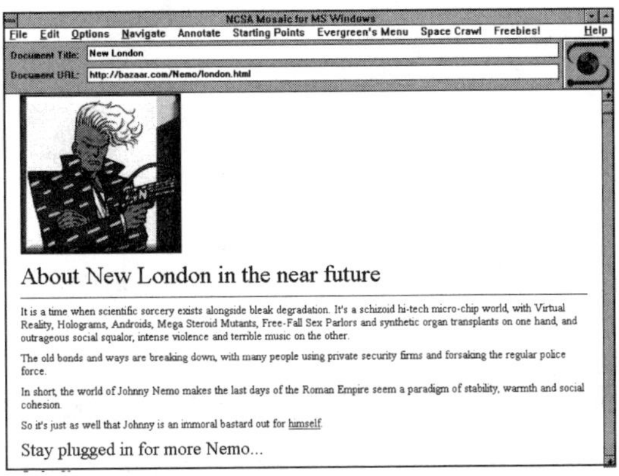

The Johnny Nemo home page

Virtual Happy Hour

It had to happen eventually. Now when you want to belly up to the bar, you can do it in cyberspace. Miller Genuine Draft has introduced the MGD Tap Room, a virtual pub where you can mingle with a virtual In Crowd and talk about In Music, In Fashion, In Art, and In Sports while you take In a few virtual beers. The downside is that no one will actually offer you a real beer, but then you're virtually assured that no one will throw up on your loafers, either.

Updated on the first of each month, the information at the MGD Tap Room is compiled by an impressive array of writers from alternative weeklies around the country. While this site is a lot of fun, let's hope it never replaces the real thing.

Getting There

`http://www.mgdtaproom.com`

Hot Links

- Pastap
- SpeakEasy
- TapTalk

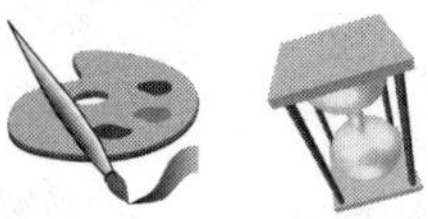

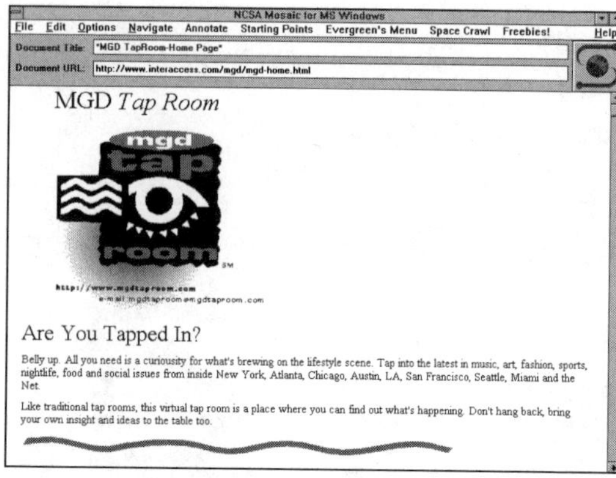

MGD Tap Room's home page

Who's This Week's Geek of the Week?

Geek of the Week is a weekly half-hour "talk radio" program on the Internet you can download and listen to on your computer. "How can I do that?" you ask. With a sound card and *lots and lots* of memory. Each show features a prominent member of the technical community to discuss issues related to the Internet, networking, and computing—definitely an intelligent alternative to today's trade press. Some past guests have included Milo Medin of the NASA Science Internet, David Crocker of Silicon Graphics, and Jeff Case (a.k.a. Dr. SNMP).

Along with the featured guests, you'll be subjected to—er, presented with—weekly featurettes, including Name That Acronym, The Incidental Tourist, and restaurant reviews from out-of-the-way places. Radio junkies, enjoy!

Getting There

`http://www.cmf.nrl.navy.mil/radio/ITRgeek.readme.html`

Hot Links

- Legal Stuff
- Name That Acronym
- Book Byte

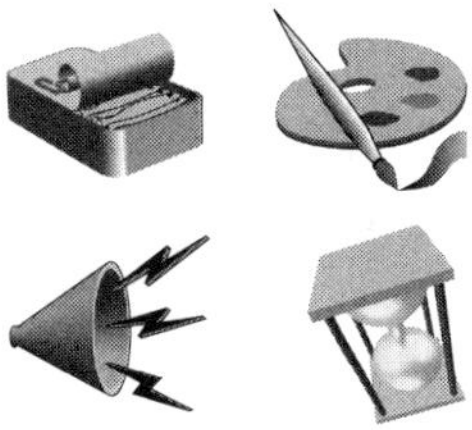

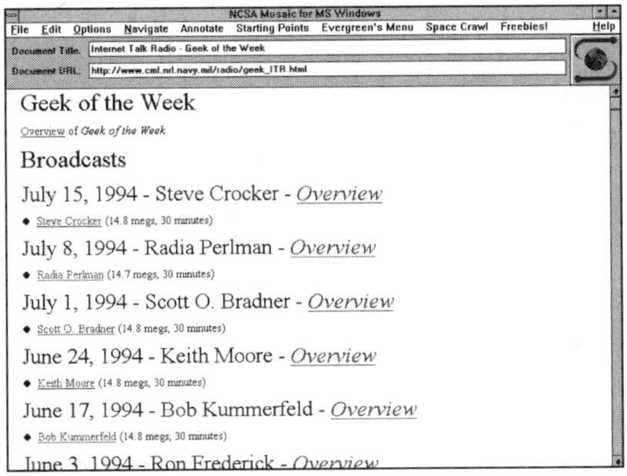

The Geek of the Week home page

The Doctor Is In

Doctor Fun, a single-panel cartoon updated daily on the Net, has been a reading requirement for many Web users since it was launched in September 1993 with "Clothes Make the Spam." Since then, Dave Farley's cartoon, drawn entirely online, has become one of the most popular Web features.

Described as sort of an online Far Side, Dr. Fun is only available on the Internet, so log on and get your daily dose of the Doctor.

Getting There

`http://sunsite.unc.edu/Dave/drfun.html`

Hot Links

- Today's Doctor Fun
- Doctor Fun Archive

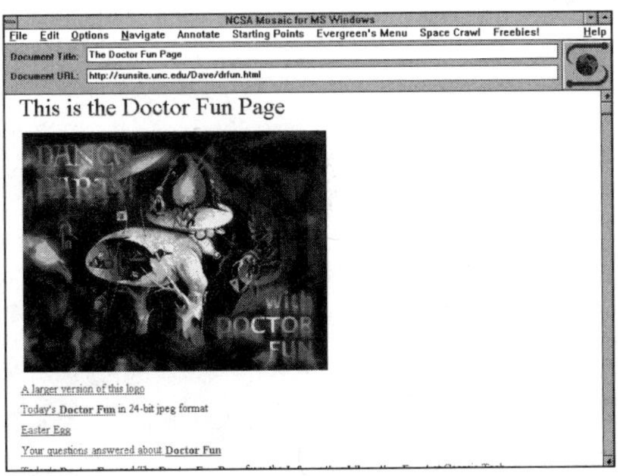

The Dr. Fun home page

Games

CSUSM Games to Download

Tell the truth: Did you really buy that computer to be more productive and efficient? Of course not. You bought it to play time-consuming, efficiency-eating, mindless video games.

Having no games on your computer is like having no speakers on your stereo; what's the point? Dig deeply enough in the hidden subdirectories of even the most straight-laced computer user and you're sure to find a couple of games. Rumor has it that the self-annointed grand daddy of the Info Highway, veep Al Gore himself, plays a couple of quick hands of Solitaire between funerals for foreign dignitaries.

Al may not know about this site yet, so I'll clue him in. There are megabytes of games to choose from: shoot 'em ups, gambling programs, cards, arcade-style action adventures, mindless utilities, and lots more. All it will cost you is the time to download the games, so you might want to do it at the office. Even your boss has to admire that kind of resourcefulness.

Getting There

`http://coyote.csusm.edu/cwis/winworld/games.html`

Hot Links

No links, but with all the games you'll find here, why go anywhere else?

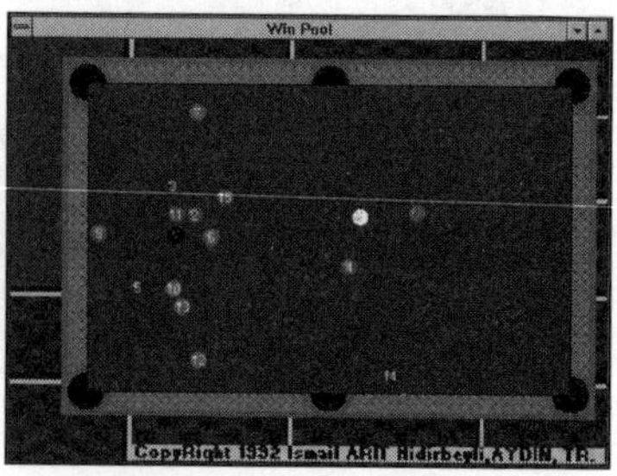

Play a little 8-ball with this neat little billiards program

Zarf's List

Sure, you could browse the Web till the electronic cows come home looking for hot games to download, if you enjoy that kind of thing. But with jillions of gigabytes to sift, you'll end up wading through a lot of muck just to find a few jewels. Why not let someone else do the work for you? That's what I did. (I'm not a masochist, after all.) There are many sites on the Web that serve mainly as pointers to other sites on a particular subject.

One of the best gaming sites I found was *Zarf's List of Interactive Games on the Web.* The listings here are actually divided into two sections: interactive games and interactive toys, the distinction being that, when playing with toys, you don't have any final goal in mind, such as saving mankind or at least getting the highest score before you're turned into charcoal.

The games available here include Battleship, Minesweeper, Shoot the Spy, and an ESP test (or did you already know that?). Toys include a biorhythm reader, virtual frog dissections, and a dream interpreter.

Getting There

http://www.cs.cmu.edu:8001/afs/cs.cmu.edu/user/zarf/www/games.html

Hot Links

- Guess the Disease
- Lite Brite
- The Magic 8-Ball
- Other Stuff

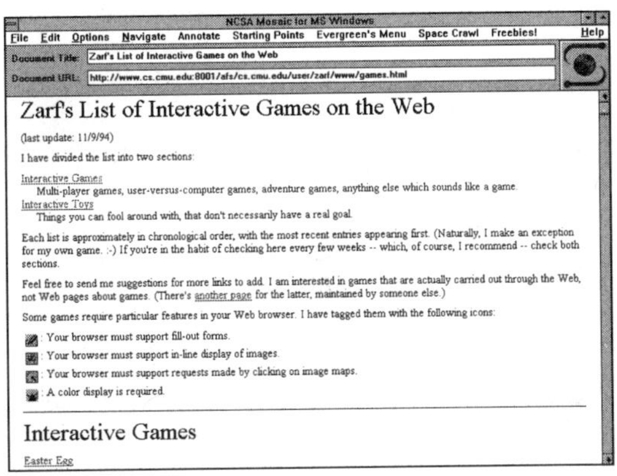

Home page for Zarf's List of Interactive Games on the Web

You're Doomed

In a nutshell, Doom is a three-dimensional action adventure feast in virtual reality. Created by id (pronounced *id*) Software, Doom has become to PCs in the '90s what Pac Man was to singles bars in the '80s, except with a lot more blood and gore.

In Doom, you take the role of space marine, recently stationed on Mars—armpit of the galaxy—with the boring task of guarding radioactive waste facilities for the Union Aerospace Corporation. Keeping with the tradition of all successful video games, hell quickly breaks loose and you soon find yourself battling for your life against grotesque and evil aliens.

This Web site points you to the best places to download free copies of Doom, get the latest info and updates, connect with other Doomophiles, and download FAQs and art.

Getting There

`http://www.cs.umd.edu/~lgas/computers/doom.html`

Hot Links

- DoomGate
- FTP Sites
- Doom Binaries

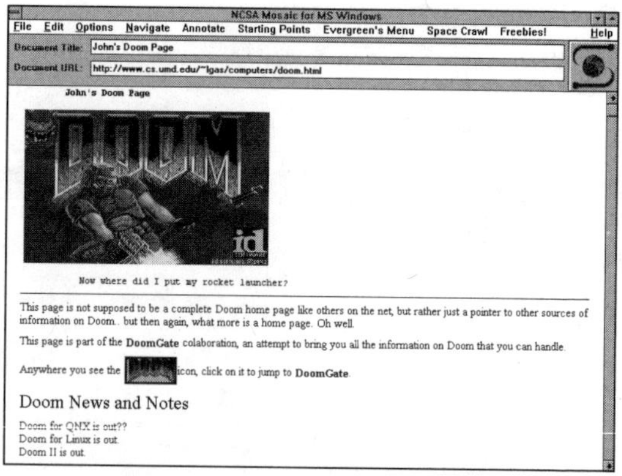

One of the many Doom home pages on the Web

Help for Nerds

At last, help for anyone suffering from the pain and itching—oh, wait. Wrong sufferers. Here's help for anyone afraid they may suffer from the humiliating disease of nerdity. While there *is* help for those diagnosed early enough, if left unchecked nerdity can spread quickly and is often transferred from fathers to sons (for some reason it is found most often in men).

Those who do suffer can still lead surprisingly normal lives, and many have become very successful (Bill Gates, Ross Perot, Elmer Fudd, to name a few). Take this test and find out if you're destined to spend the rest of your life wearing leisure suits and watching reruns of Dobie Gillis. Good luck!

Getting There

`http://gonzo.tamu.edu/nerd.html`

Hot Links

Advanced Nerd Test

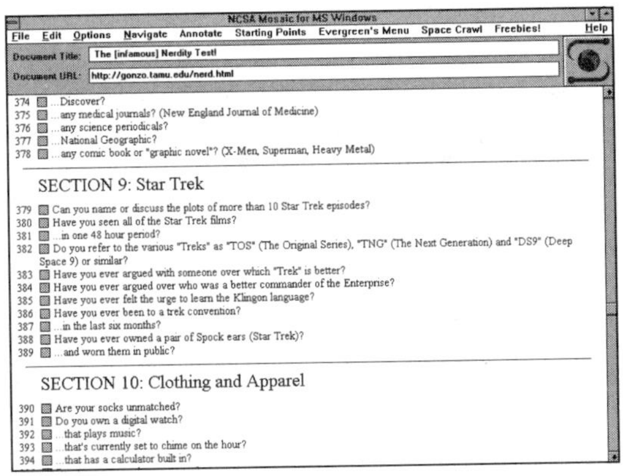

A page lifted from the Nerdity Test

Let the Games Begin

This Web page has lots of game, recreation, and sports info. You'll find links to popular board games (like chess, backgammon, and othello), card games (bridge and poker), role-playing games, dancing (like the International Association of Gay Square Dance Clubs, though this might be stretching it a bit on the games theme), pastimes (fishing, kiting, skydiving), and more.

Getting There

`http://www.cis.ufl.edu/~thoth/library/recreation.html`

Hot Links

- The Virtual Pub
- World Wide Windsurfing
- Outdoor Participatory Sports
- Foosball Archive

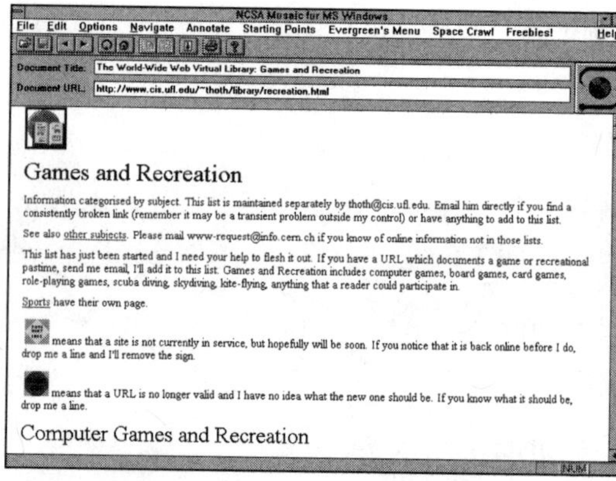

One of about a billion game pages on the Web

Government

Bean Counting Online

The Bureau of the Census has its finger on America's collective pulse more than any other government agency. From its fingertips to yours comes all the information compiled from the U.S. Census, plus a few extra bells and whistles.

Click on the PopClock to get an *up to the second* estimate of the U.S. resident population xxx,xxx,xxx as of xxx). If you have the time, check out the weekly radio broadcast of *Window on America*, produced by the Public Information Office of the Census Bureau, broadcast in English and Spanish.

Trivia lovers will get their fill of interesting factoids about the U.S. population. (Did you know that Americans consume about 22 pounds of candy a year per person? *That's* a sweet tooth.)

Getting There

`http://www.census.gov`

Hot Links

- Radio Broadcast
- Art Gallery
- Excellent Sites

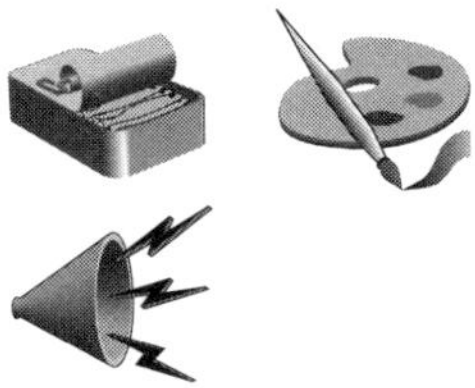

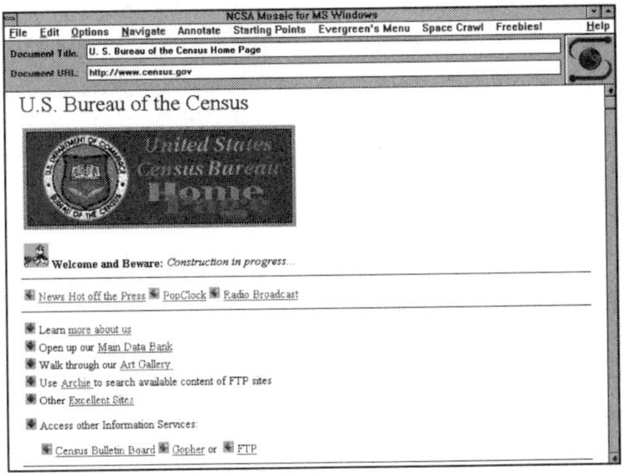

The U.S. Census Bureau's home page

The Mother of All Libraries

The Library of Congress has been wired into the Internet for several years now, but only recently has it been available through the World Wide Web. "So what's so different about LOC on the Web?" you ask.

And I'm glad you *have* asked.

From within the Web, you have direct and super-easy access to the LOC's online data and exhibits, including photographic and sound collections from the American Memory Project, the African-American Culture exhibit, and History exhibit, to name a few.

You can also get instant analyses on many foreign countries through the Country Studies/Area Handbook Program. These handy links give you the latest data on the political, economic, and social climates of several foreign countries, plus analyses of their national security systems. Now you can know (almost) as much about foreign affairs as your favorite (or least favorite) local congressperson. Ever considered running for office?

Getting There

`http://lcweb.loc.gov/homepage/lchp.html`

Hot Links

- Exhibits
- American Memory
- Global Electronic Library

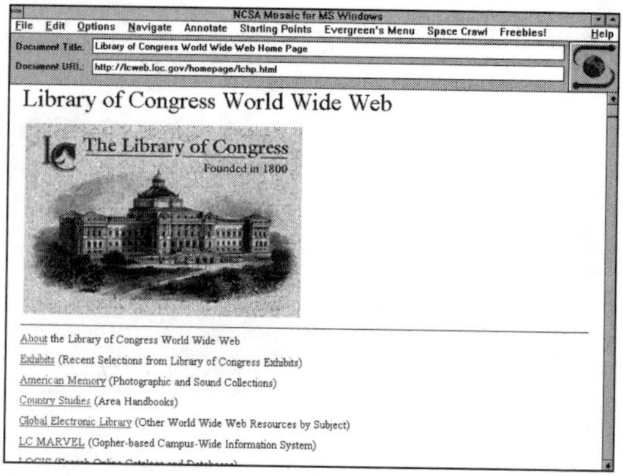

The Library of Congress's home page

Kennedy Home Page

Close though it was, Teddy Kennedy pulled another win from his hat, so it's back to business as usual for the senator. Part of that business is keeping Web-walking constituents updated on the happenings in Washington.

This Web page provides Sen. Kennedy's voting record, press releases by the senator's office, information on where Massachusetts voters can go for more information, and links to other Senate and House sites.

Getting There

`http://www.ai.mit.edu/projects/iiip/Kennedy/homepage.html`

Hot Links

- Online Senate Documents
- US FY95 Budget
- US Senate
- US House

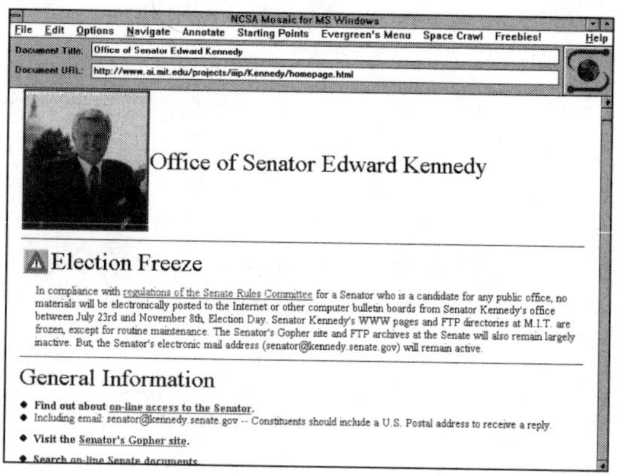

Sen. Kennedy's home page

Hop Onboard NavyOnLine

Landlubbers who want to keep abreast of what's happening on the Defense Department's high seas can check out this interesting site in Netdom. NavyOnLine offers the drydocked set the latest information on what's going on with the men and women who spend their duty time defending the seven seas.

Get the latest research data and current events from NavyOnLine, including Navy news from the Navy News Service and a fascinating look at the Naval Research Laboratory (founded by Thomas Edison in 1923 for those of you who still remember the Depression as an economic event rather than a psychological malaise). There are some cool pictures of naval ships being built at the Naval Surface Warfare Center, plus tons of other information about the U.S. Navy. This is a great site for Naval ship buffs.

Getting There

`http://www.ncts.navy.mil/`

Hot Links

- Space and Naval Warfare Systems Command
- Department of Defense Resources
- Office of the Secretary of Defense

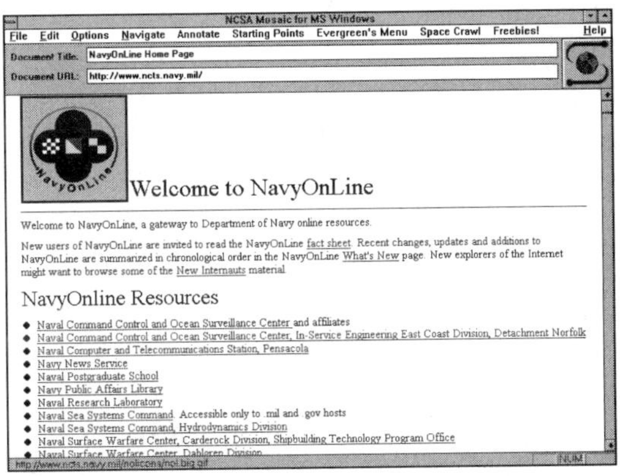

NavyOnLine's home page

Fight for Your Rights

Named for human-rights pioneer Diana Vincent-Daviss, Diana is the University of Cincinnati's database of hundreds of human-rights and other legal documents available on the Web for your perusal. Diana was created to "promote the creation, preservation, organization, and dissemination of primary and secondary electronic legal materials critical to human-rights research," according to Taylor Fitchett, UC's law library director.

Much of the database contents are documents from the U.N. and the O.A.S., although documents from several other sources are included. Putting the entire contents of Diana online for Web researchers is a work in progress, so wear your hard hat and please be patient.

Getting There

`http://www.law.uc.edu/Diana`

Hot Links

- Primary Human Rights Sources
- Secondary Human Rights Sources

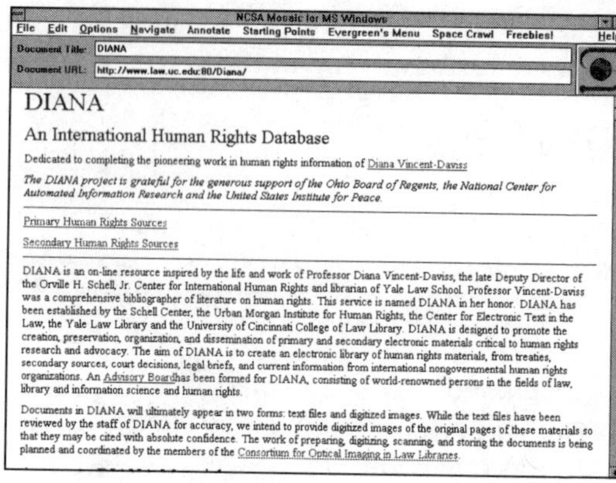

The University of Cincinnati's human-rights home page

Whitehouse Online

A recent media gala at the White House, complete with a speech by Al Gore and a hearty cyber-welcome from the president, kicked off the introduction of the White House in cyberspace. According to Vice President Al Gore, the White House Web site will bring "the entire federal government to your desktop computer." I doubt it would all fit, but it doesn't matter. At press time, it was up and running, albeit with a few bugs still to work out (sounds like a metaphor for our government).

You can listen to a welcome speech from the president, view an electronic photo album, get White House tour information, register as an online guest, even hear an audio file featuring Socks, First Cat.

Once the bugs are worked out, this should be a fun, informative site (and if health care reform is ever accomplished, I'm sure that will be fun and informative as well).

Getting There

http://www.whitehouse.gov

Hot Links

- FedWorld
- Interactive Citizens Handbook

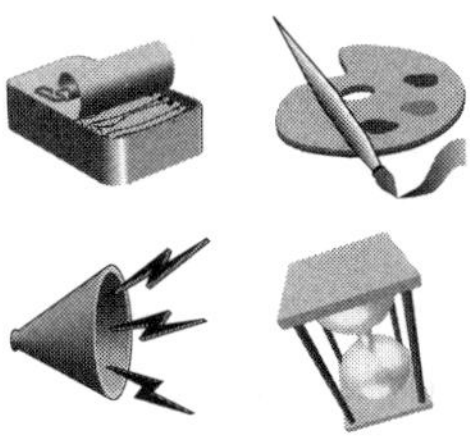

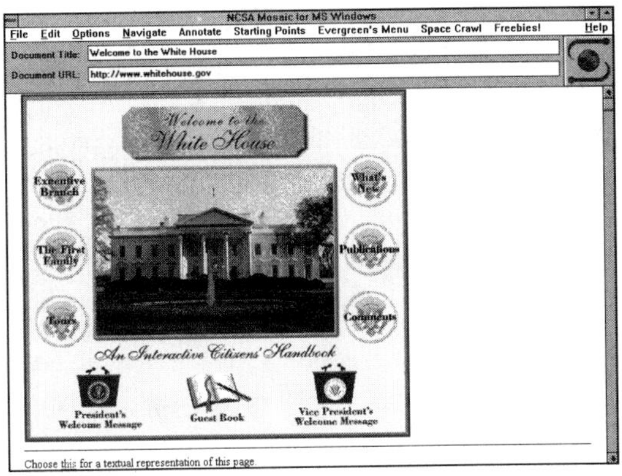

The White House comes to the Web

Health

Help for Cancer Patients

Winner of the Best of the Web '94 Award for Best Professional Service, OncoLink is a great source for dozens of cancer-related topics. The first multimedia oncology information resource placed on the Internet, OncoLink was established as a clearinghouse for information relevant to the field of oncology and is used to educate health care personnel and cancer patients and their families, and to rapidly collect information pertinent to oncology.

Check out some of the great book reviews such as the one for *The Breast Cancer Companion*, information on pain management, and amusing ways to handle stress, to name a few of the many ways to put this site to good use.

Getting There

`http://cancer.med.upenn.edu/`

Hot Links

- Book Reviews
- Frequently Asked Questions About Cancer
- Other Cancer Resources

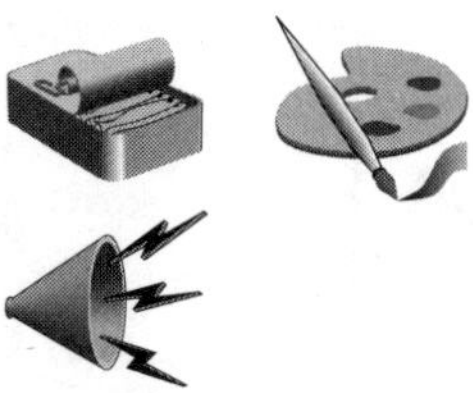

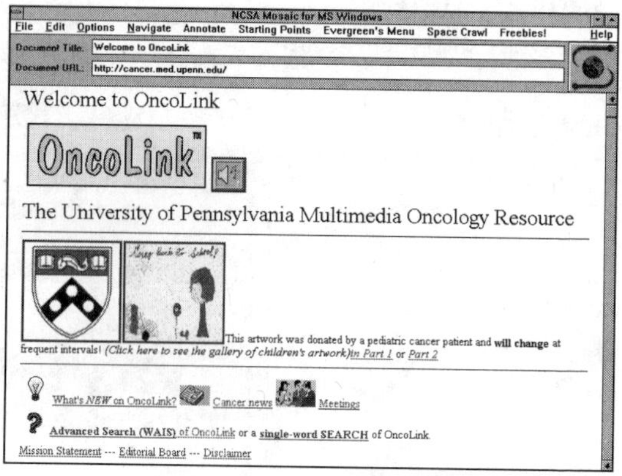

Cancer information can be found through OncoLink

Good for What Ails Ya

Good Medicine Magazine is an informative and entertaining bi-monthly guide to better health and preventive medicine through the interaction of traditional and holistic medicine (that means pills with lots of holes in 'em, right?). This Internet version of the magazine gives you a glimpse at what you can expect in every hardcopy issue.

Recent articles have included information on aromatherapy, the art of breathing (and you thought you already knew that one), and an in-depth guide to herbs. Check out a copy: If you can't be wealthy and wise, at least stay healthy.

Getting There

`http://none.coolware.com:80/health/good_med/`

Hot Links

- Publishing Information
- Coolware

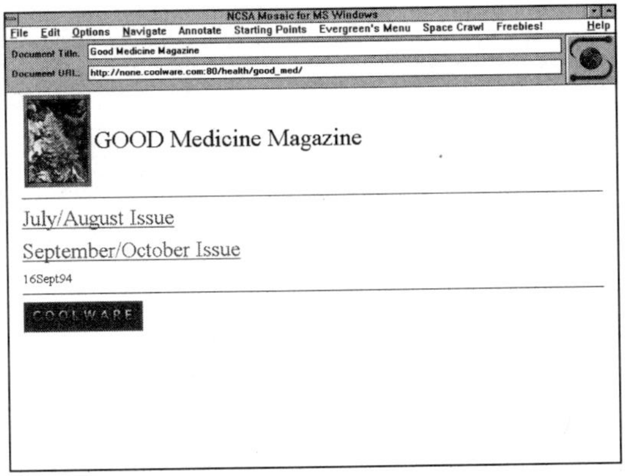

Home page for Good Medicine Magazine

Nightingale Nights

I suspect that if you've ever had a question about the field of nursing (like "Whatever happened to those cool Florence Nightingale clip-on caps they used to wear?") you'll find your answer here. The College of Nursing at the University of Tennessee at Knoxville is home to this comprehensive guide to nursing-related Web sites. With only about a billion pointers to information about the nursing profession, this site is by no means complete, though it does come close.

You'll find information on the prognosis for national health care (and it ain't looking good), nursing programs offered at other colleges, professional publications available on the Net, and many other health-related sites.

Getting There

`http://nightingale.con.utk.edu:70/0/homepage.html`

Hot Links

Too many to list, but they include the politics of health care, nursing publications, education resources, and much more.

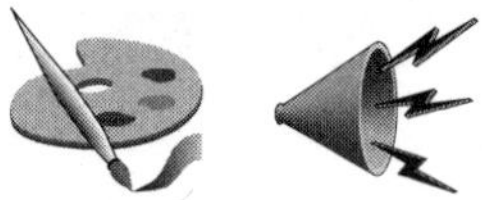

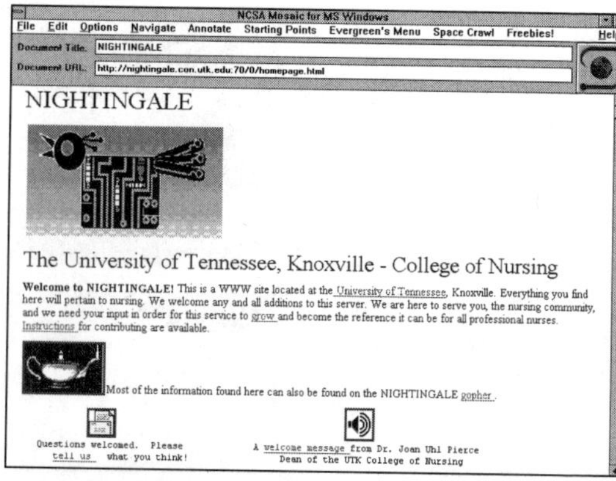

Information for the nursing profession can be found on the Nightingale home page

Stomach This!

Access this Web site and feel the burn. It may not look like much, but it contains *abs*olutely the best information you'll find for being able to see your shoes again. The Abdominal Training FAQ contains tips designed as an introduction to abdominal training to help you on your way to better fitness, or to at least look good in a pair of boxers again.

Getting There

`http://clix.aarnet.edu.au/misc.fitness/abdominal-training.html`

Hot Links

- Stretching FAQ
- Ab training FAQs

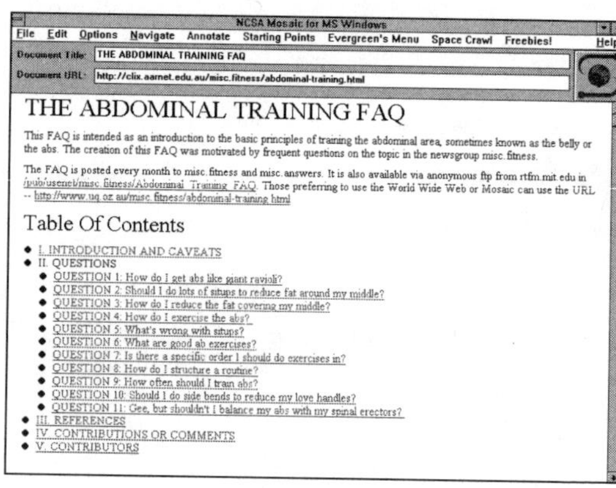

Flatten your stomach with help from the Abdominal Training FAQ

Take Your Cyberpet to the NetVet

This archive was originally created by Ken Boschert, DVM, to provide information and resources on all-things animal, especially for biologists, zoologists, and veterinarians. But it's grown to become more all-encompassing. Here you'll find online issues of *Discover* magazine, *Environmental Magazine, Issues in Science and Technology, Journal of Neuroscience*, subscription sites for professional organizations and newsletters, and a variety of other scientific and medical information.

Getting There

`http://netvet.wustl.edu/On:\e-zoo.html`

Hot Links

- The Electronic Zoo
- NetVet Gopher Server
- Selected World Wide Web Sites

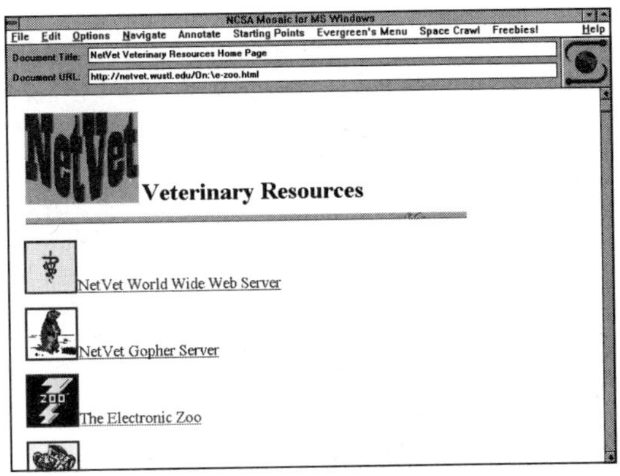

Veterinary resources can be found through the NetVet home page

History

Do You Remember When . . . ?

You may think Congress can't do anything right, but at least their library's on the ball: Direct from the special collections of the Library of Congress, it's the *American Memory*, a great Web hangout for students of all ages. Created from the enormous archives of the LOC, this special exhibition provides a fascinating glimpse back in time, with these four outstanding exhibits on American history:

- *The Nation's Forum* contains 59 sound recordings of speeches by American leaders from the turn of the century, including Warren G. Harding, James Cox, and Franklin D. Roosevelt. Speeches range from one to five minutes.
- *Selected Civil War Photographs* contains over 1,000 photographs of troop encampments, battle scenes, and portraits of Confederate and Union officers. Most of the photographs were taken by famed Civil War photographer Matthew Brady.
- *Carl Van Vechten Photographs* consists of nearly 1,500 photographs taken by Van Vechten between 1932 and 1964. The bulk of the collection consists of portraits of celebrities. A much smaller portion is an assortment of American landscapes.
- *Color Photographs from the FSA and OWI* is actually two collections of color photographs taken by the Farm Security Administration and the Office of War Information between 1939 and 1945. The FSA collection contains over 600 photos depicting farm laborers and life in rural America, Puerto Rico, and the Virgin Islands. The OWI collection of nearly 1,000 photos focuses on women factory workers, railroads, aviation training, and other aspects of World War II mobilization.

Getting There

`http://rs6.loc.gov/amhome.html`

Hot Links

- Library of Congress Home Page
- Civil War Time Line
- How to Order Photographic Prints

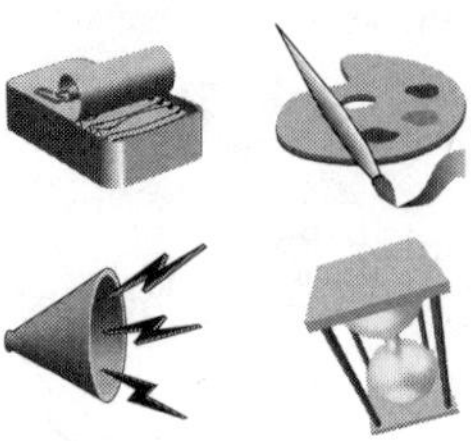

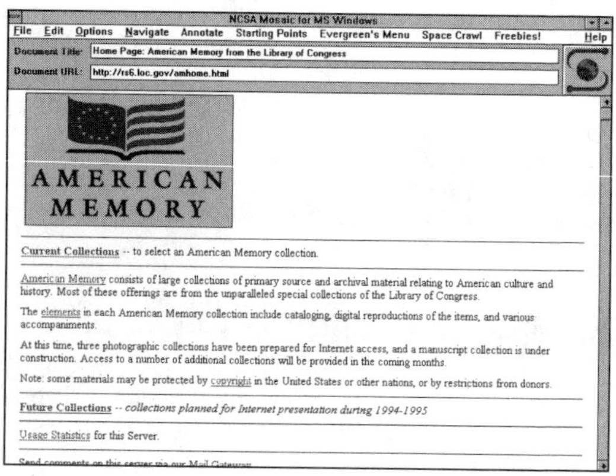

The American Memory home page

We the People...

A nominee for Best of the Web '94 for Document Design, this site has brought the United States Constitution into the 21st century with a hypertext version. One click of the mouse takes you to the Preamble, another will list all the signers. What's especially handy are the links between provisions in the Constitution that have been amended or somehow affected by other amendments, for instance slavery (Article IV, Section II) and its abolition (Amendment XIII)—your boss notwithstanding.

Getting There

http://www.law.cornell.edu/constitution/constitution.overview.html

Hot Links

- Signers
- Amendments

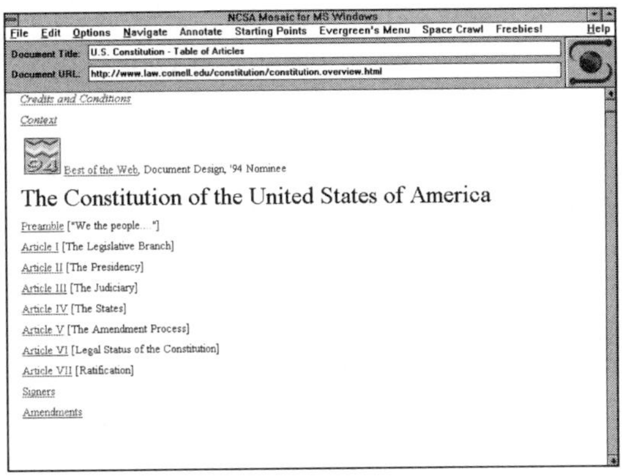

Hypertext version of the U.S. Constitution

The Original Washington Insider

Here's a brief look at our first president, including his early life and career, his role in the French and Indian War, Virginia politics, the American Revolution, his presidency, his life afterward, and how he got across the Delaware with all those hard-luck soldiers shoehorned into such a small boat. While there's nothing here about chopping down cherry trees or having wooden teeth, you'll still get an interesting look at the Father of Our Country. Great for teachers and for students who have a history report due first thing tomorrow morning.

Getting There

http://sc94.ameslab.gov/TOUR/gwash.html

Hot Links

- Tour Map of Washington D.C.

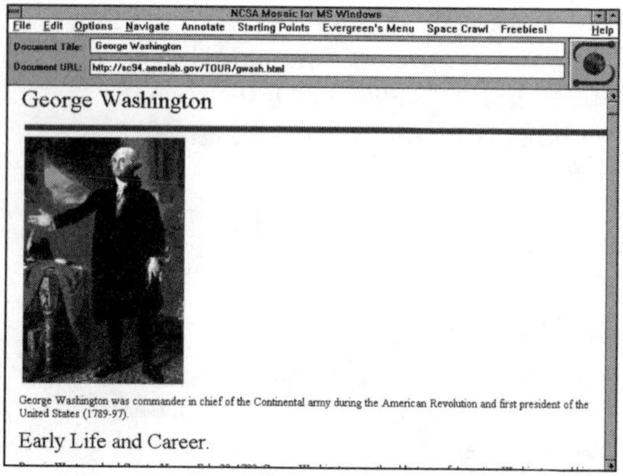

The life of George Washington is examined at this Web site

D-Day Archive

Dooms Day, *Decision Day*, even *De Day* as some soldiers from Brooklyn called it. Regardless of what the *D* stood for, at 6:30 a.m. June 6, 1944, every soldier on the Normandy coast knew what it meant. So began what has been called by some historians one of the greatest battles in history.

Get the real story of D-Day at this site from many who were there as reprinted from *Stars and Stripes*. You can also download original newsreels of the invasion, as well as photos, maps, and sounds. Read the pep speech Ike gave to his boys before the guns started blazing. There are also loads of maps and battle plans, government and military archives, and much more.

In addition, there are newsreels of the Germans marching into Paris and a V1 bombing of London, as well as historic speeches you can listen to by Churchill, Hoover, Chamberlain, and Truman.

Getting There

http://192.253.114.31/D-Day/Table_of_contents.html

Hot Links

- Government and Military Archives
- Stars and Stripes Newspaper
- Army and Navy News Reels
- Famous Speeches
- Maps and Battle Plans

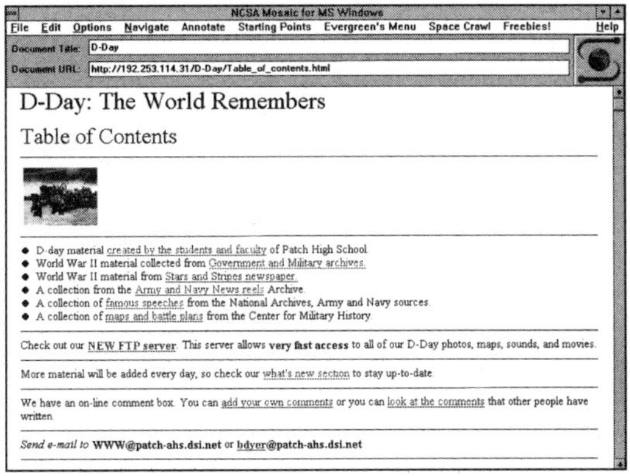

Web page commemorating the 1944 Allied invasion of France

Internet Help

NCSA Software Development Group

Get in the fast lane on the Information Highway (oops, I promised myself I wouldn't use any of those tired metaphors) by downloading the latest, greatest software for the Web. Through NCSA's software developers, you have access to lots of great Web tools, like the latest version of Mosaic, Audible Collage, PC Show, and Telnet. There are versions for Windows, X Windows, Macintosh, and (gasp!) DOS.

Getting There

`http://www.ncsa.uiuc.edu/SDG/Software/SDGSoftDir.html`

Hot Links

- Macintosh
- PC
- UNIX

- Software tools for data sharing and transfer
- CD-ROM

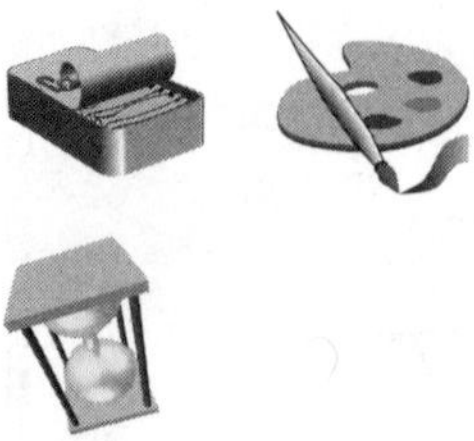

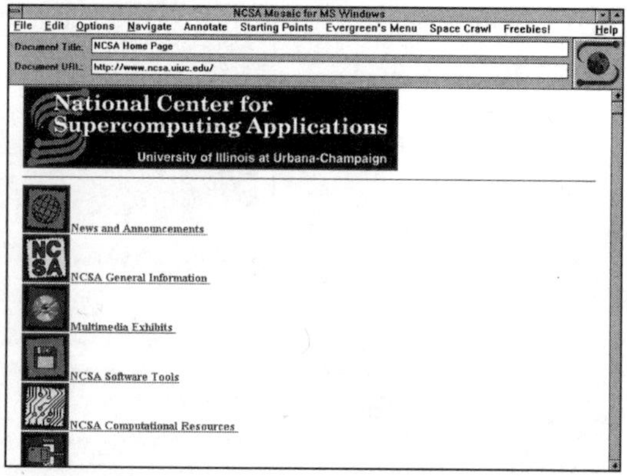

NCSA Software Development Group home page

A Navigator for Network Newbies

Dipping your big toe into the ocean of information available on the Web can be a bit intimidating the first time. The Global Network Navigator is a great place to begin when you finally make the plunge. There are lots of tips and resources for newbies, as well as many fun and helpful things to assist you in your cyber-travels. And you don't have to wait two hours after eating to get started.

Check out the Travelers' Center for help planning vacations or business trips. The Personal Finance Center teaches you how to track your finances and offers other help with your money. You'll even find valuable information on selling your home.

Finally, connect to the *Whole Internet Catalog* for sage advice about navigating the Net and pointers on finding the resources you're looking for.

Getting There

`http://nearnet.gnn.com/gnn/GNNhome.html`

Hot Links

- Travelers' Center
- Personal Finance Center
- Digital Drive-In

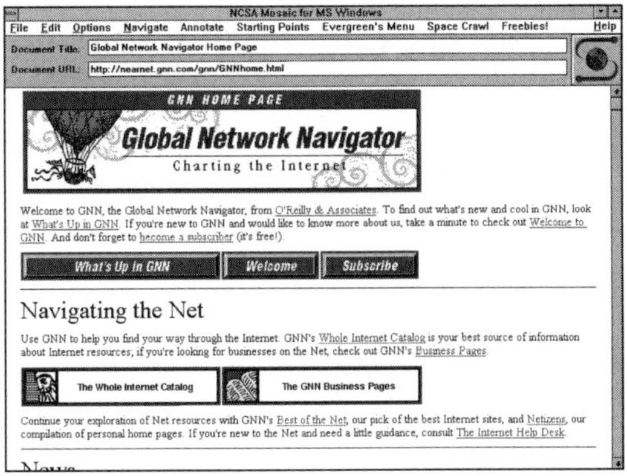

The Global Network Navigator's home page

In the NIC of Time

Tired of answering FAQs from novice Internauts and want to tell them where to *really* go? What? You say *you're* still new to cyberspace? Well, take a look at this: The InterNIC Info Guide is a comprehensive online information service that brings you information about getting started on the Internet and resources that you can access online. Get valuable information about new services such as *The Scout Report* and an online hypertext version of the NSF Network News.

Getting There

`http://www.internic.net/infoguide.html`

Hot Links

- Scout Report
- Internet Resources
- Web Picks

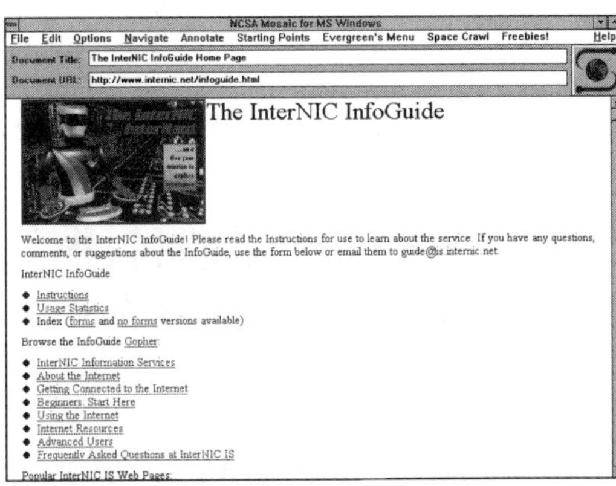

The InterNIC InfoGuide home page

FREE $TUFF from the Internet Online

My gift for shameless self promotion aside, this is truly a one-of-a-kind Web site to help you find the hidden treasures buried in cyberspace. Like my hardcopy book of the same name, this online version of *FREE $TUFF from the Internet* takes you to all the best Internet sites you can access to find tons of free goodies to download or send away for.

Read the text to find out where all the great stuff is located, then click on the hyperlinks to get there instantly. You'll find a huge collection of GIFs, catalogs, newsletters, government publications, games, puzzles, posters, and more. The most fun you can have with your computer on!

Getting There

`http://power.globalnews.com/articles/txt/freestuf/contents.htm`

Hot Links

- Books and Literature
- Kid Stuff

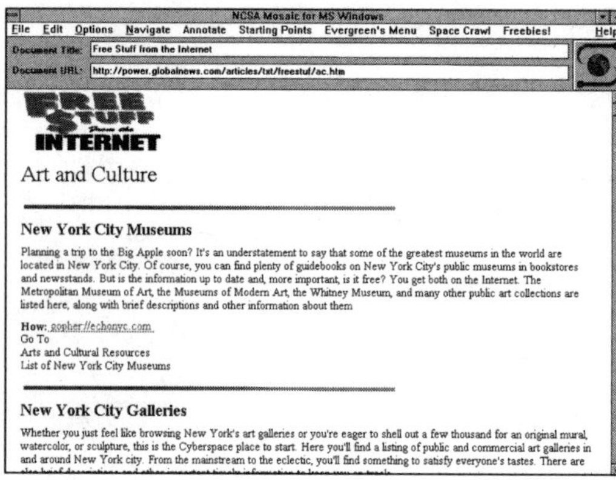

FREE $TUFF from the Internet home page

Lists of Links and Links of Lists

Scott Yanoff's Special Internet Connections List is an especially rich Internet "list of links"—that is, a document listing URLs of interesting and useful resources on the Internet. Scott has been maintaining the list since 1991, and it consists of a large HTML page with a table of contents at the top, followed by the links in alphabetical order with a short description of each.

Topics include art, astronomy, news servers and journals, games, chat, physics, business/financial, law, literature, history, gopher sites, space, and mucho more. This is one of those places that as a great Internet "bunny slope" when first getting your bearings in Netdom.

Getting There

http://www.uwm.edu/Mirror/inet.services.html

Hot Links

Too many to list. See for yourself.

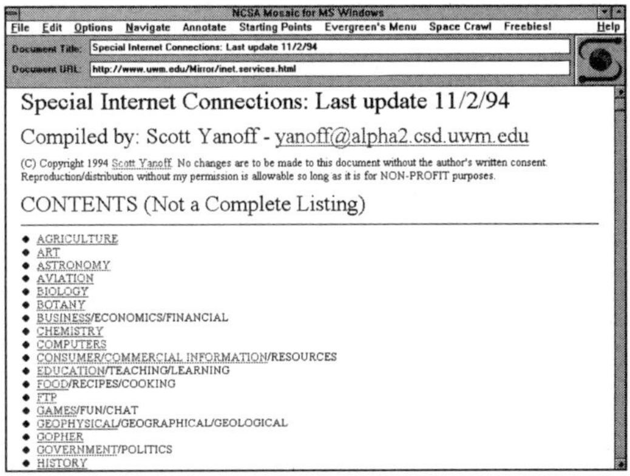

Yanoff's Special Intenet Connection's home page

The Web Comes to a Crawl

If you aren't already using WebCrawler, run, don't walk, to this site and place it on your menu. The WebCrawler is a program that runs through the Web visiting as many sites as it can to create a master index of what's out on the Web. While not an exhaustive search utility (but then the Web has no such thing), the WebCrawler is fast and you'll quickly find yourself relying on it heavily for guidance in your Web travels.

Note that the WebCrawler isn't perfect, unless there's some strange rhyme to its reason. For instance, search for the word *Internet* and you'll come up empty, as you will if you search for *Web*. Search for *humor*, though, and you'll get plenty of hits, including the transcripts to the testimony from O.J. Simpson's Grand Jury hearing. Go figure.

Getting There

http://www.biotech.washington.edu/WebCrawler/WebQuery.html

Hot Links

How much time have you got? Count 'em and let me know.

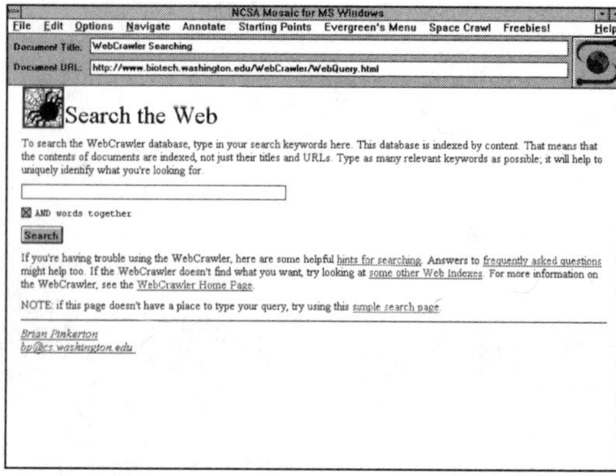

The WebCrawler search utility

Searching the Galaxy

The EINet Galaxy is a network search utility designed to help make finding information buried on the Internet easier to dig up. Commercial and public information are included in its database organized by topic.

Getting There

`http://galaxy.einet.net/`

Hot Links

- New Stuff
- Space Telescope Science Institute

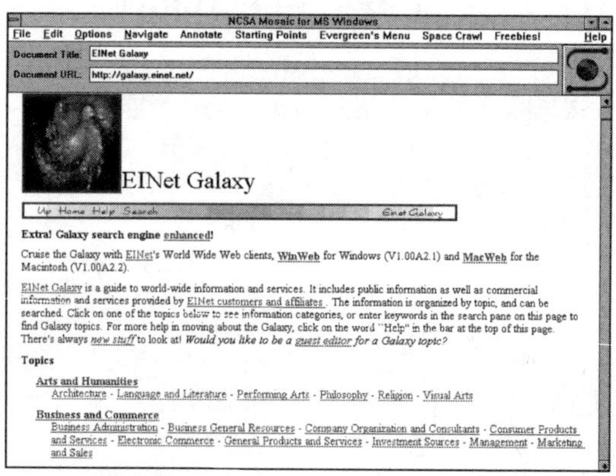

EINet Galaxy's home page

A Library for Virtual Bookworms

From those crazy guys that brought you the World Wide Web (CERN) comes The WWW Virtual Library. This library may not contain a single book, but that doesn't seem to matter in cyberspace. You'll find pointers to hundreds of Internet resources arranged according to subject area.

From Aboriginal Studies to International Affairs, Religion, and Unidentified Flying Objects, this library is a browser's paradise. There's even information about how you can put your own data on the shelves—try *that* at the Library of Congress.

Interested in helping to maintain some of the information stored here? CERN would like to talk to you about becoming a WWW Virtual Library Administrator. The pay is low, but you'll be more than compensated with long hours and no weekends. If you're still reading, they *definitely* want you!

Getting There

http://info.cern.ch/hypertext/DataSources/bySubject/Overview.html

Hot Links

Huge variety, too many to list

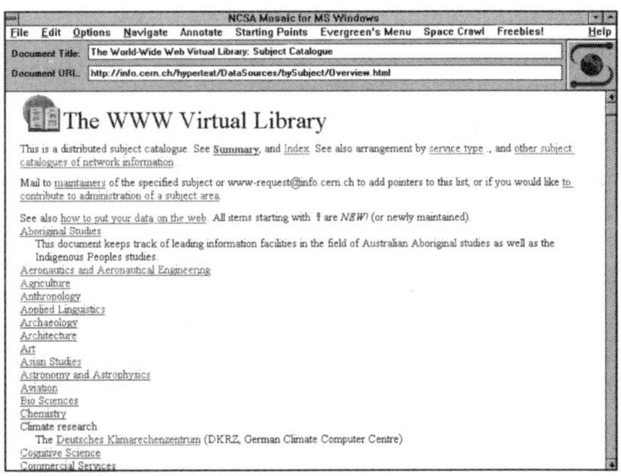

The Web's Virtual Library from CERN

Kids

Just for Kids

Interesting Places for Kids. The name pretty much says it all. This site is a compilation of the where and what of things on the Web for those whose feet don't quite reach the floor when they're sitting at their computers.

The link names might sound a bit stuffy (Art and Literature, Museums, and so on) but the links themselves are definitely geared toward kid-dom. Kids will find some fun games to play online (hangman and information on juggling, among others), as well as other links to fun sites and sounds on the Net.

Getting There

`http://www.crc.ricoh.com/people/steve/kids.html`

Hot Links

- The Adventures of Cybercat
- Worldwide WWW Information
- metaverse.com

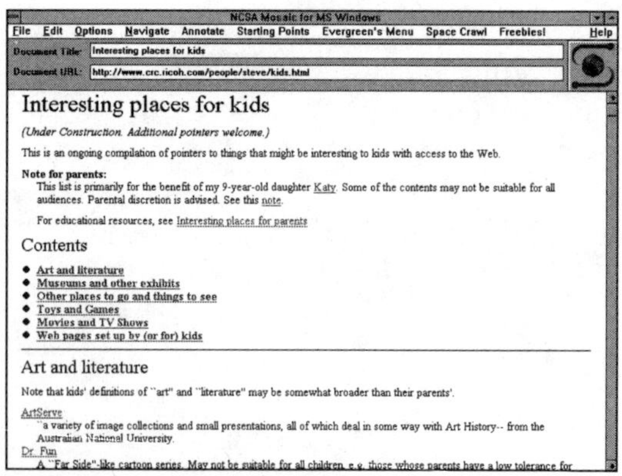

The Interesting Places for Kids home page

Animaniac Mania

From the collective brains of Steven Spielberg, Warner Brothers, and Fox Television comes the Animaniacs. This site will bring you what I venture to say will be all you ever wanted to know about this gang of looney toons (not to be confused with the other Looney Tunes).

While I can't personally vouch for the quality of the show (being much too busy writing this book to enjoy myself), powers higher than me have said it is a must-see for kids. Don't they just have all the fun. As for its marathon of a URL, I hope you only have to type it once.

Getting There

`http://www.cs.cmu.edu:8001/afs/cs.cmu.edu/user/clamen/misc/tv/Animaniacs/Animaniacs.html`

Hot Links

- The Nifty Animaniacs Reference File
- Animaniacs Lyrics
- List of Segments
- List of Characters

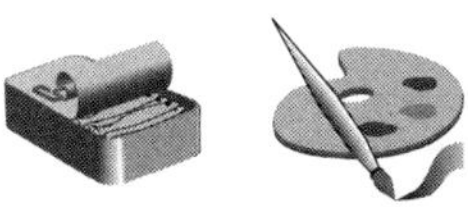

Cyber Junior High

"It's not just a school, it's an adventure." With those words, sixth through ninth graders checking out cyberspace Middle School are thrust out onto the Web to learn about all the Internet has to offer. Kids will find hundreds of links to a multitude of interesting things, like online museums located in the U.S., Australia, and Russia; study aids and research information; and links to schools around the country.

Typing was about the most high-tech class you could take back when I was in high school. Catch a ride at the Bus Stop to see what today's kids are learning. At Champaign Centennial High School in

Illinois, they're teaching hypermedia and multimedia, and students developed their own Web page that's used by other students to plug into cyberspace.

Talk about your high-tech note-passing! At some elementary schools, kids have their own E-mail accounts that they can use to communicate with each other. There are even educational resources for teachers to learn how to get the most use out of the Internet in their classrooms. No longer will kids be able to claim the dog ate their homework. Maybe now it'll be "I had a BIOS error booting my hard drive and your server was down when I tried a remote logon." The more things change . . . .

Getting There

`http://www.scri.fsu.edu/~dennisl/CMS.html`

Hot Links

- Surf City
- Topics of Interest
- Virtual School Bus
- Educational Resources for Teachers

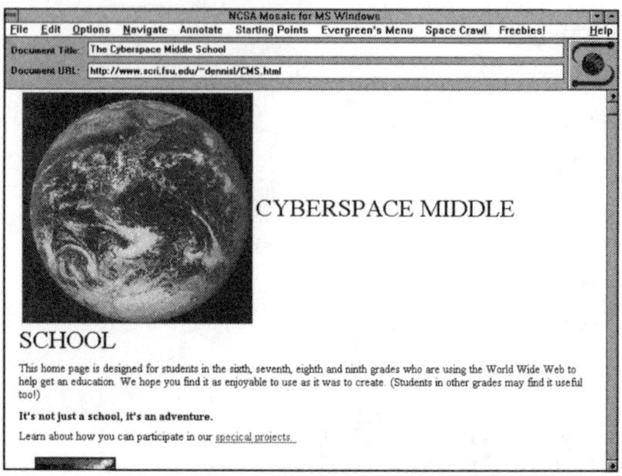

The Cyberspace Middle School home page

That Purple Dinosaur You Love to Hate

Is Barney really a demon from hell? Strong evidence says yes, but only his mother knows for sure. Yep, It's Barney's Page provides some of the purplest black humor ever slung at an extinct carnivore. See Barney as you've never seen him before: impaled on a spike or maybe as roadkill. You get the picture.

There are also Barney songs you can sing along with, real Barney audio clips, and plenty of Barney cartoons. Need more punishment? Then go watch the real thing. That'll teach ya.

Getting There

`http://www.galcit.caltech.edu/~ta/barney/barney.html`

Hot Links

- Barney's Photo Album
- Barney Target for Shooters
- Barney Sound Clips

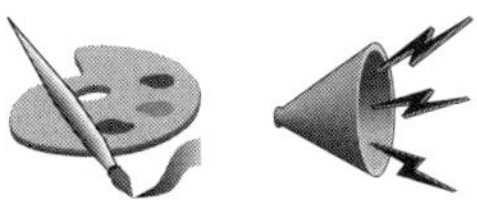

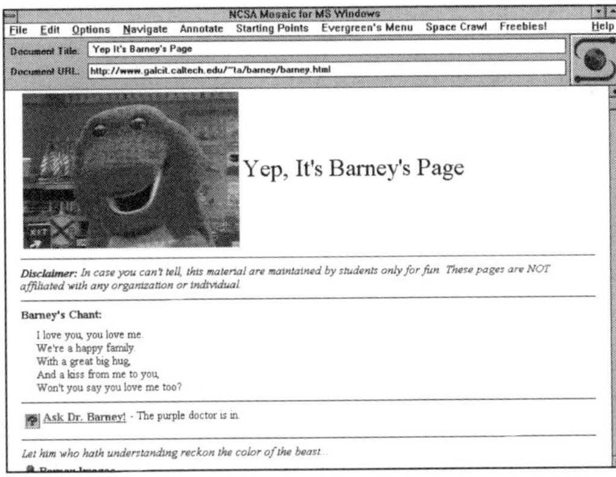

Barney's home page

Keep It Up

Trying to balance your work, play, family, and friends? Hey, you already know how to juggle and didn't even know it. Take a break from the daily grind and give this relaxing hobby a try. Besides being a great way to unwind, juggling helps you with your coordination, balance, and self-esteem; instantly makes you more attractive to the opposite sex; and cures baldness (just making sure you're paying attention).

The Juggling Information Service is your one-stop shop for juggling tips, tricks, information, and inspiration. This site links all (or at least all known) juggling sites on the Internet into one huge "Web o' Juggling." In addition to dozens of links to juggling home pages on the Web, this site has juggling software you can download, pictures, and links to other fun sites (like Frisbee).

Getting There

`http://www.hal.com:80/services/juggle/`

Hot Links

- Picture Gallery
- Movie Theater
- Juggling Software

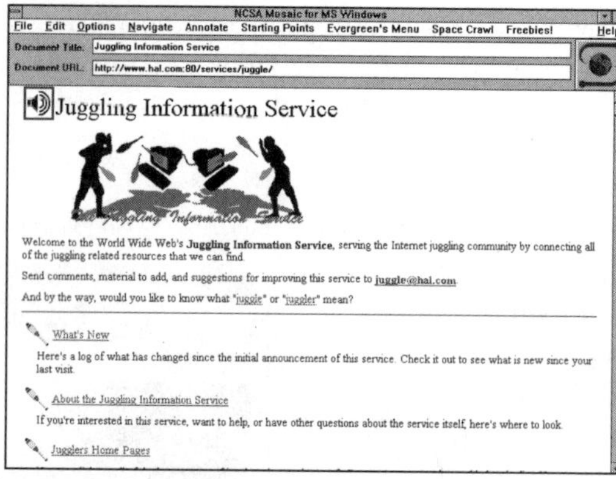

Juggling Information Service home page

Blue Dog Can Count!

Kids of all ages will love this one. It's totally offbeat—the sort of thing that makes the Internet and Mosaic so gonzo great. Yes, it is a blue dog who can do arithmetic. Enter a simple formula (such as 5 + 6), and Blue Dog will bark out the answer. Try it—that's all I'll say, other than to point out (as the page does not) that you must have multimedia-capable hardware for it to work.

Getting There

`http://hp8.ini.cmu.edu:5550/bdf.html`

Hot Links

- Void

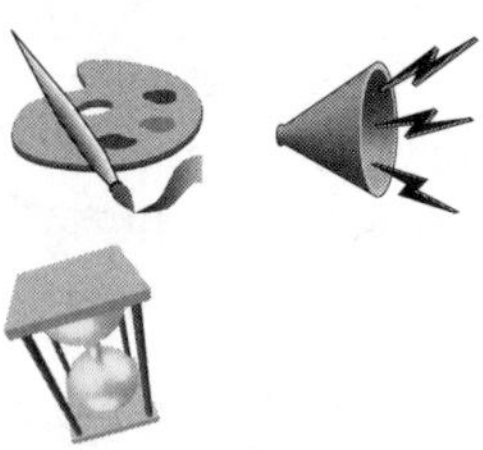

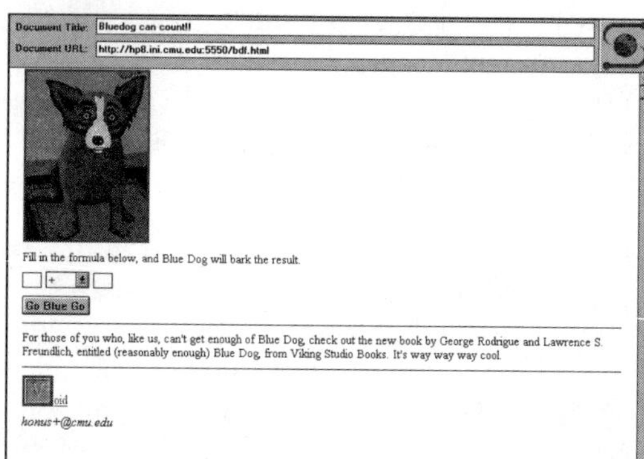

Blue Dog's home page

Caution, Hedgehog Crossing

If you're the type whose eyes start to blister from staring unblinkingly at your television screen while playing video games, take a break. Boot your computer and plug into this site where you can stare unblinkingly at your monitor while you check out the latest video games from Sega. Game-o-philes will love Sega Web, Sega's venture into cyberspace that shows off their new products with video clips, screen shots, and hints to get you through the rough spots.

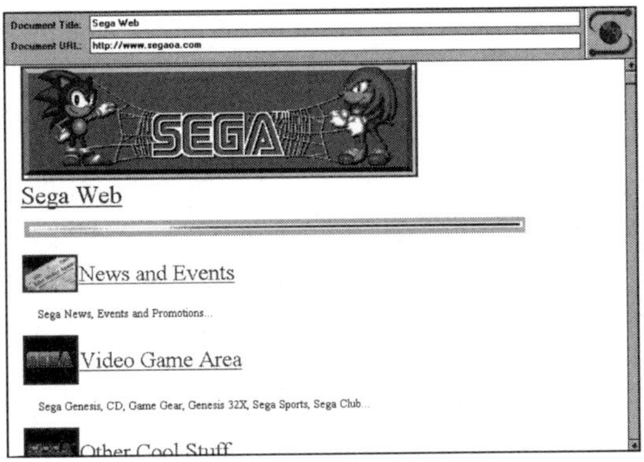

The SEGA home page

Getting There

`http://www.segaoa.com`

Hot Links

- Other Cool Stuff
- Elsewhere

Law

Legal Eagles on the Web

If the extent of your experience with the law is watching Call-an-Ambulance-Chaser commercials on afternoon TV, count yourself lucky (albeit ill-informed). But if you ever need legal help, here's a good place to get an overview. You'll find links to many law-related sites on the Net, including mailing lists you can subscribe to and places to download documents relevant to your needs. There are lots of government links here, as well as a searchable database of Supreme Court decisions.

Getting There

`http://www.law.cornell.edu/`

Hot Links

- Supreme Court Decisions
- E-mail Addresses of Faculty and Staff and US Law Schools
- Legal Information Institute

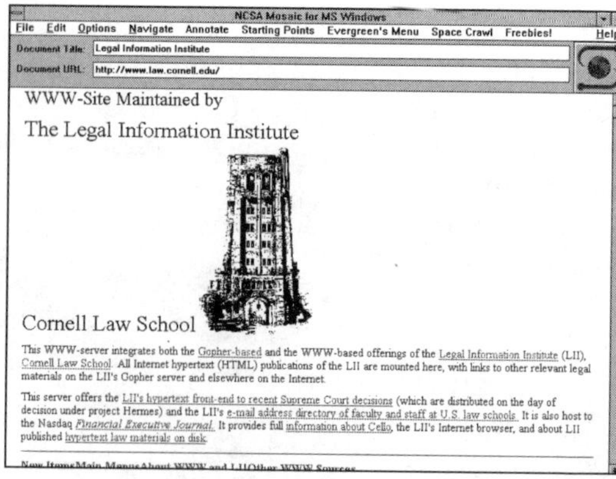

The Legal Information Institute's home page

Did You Hear the One About . . . ?

I may be out of order, but I couldn't resist (and it is law related—sort of). Here's a collection of lawyer jokes that will appeal to your funny bone, compiled from different sources on the Internet. Objectionable? Probably. Funny? Yes, but unfortunately not to those who could sue me.

I hate to make fun of a particular group, but it's hard to feel sorry for the type of guy who drives a Mercedes to his yacht club. In any case, these jokes are a regular hoot and a habeus holler. Enjoy.

Getting There

`http://deputy.law.utexas.edu/jokes1.htm`

`http://deputy.law.utexas.edu/jokes2.htm`

Hot Links

- Humor Web Page
- Humor Gopher Archive
- Land of the Lost

Trade Law

Trade law may not be on your A list of great reads, but if you now invest or plan to invest money abroad, you'll probably benefit from a refresher course in what makes the world economy tick.

This site provides a timeline of trade laws and agreements between the United States and other countries. Spanning the late 1800s through the present, this site includes the full text of some the more important (or at least more meaningful in today's terms) agreements, including GATT, NAFTA, and the Maastricht Treaty.

Getting There

http://ananse.irv.uit.no/trade_law/nav/trade.html

Hot Links

- Hague Convention
- Universal Copyright Convention
- Patent Cooperation Treaty

World trade history and agreements

If It Pleases the Court

The U.S. Supreme Court is the country's highest Federal court, with jurisdiction over all other courts in the nation. Now is that power or what? Get the facts on the nine justices who make up this legal body, including their personal and professional backgrounds, how they rose to power, who nominated them, and more.

Getting There

http://www.law.cornell.edu/supct/justices/fullcourt.html

Hot Links

Click on the picture of the judge you want information on (or click on his or her name).

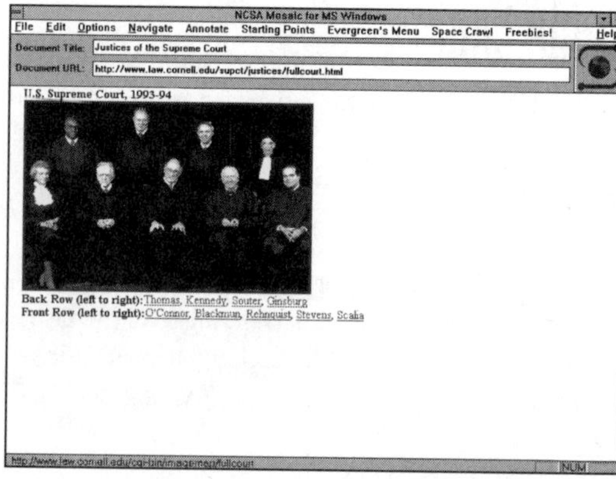

If it pleases the Court, here are the bios for each of the present Supreme Court Justices

O.J. Simpson Case Examined

Perhaps the most publicized murder trial of the century, the O.J. Simpson case has been felt deeply by anyone familiar with the former NFL great. Now the *San Francisco Examiner* has made its news articles of the Simpson case available to read and download from the Web through its online newspaper, the *Electric Examiner.*

This site gives you the most recent chapters in the Simpson story, as well as access to numerous articles published throughout the investigation. Is he innocent? Is he guilty? It's in the hands of the jury now… .

Getting There

`http://sfgate.com/examiner/simpsonhome.html`

Hot Links

The Official Unofficial OJ Simpson Home Page

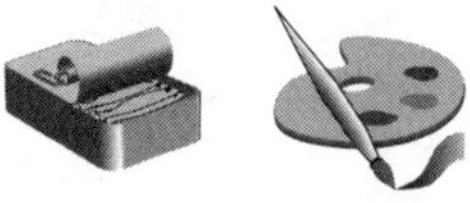

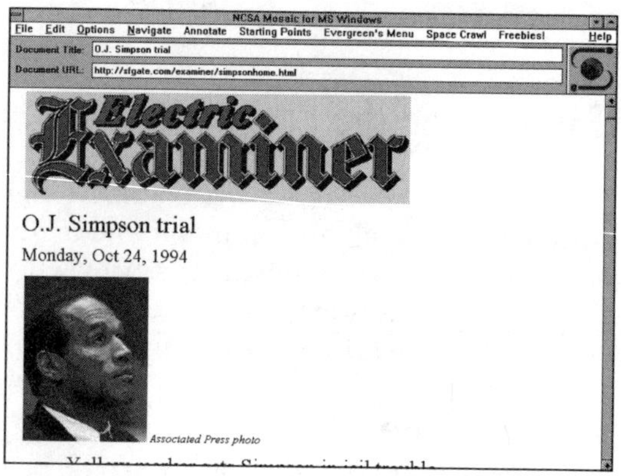

The O.J. Simpson page at the Electric Examiner

Nolo Contendere This!

Nolo Press, publisher of self-help legal books and software, has put its shingle out on the Web. Learn how to take the law into your own hands with information about living trusts, getting along with your neighbors, personal injury claims, and more.

Of special interest are the briefs that have had all the legalese surgically removed. What's left are valuable essays on copyrights, obtaining patents, and more.

Getting There

`http://gnn.interpath.net/gnn/bus/nolo/index.html`

Hot Links

- Legal Briefs
- Catalog
- Lawyer Jokes

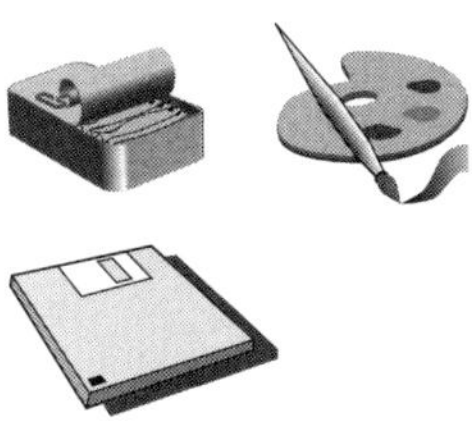

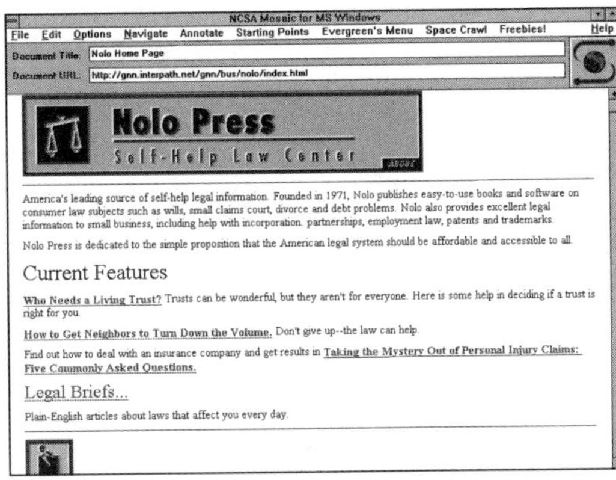

The Nolo lowdown for self-help legal information on the Web

Movies and Videos

Star Wars Home Page

May The Force be with you, and may you Have a Lot of Time on Your Hands when accessing this site, because you'll need it. Loading takes a while, but it'll be worth it to all you Wookiephiles and Vader Heads. You'll get news about upcoming movies and video games (have you heard about the Doom spinoff *Dark Forces*?), sound effects libraries, pictures for downloading, and a galaxy full of all-things Star Wars.

Getting There

`http://stwing.resnet.upenn.edu:8001/~jruspini/starwars.html`

Hot Links

Lots of links, including Star Wars bloopers, a guide to related comic books, and where to find merchandise

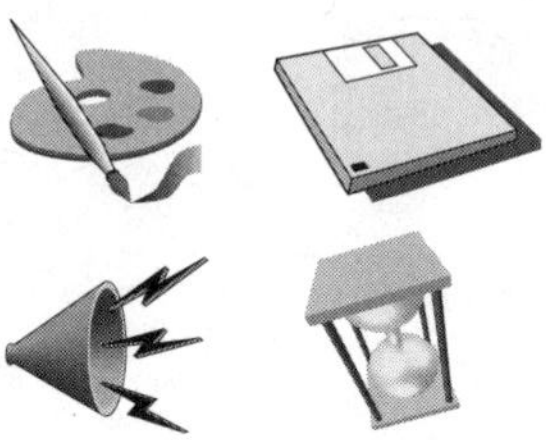

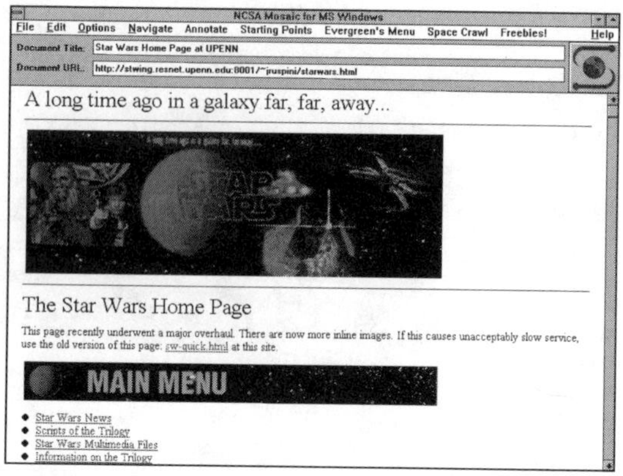

The Star Wars home page

All You Need Is the Popcorn

Cardiff's Movie Database Browser offers an amazing store of information on all the movies you've ever heard of, and plenty you haven't. It's completely free to access, can be searched on several different criteria, and allows you to vote a value from 1 to 10 for your favorite (or not-so-favorite) movies.

You can search by movie title or by name (such as by actor, actress, director, and so on). What's in the database is quite accurate, as much as I've checked; however, there are some holes in the more obscure spots, like costume designers for Grade Z horror flicks of the 1950s (*My Mother Was a Werewolf*, and the like). This database has been compiled 100 percent by volunteers, and if you know how to fill one of the "holes," you are enthusiastically invited to do so.

Getting There

`http://www.msstate.edu/Movies/moviequery.html`

Hot Links

- Top 40 Films
- Bottom 40 Films
- Academy Awards

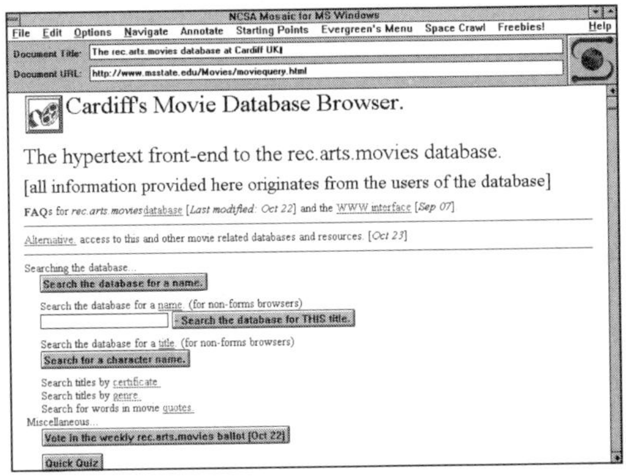

Cardiff's Movie Database Browser home page

Blade Runner

One of the Internet's most talked about movies, *Blade Runner* has gone from box office failure to cult classic since its release in 1982. Get all the inside info on the production and following of this remarkable movie.

Followers of *Blade Runner* will want to check out this site, complete with sequel information (why does Hollywood always insist on ruining a good thing?) and answers to your frequently asked questions—even film clips and sound files in AU format (Windows users will want to convert these to WAV).

Getting There

`http://kzsu.stanford.edu/uwi/br/off-world.html`

Hot Links

- The Blade Runner FAQ
- Images
- Sounds

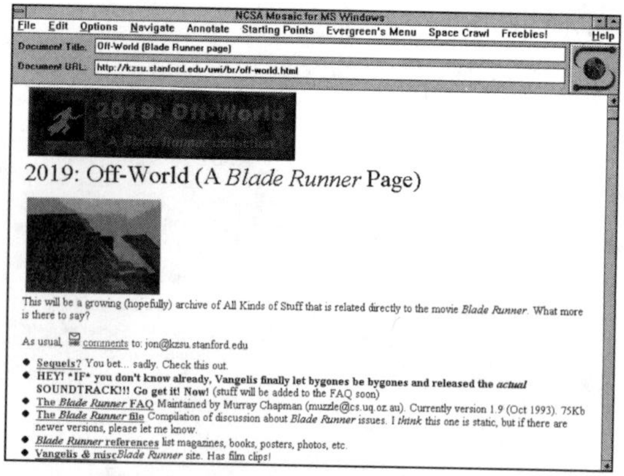

One of several sites devoted to Blade Runner

Why I Oughta . . .

I wonder how many eyes were poked out and heads cracked open by kids imitating the antics of The Three Stooges in the '30s and '40s? But, hey, comedy isn't pretty.

Do the Curly Shuffle over to this Web site to get your dose of slapstick fun from Larry, Manny, Moe, and—no, wait. That's the Pep Boys. Anyway, you'll find plot synopses from Stooge one-reels and full-length movies, trivia (did you know Curly was a professional ballroom dancer before achieving Stoogedom?), biographies, sound bites, and more. Woowoowoowoo!

Getting There

`http://sweetums.nmsu.edu/stooges.htm`

Hot Links

- Trivia
- Sound

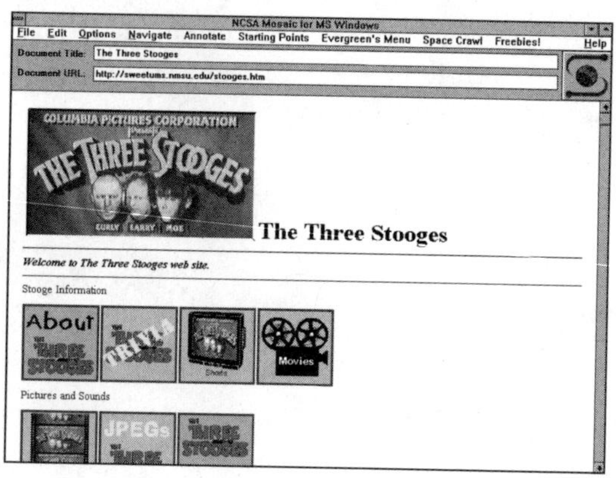

A page for Stooge-o-philes

Music

A Hunka Hunka Burnin' Elvis Info

"Only those who believe in The King should read on." So proclaims the Elvis Aron Presley Home Page, a web site for true Elvis devotees. You'll get more than your fill of all things Elvis at this site, including an online tour of Graceland and a collection of photographs that capture The King in "all his glory."

Had enough? I didn't think so. There are also samples of Elvis tunes you can download to your Mac or PC and a list of things you *never* wanted to know about The King. There's even software, including an Elvis Detector in case The King is hiding somewhere in the vicinity of your computer. Long live The King in cyberspace!

Getting There

`http://sunsite.unc.edu/elvis/elvishom.htm`

Note: This page is temporarily in legal limbo while the author determines what she can and cannot offer without violiating copyright law. However she promises that the page will return shortly—and better than ever.

Hot Links

- Elvis Biography
- Memphis Page

Aloha from the Internet

Sounds of the Underground

Sure there are music archives on the Internet. Why heck, there are dozens of sites where you can discuss the latest bands till your fingers fall off. Some of those sites even have audio samples of a few bands. But here's a site that finally gives listeners of alternative music what they want.

Calling itself the first free hi-fi music archive on the Net, the *Internet Underground Music Archive* is an online library of songs by alternative bands you can download, along with group bios, images, and reviews. You can even leave your own review if you want and download catalogs from the different labels listed here. Now you can try *before* you buy.

Getting There

`http://www.iuma.com`

Hot Links

- TeenBeet
- Bedazzled
- Warner Bros.

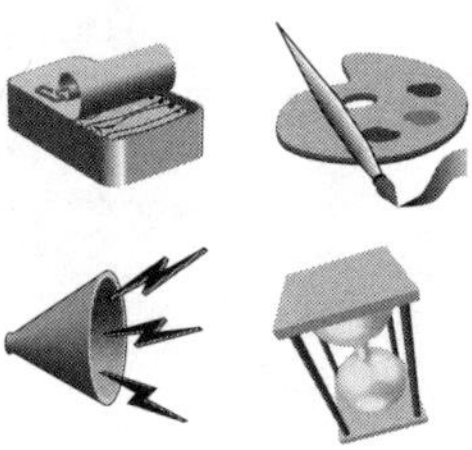

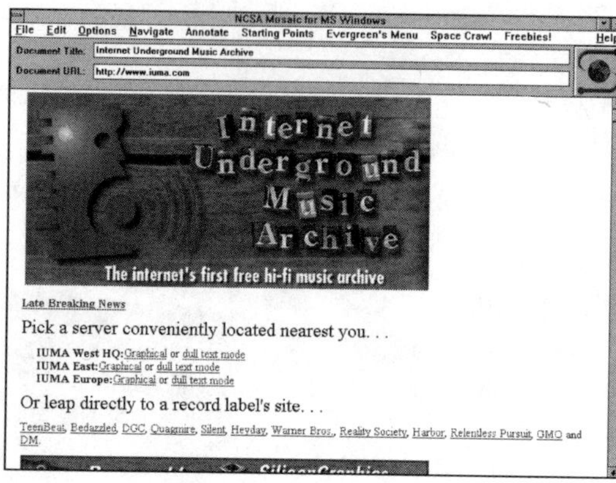

Underground Music Archive home page

Megadeth, Arizona

Where in the hell is Megadeth, Arizona? Locals will tell you it's anyplace near Phoenix in the summer, and they'd be half right. (Of course, some people think Phoenix in the summer *is* hell.) Actually, Megadeth, Arizona, is a Web site named in honor of a record studio on the outskirts of Phoenix where heavy metal rockers Megadeth recorded their latest album *Youthanasia.* (Do you really think I could make this stuff up?)

Kind of a *Rocky Horror Picture Show* meets *Psycho*, Megadeth, Arizona is a tourist trap from hell offering everything but the world's largest ball of string. And it's certainly a heavy metal fan's paradise—or should I say purgatory? Fans can download a song from the group's new album, get video clips of the band, send electronic fan mail, check their *horrorscopes*, and browse the souvenir shop.

Getting There

`http://bazaar.com/Megadeth/megadeth.html`

Hot Links

- Visitor's Bureau
- Youthanasia
- KDETH 101
- Hall of Records

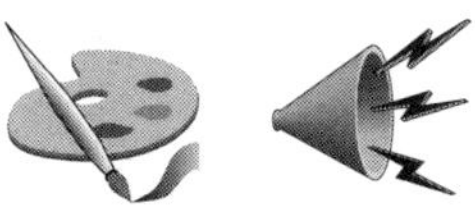

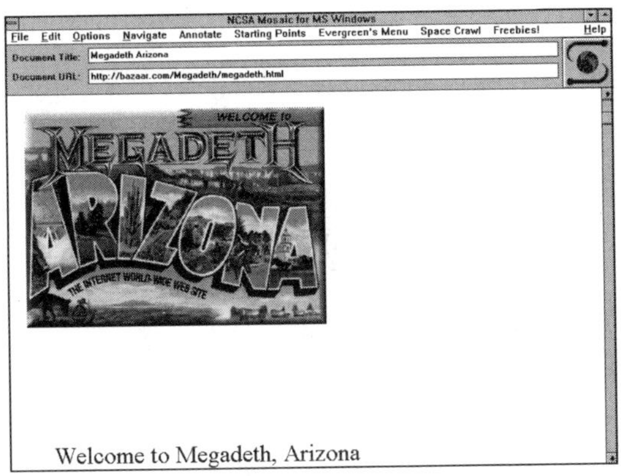

Welcome home to Megadeth, Arizona

Something Weird on the Web

Ten years worth of Weird Al Yankovic should be enough for anyone, and that's what you'll get at Daniel's "Weird Al" page. Get the complete lyrics of Weird Al's songs, including such true classics as Eat It, King of Suede, and Bohemian Polka. Check out the sound files, too.

Daniel may have a slightly skewed sense of musical appreciation, but then if Prince or Snoopy Fresh-Jazz Doggy-Dog Doo (whatever) can have legions of undying fandom, who am I to judge?

Getting There

http://cristl.see.plym.ac.uk/dfsmith/index.html

Hot Links

- Album Covers
- Dr. Demento

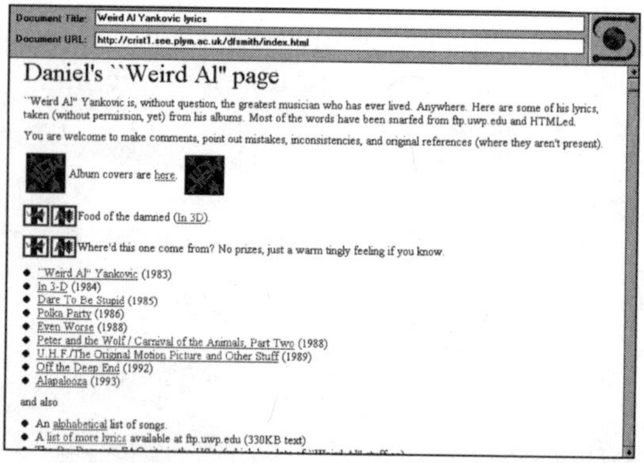

Homage to Weird Al

WebTV Music Videos

Music video junkies can still get their recommended daily allowance of rock and roll by downloading the videos at this site. Remember Deborah Harry? The original new wave sweetheart with the heart of glass is alive and well and bringing down the virtual house in cyberspace. You can also get music files of Eric Clapton, Michael Jackson, and other music giants.

So turn off the TV before those music videos rot your brain, then get on your computer and do something productive—like watching music videos online. At least you won't have to put up with the obnoxious VJs and acne commercials.

Getting There

http://w3.eeb.ele.tue.nl/mpeg/movies/music/index.html

Hot Links

- Debbie Harry
- Michael Jackson
- Tears for Fear

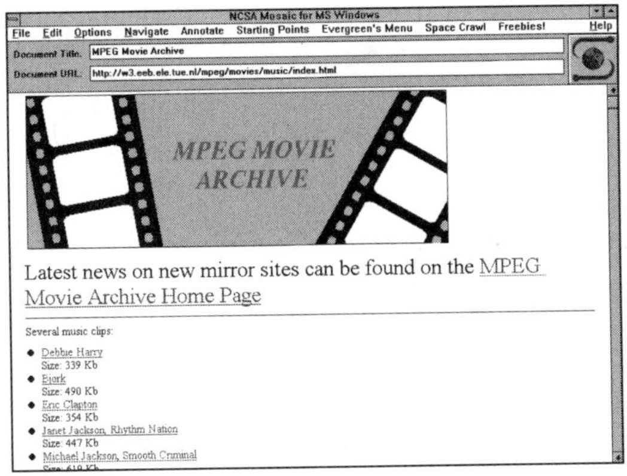

The MPEG Movie Archive home page

Satisfaction on the Web

The Official Rolling Stones Web Site is one of the best rock-fan hangouts yet erected on the Web—and certainly, if you're looking for drawings and photos of tongues, there will never be a better one. Seriously, the page presents promo audio clips from the Stone's new CD, *Voodoo Lounge*, along with pictures of the band and lots of other things relating to the Stones, their current tour, and recent recordings.

To celebrate the new *Voodoo Lounge* CD, voodoo images of various sorts are available in the picture archive, along with audio clips for those endowed with multimedia hardware.

Getting There

`http://www.stones.com/`

Hot Links

- Our Picture Collection
- Sound Samples from Voodoo Lounge
- Merchandise Catalog

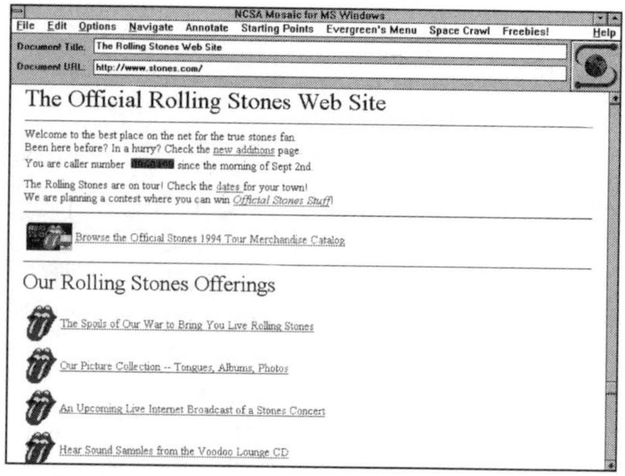

The Official Stones home page

Religion and New Age

Gimme That Old-Time Interactive Religion

In the beginning ARPANET created the Internet. And the Internet was without form, and void of 25 million people. And the Spirit of Progress said let there be TCP/IP connections and it was good.

Maybe that quote isn't covered here, but you will find a great melding of old time religion and real time technology at this site. This online version of the King James Bible is fully searchable so you can type keywords and get hundreds of "hits." Great for searching for quotes and inspirational verses that you just can't put your finger on.

Getting There

`http://etext.virginia.edu/kjv.query.html`

Hot Links

Thousands of possibilities, depending on the keyword you search for

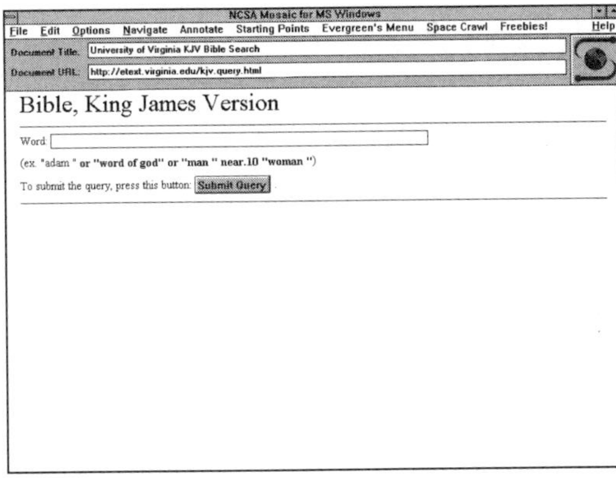

Online Bible lets Web surfers search for salvation

Jewish Resources

The variety of religious resources on the Internet is voluminous, with information and resources for every major (and dozens of minor) religious group to access. Judaism is no exception. Here's an exhaustive and well thought out list of resources for the Jewish community.

In addition to an exceptional Top Ten List of links, there are many other pointers to Jewish-related Internet sites, like The Anne Frank Web Site, the Israel Information Service, and an online bookstore. Shalom!

Getting There

http://escape.com/~indigo/jewish.html

Hot Links

- Jerusalem One
- The Anne Frank Web Site
- The United States Holocaust Memorial Museum

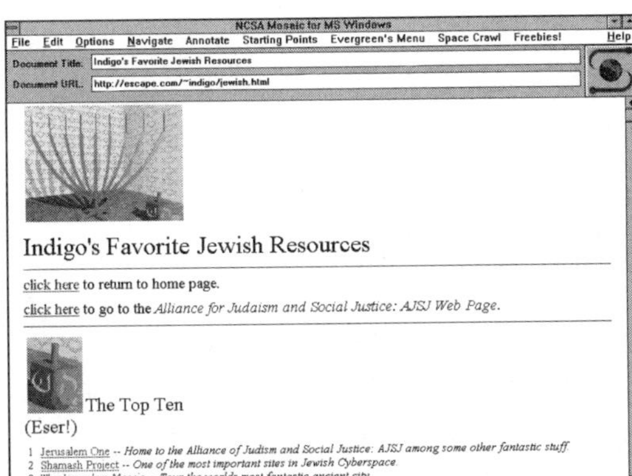

Hot links to Jewish resources on the Web

Christian Resource List

Afraid of spending eternity in Hell (no, I'm not talking about Microsoft Customer Support)? Even Web users need saving (some might say *especially* Web users). Here's where you can find hundreds of links to Christian-related documents on the Web. There are several versions of the Bible, links to discussion groups and FTP sites, and answers to many of those nagging questions about organized religion.

You can also find religious study guides and outlines, links to other Web sites, and a lot more, and information on accessing online exhibits of religious artifacts.

Getting There

http://saturn.colorado.edu:8080/Christian/list.html

Hot Links

- The King James Bible
- Christian Music Artists
- Newsgroups

TEXT

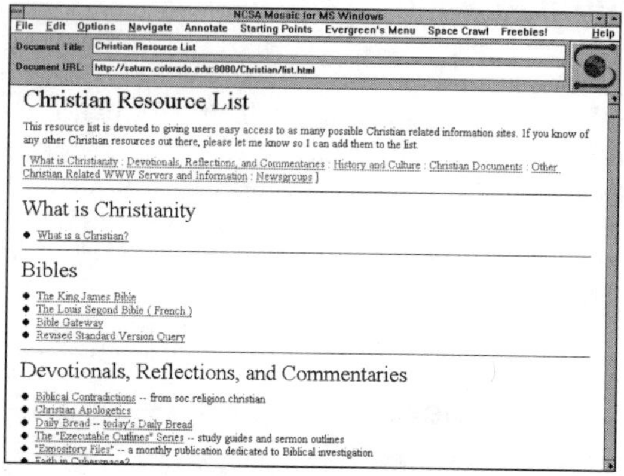

Online Bible lets Web surfers search for salvation

World Religions

Many westerners are shocked to find out that Christianity is *not* the world's most dominant religion. That title belongs to Buddhism. Other big players in world religion are also represented here: Hinduism, Judaism, Christianity, Islam, and Baha'i Faith.

In addition to some of the history and dogma of these religions, this site includes links to some of their major writings, too. Access and download the text to the *Bhagavad Gita*, the *Dead Sea Scrolls*, *The Bible*, and many important church documents from early Christianity.

Getting There

http://www.biologie.uni-freiburg.de/~amueller/religion/

Hot Links

- The Secular Web
- Human Rights
- Planet Earth

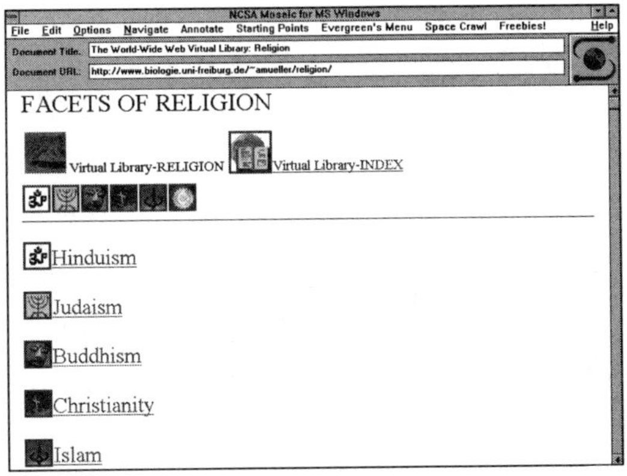

The Facets of Religion home page

If the Spirits Move You

Spirit-WWW is a Web-based collection of resources for the paranormal/ New Age/metaphysical subculture. There are a number of articles on channeling of higher entities, out-of-body experiences (OBEs for those in the loop), yoga, UFOs, theosophy, Eastern philosophies, light studies, healing and alternative medicine, new age music and music reviews, spirit-related art, and even movies.

As good as the page is, connections to the host machine can slow you down to a crawl, and regardless of how fast your own link is to the Internet, accessing Spirit-WWW can be like raising the dead. Use the time to meditate.

Getting There

http://err.ethz.ch/~kiwi/Spirit.html

Hot Links

- Channeling
- UFO Phenomena
- Electric Mystic's Guide

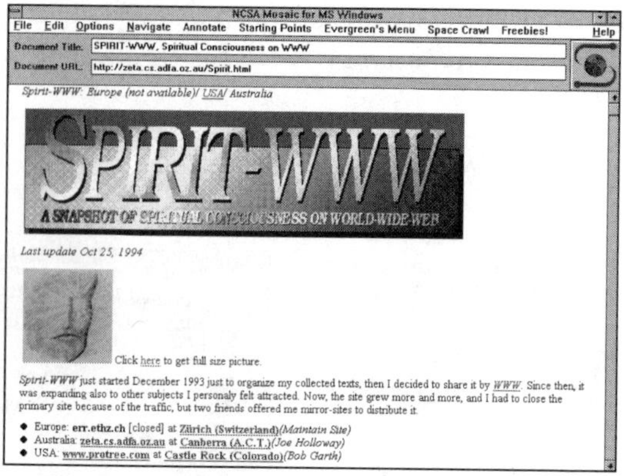

The Spirit-WWW home page

Electronic Salvation

Contrary to the opinions of the uninitiated, the Internet's population is not formed from a pool of perverts, sinners, pedophiles, and malcontents. Religion in all its forms is actually quite prevalent in cyberspace.

At this site, you have your pick of dozens of links to religious and philosophical sites on the Internet. Especially useful are the Christian Resource List and Jerusalem One, both of which will point you to many more sites. Both can be found in the Collected Works link.

You'll also find guides like *CyberMuslim: The Guide to Islamic Resources on the Internet* and *The Electric Mystics' Guide to the Internet*, as well as software with a religious tilt.

Getting There

`http://dewey.lib.ncsu.edu/disciplines/religion.html`

Hot Links

- Finding God in Cyberspace
- Judaism and Jewish Resources
- Electronic Journal of Analytic Philosophy
- Software for Theologians

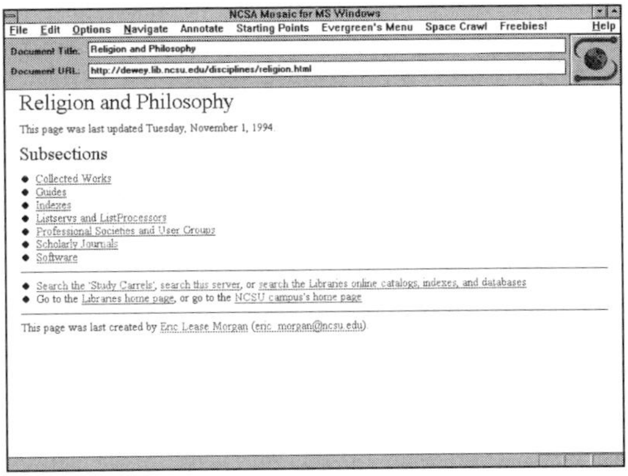

Religion and Philosophy are thriving on the Web

Jerusalem Mosaic

Jerusalem's long and fascinating history is explored at the Jerusalem Mosaic Web page. From its holy and violent past to its present promises of peace, Jerusalem has been called the most dramatic city in the world.

This site brings you the sights, sounds, and faces of Jerusalem, including maps, pictures, songs, and the people who call this city home.

Getting There

`http://shum.cc.huji.ac.il/jeru/jerusalem.html`

Hot Links

- Song of Jerusalem
- Jerusalem from the Sky
- Main Events in the History of Jerusalem

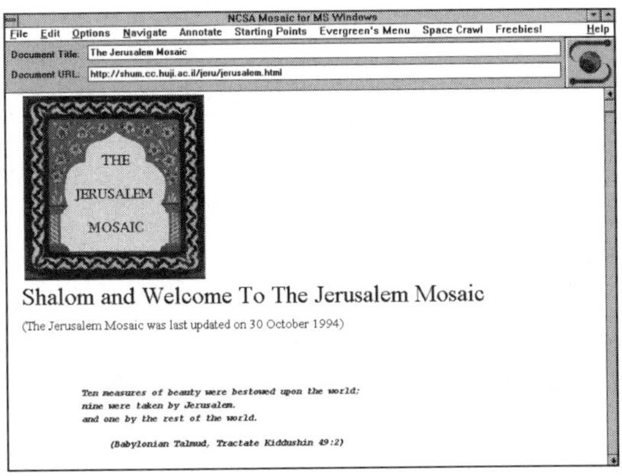

The Jerusalem Mosaic home page

Science

Virtual Biology 101

No muss! No fuss! And you won't go home smelling like formaldehyde! Learn all you ever wanted to know about frog innards without ever having to actually croak one. You have your choice of two separate virtual frog dissections, one (from Lawrence Berkeley Laboratory) using computer-generated images of a frog, and the other (from the University of Virginia) using actual photographs and even movies of a dissection of a real frog.

Both simulations are free—with the caution that like all good simulations, these suck resources like a vacuum. You'll need plenty of RAM, and plenty of patience on any link slower than ISDN speed. Even at 28.8 Kbps, you'll wait several minutes for some of the bitmaps to move down the line, especially at times of the day when Net traffic is bumper to bumper.

These are excellent prototypes of the cutting edge (as it were) educational software that will be widely used over our eventual Information Superhighway.

Getting There

`http://curry.edschool.Virginia.EDU:80/~insttech/frog/menu.html (University of Virginia)`

`http://george.lbl.gov/ITG.hm.pg.docs/dissect/info.html (Lawrence Berkeley Laboratory)`

Hot Links

- Skin Incisions
- Muscle Incisions
- Internal Organs

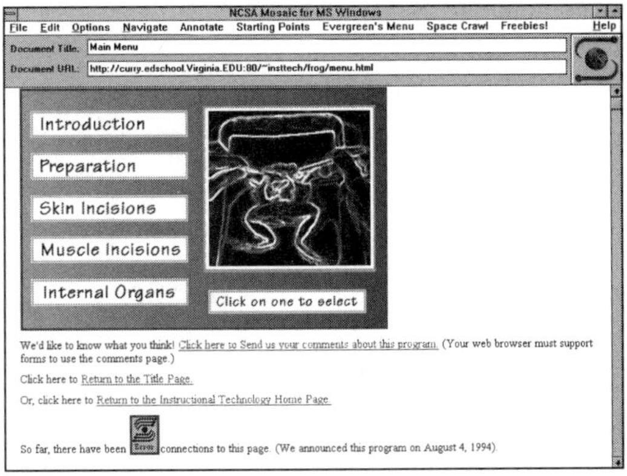

Non-elective surgery (at least for the frog) on the Web

The Universe Is Yours to Download

Celebrating the 25th anniversary of the Apollo 11 moon landing, NASA is now flying high in cyberspace. But NASA isn't resting on its rocket-booster laurels. They're eager to justify the value of their existence, so *you* decide whether NASA is using its funding wisely.

Here's a Web site showing how much of space technology has been applied to the exploration and documentation of Mother Earth, in addition to your galaxy and mine—that favorite of song and dance and candy bars: the Milky Way.

In fact, you can access a veritable universe of space-related info at NASA's Web site. Besides shuttle schedules (as though they'd let *you* on board) and information updates, there's information about the latest commercial technology being used in the aerospace industry, atmospheric maps showing the ozone hole over Antarctica, a browsable online atlas of Mars with a map you can zoom in on and scroll (a must-see), images and movies of the Dante II robot mission to the Mount Spurr volcano in Alaska, and much more.

There are also lots of great links to other space resources, including the Jet Propulsion Laboratory and the Goddard Space Flight Center. With NASA on the Web, you'll be tempted to remain in orbit until Jean-Luc Picard grows an afro.

Getting There

http://hypatia.gsfc.nasa.gov/NASA_homepage.html

Hot Links

- Hot Topics
- Other Space Agencies
- Other Aerospace Sources

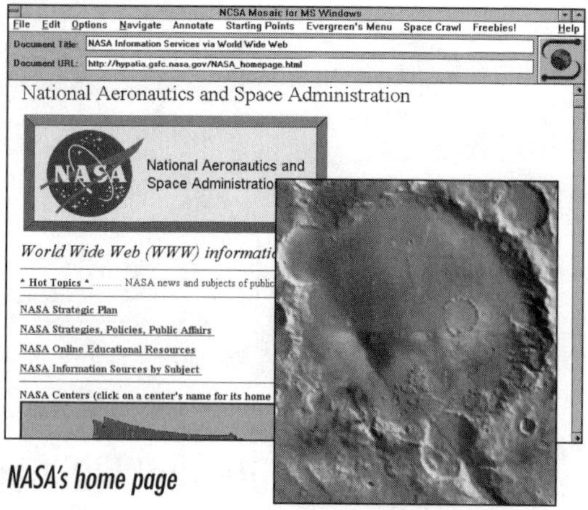

NASA's home page

Gusev Crater was probably Lake Gusev a couple of million years ago, until Mars dried up. This image was downloaded from the online atlas at NASA.

Up, Up, and Away

This site may be light on text, but who needs words when you'll be left speechless at the sight of this photographic history of powered flight? You'll witness the success of Orville (or was it Wilbur) Wright's historic first flight at Kittyhawk, North Carolina, as well as the failures of some of the also-rans like Pilcher's Beetle and Phillip's Multiplane.

It's hard to believe that less than one hundred years ago gravity still had humankind's feet cemented firmly to the ground and airline food was still a distant glimmer in some sadist's eye. Think about that next time your luggage is lost—it sure beats riding the stagecoach.

Getting There

http://hawaii.cogsci.uiuc.edu/invent/invention.html

Hot Links

- Link to Hawaii Home Document

What aviation might have looked like if not for the Wright brothers' lucidity

Look Out Below

One week in July 1994, comet Shoemaker-Levy crossed paths with Jupiter—and lost. The show was spectacular, an event like none ever observed by human eyes. The comet was torn into about 20 chunks by the tidal forces of Jupiter's massive gravitational field, and one by one the fragments blasted into the planet, leaving scars in its cloud belts that could be seen on Earth with telescopes as small as three or four inches of clear aperature.

The best views were not by human eyes at all, but with the highly sophisticated electronic imaging systems of the world's great observatories and the repaired Hubble Space Telescope in Earth orbit. Tens of thousands of beautifully detailed images are being circulated among astronomers, and the very best of these are available for free on the Web.

NASA has set up a home page for the Shoemaker-Levy event, and through it you can read about the collision and (most important for the bulk of us non-astronomers) gape at the awe-inspiring electronic images of the giant planet and its brand-new blemishes. The visible light images show distinct violent disruptions in the cloud tops, but the infrared images show searing vortices of heat energy created as the comet fragments were vaporized in Jupiter's upper atmosphere.

Those of us here today may or may not live to see anything quite this peculiar in our solar system again. Certainly we don't want to get a *whole* lot closer to an event like this—but for now, it's something you should *not* miss!

Getting There

`http://navigator.jpl.nasa.gov/s19/s19.html`

Hot Links

- News Flash
- Other Comet Shoemaker-Levy Home Pages
- JPL Home Page

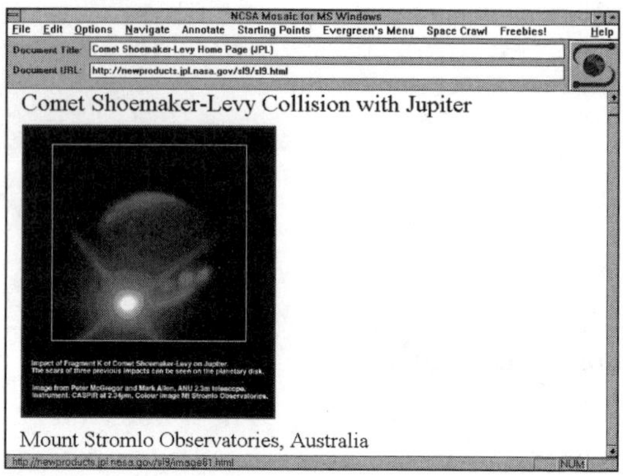

One of thousands of impact photos available on the Internet

You Must Be Dreaming

At last, a forum to discuss my recurring dream with Marge Simpson, chicken feathers, and a quart of Valvoline: dreamMosaic. This Web site is devoted to recording and correlating the dreams of Web walkers from around the world.

According to the text at this site, the plan is to "use dreams as an interface to . . . the Internet" in order to "explore the unfolding of someone else's dream to shape your travels through the Web." Uh huh.

Ultimately, say the Webmasters, the goal is to see if evidence can be found to support the theory of group dreaming, in which different people have concurrent dreams about similar events, locations, or people (or in my case, cartoon characters).

Getting There

`http://www.itp.tsoa.nyu.edu/~windeatr/dreamMosaic.html`

Hot Links

- Dreams as Interface to the WWWeb
- dreamSources
- YAHOO Dream Index

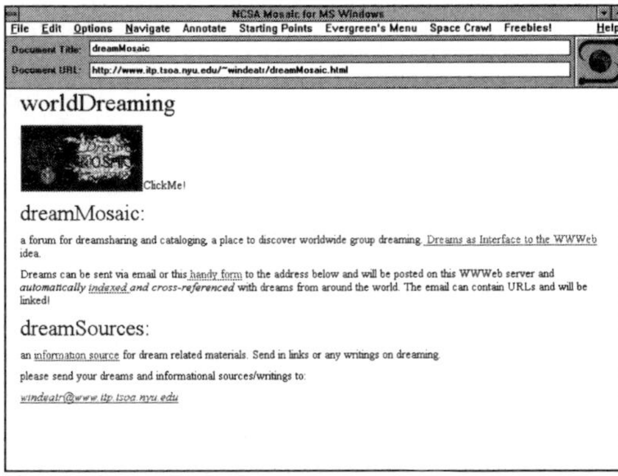

Sweet dreams recorded and discussed on the Web

Humans in Space

Just what does space travel feel like and how is the human body affected by prolonged exposure to weightlessness? The closest I've ever come to answering these questions are some lost weekends from my college days and a few mountain biking endos, but I'll save those for another book.

This Web site from the Space Biomedical Research Institute will help you to grasp the basics of space physiology and what happens to the human body in the space environment. Written as a general introduction rather than for physicists, *Humans in Space* also includes some basic science experiments that you can perform to learn the basics of space biomedicine—definitely useful in the classroom.

Getting There

`http://medlib.jsc.nasa.gov/intro/humans.html`

Hot Links

- Basics of Space Flight

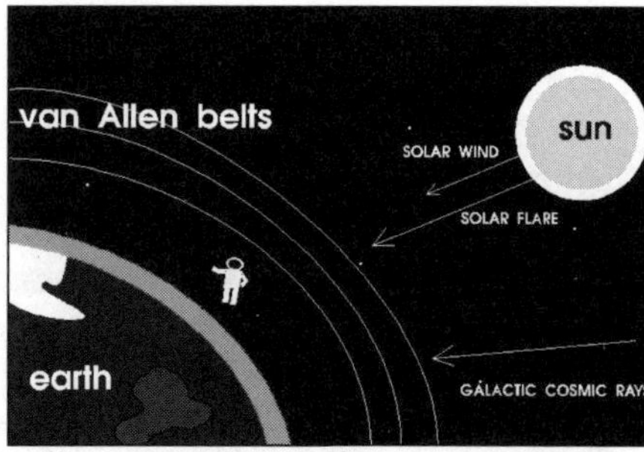

One example of some of the drawings you can download explaining the effects of space on humans

Racin' in the Sun

Here's a Web page that acts as a clearinghouse of sorts for solar auto racing. These cars, most of which were designed, built, and raced by U.S. and Canadian university students, are completely powered by energy collected from the Sun.

Get information on upcoming and past solar races, including maps of the routes, participating teams, official results, and more. There are even links to U.S. weather maps so you can make sure the race won't be rained out.

Getting There

`http://www-lips.ece.utexas.edu/~delayman/solar.html`

Hot Links

- Other Teams
- U.S. Weather Maps + Reports
- The Electric Power Research Institute

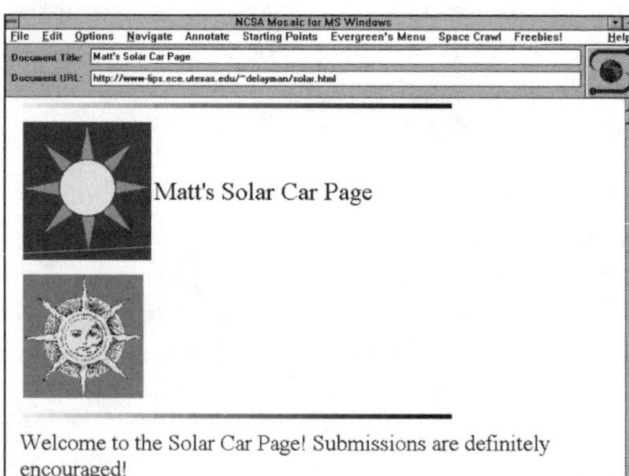

Everything under the Sun about solar racing can be found at this Web site

SHOPPING

Let's Go Shopping the Internet Way

The Internet Plaza is an online shopping extravaganza, providing interactive shopping and even allowing you to place orders online. You'll find lots of gift ideas, including an online florist, book store, gift shop, and more. There are even links to other shopping malls and services scattered throughout cyberspace. Christmas shopping has never been easier.

Getting There

`http://plaza.xor.com/stores/index.html`

Hot Links

- Visit Stores
- Foot Traffic
- Monthly Feature

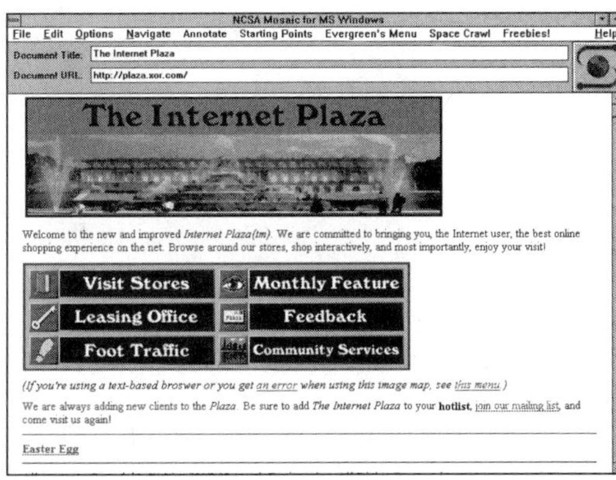

Lots of gateways to online shopping at the Internet Plaza

Skip the Crowds at the Shopping Maul

The Internet Shopping Network, the world's largest shopping mall, offers products from more than 600 companies—and it's all online. A subsidiary of the folks who brought cable potatoes the Home Shopping Network, the Internet Shopping Network is another of the Home Shopping Network's giant marketing ventures.

At the Internet Shopping Network, you can browse through online catalogs to find the best deals cyberspace has to offer. You'll find loads of products, including programs for Macs and PCs, CD-ROMs, disk drives, modems, and games, games, games. You can even have them delivered to you on the next business day. Is modern technology great or what?

Getting There

http://www.internet.net/

Hot Links

- Catalogs
- Power Shopping

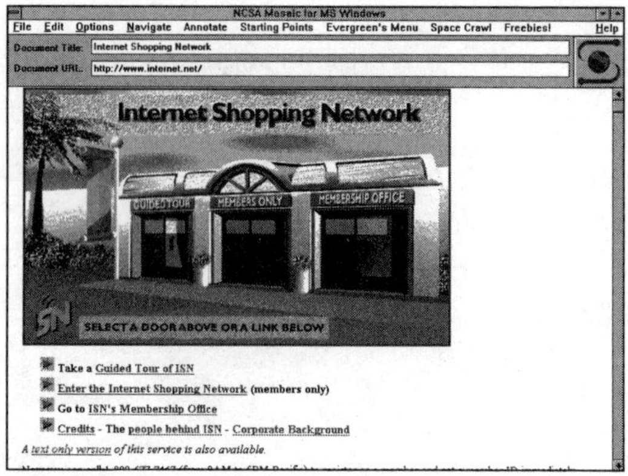

Internet Shopping Network home page

Pizza and the Net: a Perfect Marriage

You worked through lunch and you're so hungry you're about to eat your mouse. Maybe you're thinking about ordering a pizza but don't want to break your modem connection to make the call. Have I got a surprise for you. If you're in an area where Pizza Hut is test marketing its new "PizzaNet," you're in luck. Order an online pizza—or pizza online—through the Web.

PizzaNet customers get product descriptions and current specials, then place their orders (hold the anchovies). At last someone has found a practical use for the billions of dollars in research spent developing the Information Highway.

Getting There

http://www.pizzahut.com

Hot Links

- The Santa Cruz Operation
- SCO

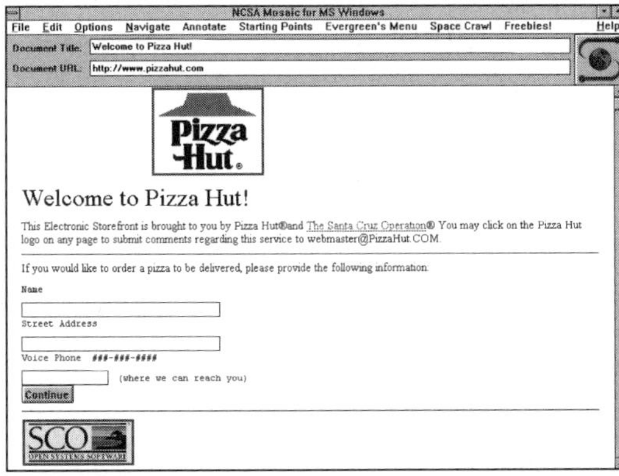

Order your pizza on the Pizza Hut home page

Suds o' the Month

Books of the month, chocolates of the month, Tupperware of the month. Why not a beer of the month? That's exactly what you get at this Web site, times 12. Cascade River's Beer page shows you how to sign up for this fun and tasty club. Each month you'll get two six packs of beer from some of America's best microbreweries. These small breweries haven't forgotten that all beers don't have to taste the same.

If you're new to microbreweries, you'll be amazed at the variety of flavors these mom-and-pop brewers produce. You'll never go back for the convenience-store specials again.

Getting There

`http://venus.mcs.com/~cascade/html/beer.html`

Hot Links

- Hot Stuff
- Beer Page
- Beer-Related WWW Pages

Beer of the Month home page

Let's Make a Deal

Looking for your hard-to-find dream car? It just might be on the Internet. AutoPages of Internet helps buyers and sellers come together in cyberspace. This service lets you browse thumbnail pictures and descriptions of some of the most beautiful cars you're likely to see for sale, like Ĺamborghinis (no home should be without one), Mercedes, and Chevy Vettes (sigh). Click on the car you're interested in for more information.

If there is such a thing as reincarnation, I want to come back as a Rolls.

Getting There

`http://www.clark.net/pub/networx/autopage/autopage.html`

Hot Links

- Exotic Cars
- Classic Cars
- Car Dealers

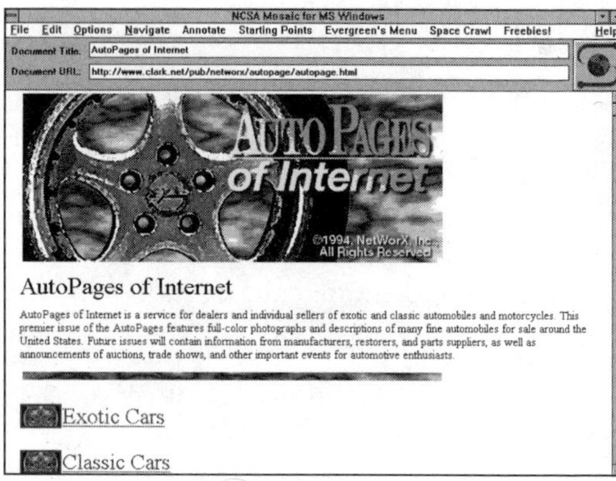

AutoPages of Internet home page

Shop Till You Drop

Where else are you going to find contemporary Russian fine art, personal body alarms, and "the original burp gun" all under the same roof? The Branch Mall, of course. The Branch Mall has it all, at least everything *I've* ever heard of. You can order flowers online, join the Treat-of-the-Month club for cats and dogs, and buy Fuller brushes at dealer discounts. Happy bargain-hunting.

Getting There

`http://branch.com`

Hot Links

- Clothing
- Travel

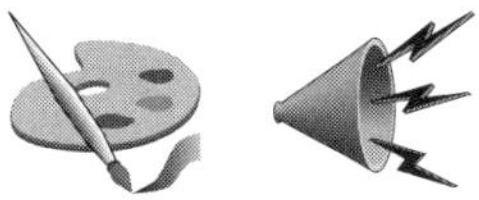

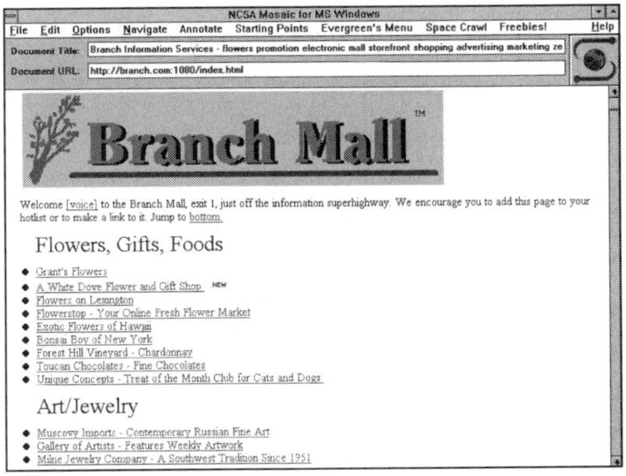

The Branch Mall home page

Sports, Hobbies, and Recreation

A Quick Fix for Sports Junkies

Yank yourself away from ESPN long enough to log on here; you'll be glad you did. Voted Best Entertainment Site in the Best of the Web '94 contest, the WWW Sports Information Server is up, running, and available to give you the latest information on America's most serious, most civil, and most culturally uplifting pastimes: basketball and football.

Yup, this service provides extensive coverage of the NBA and NFL, including the latest scores and schedules. You'll find up-to-date league standings and box scores for all the season's games, plus player-by-player stats for every team. There are even histories of NBA awards like Rookie of the Year and MVP; great for trivia (or is that trivial?) buffs.

Getting There

http://www.mit.edu:8001/services/sis/sports.html

Hot Links

- Cybersports NBA Page
- Sports Section
- Playoff Chart
- Super Bowl History

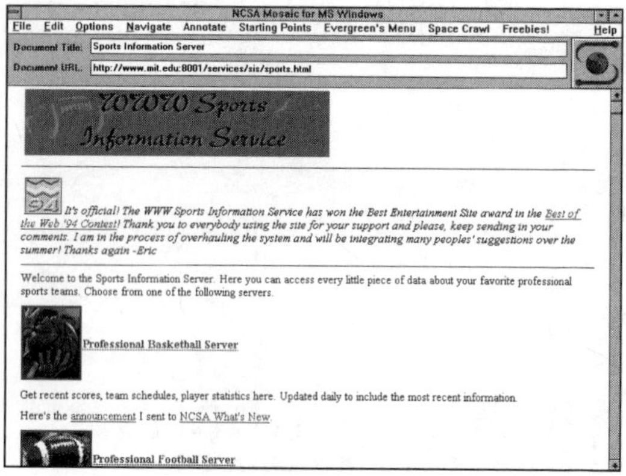

Sports Information Server home page

Mountain Biking—Because It's There

Open to anyone on two wheels, Team Internet is a registered member of the United States Cycling Federation and the National Off Road Bicycling Association. Bikers who join can use the club name on racing license applications and plans are in the works for affiliations with other national organizations.

And don't forget about the team jerseys. Although not guaranteed to shave minutes off your time trials or downhills, these snazzy uniforms will definitely make you *look* faster in the pack. Join up and find out what other perks come with membership.

Getting There

http://www.sce.carleton.ca/rads/greg/team-internet/

Hot Links

- Global Cycling Network
- Race Results
- National Collegiate Cycling Association

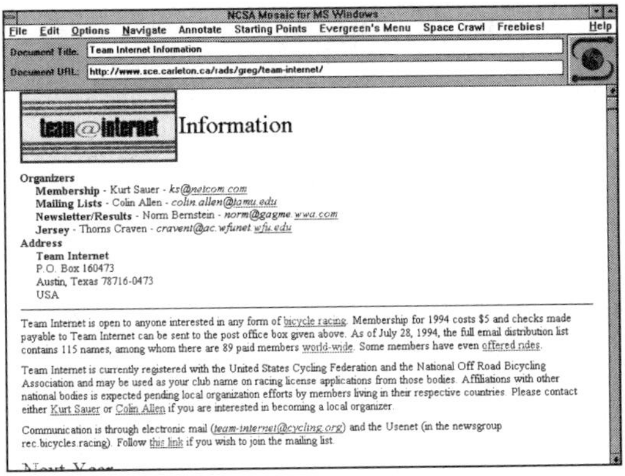

Team Internet home page

Drive for Show, Putt for Dough

If you love golf, the 19th Hole is for you. At the time this book was published, Jimbo Odom, this site's WebMaster, was on a temporary sabbatical, though he promises to be back soon. And it should be worth the wait. When things get back to normal, you'll find the latest tour schedules and results, rankings for the top 100 pros, the rules of golf, a great archive of scorecards, the *Golf Digest* record book, and more. There are even GIFs of the hottest courses, a golfer's FAQ, and a list of other great golf pages on the Web.

Getting There

`http://dallas.nmhu.edu/golf/golf.htm`

Hot Links

- Rules of Golf
- Scorecard Archive
- Golf Art / Pictures

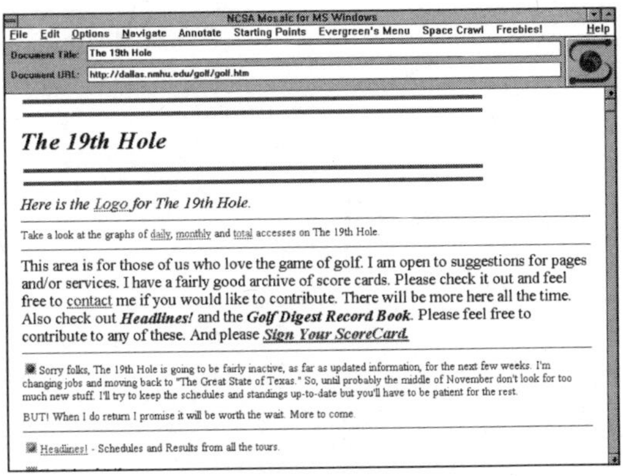

19th Hole home page

Start Your Engines

Did you know that the Indianapolis 500 attracts the largest audience of any sporting event? This site will show you why. It's a great place for automotive racing enthusiasts to learn about their favorite drivers and the cars they race. The r.a.s. Racer Archive provides news and information on Formula One, Indy car, and NASCAR racing.

This site has a lot of photos and drawings of cars and drivers, as well as historic racing machines. If you're running a machine that's "memory challenged," you might have to wait a little, but it's worth it.

Getting There

`http://www.eng.hawaii.edu/Contribs/carina/ra.home.page.html`

Hot Links

- 1994 Formula 1 World Championship
- 1994 CART PPG IndyCar Championship
- r.a.s. Racing Gallery

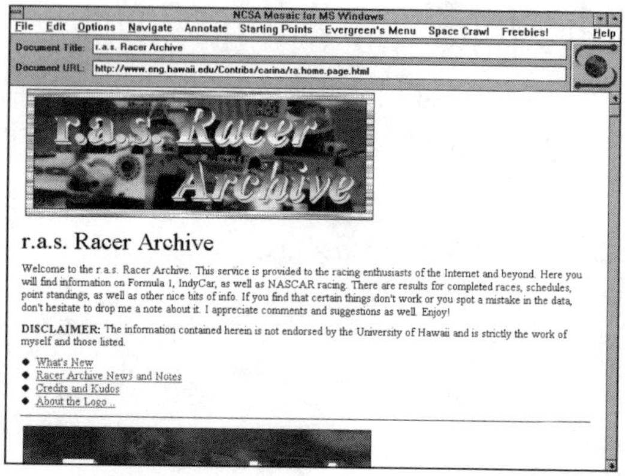

r.a.s. Racer Archive home page

Let's Go Fly a Kite!

"Jason's Web Kite Site" is an Australian nexus for things that fly on strings. Most people don't realize it, but kites have followed technology into the 21st century, and are no longer a couple of willow switches with newspaper glued on. Today's kites use exotic materials like carbon fiber rods (or for teeny weeny little kites, solid boron rods no thicker than needles!) and ripstop nylon. They can be big, too—sometimes eighty or a hundred feet long.

Jason's kite photo collection gives a pretty good feel for the diversity of modern kites. It's presented as a list of thumbnails, which you can click on to download the full-sized images. The page also provides pointers to some kite newsletters, newsgroup rec.kites, and other kite sites elsewhere in the world.

Getting There

http://www.latrobe.edu.au/Glenn/KiteSite/Kites.html

Hot Links

- Single Line Kites
- Dual Line (Stunt) Kites
- Kite Buggying

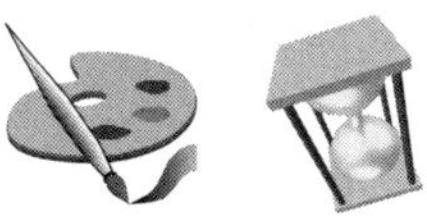

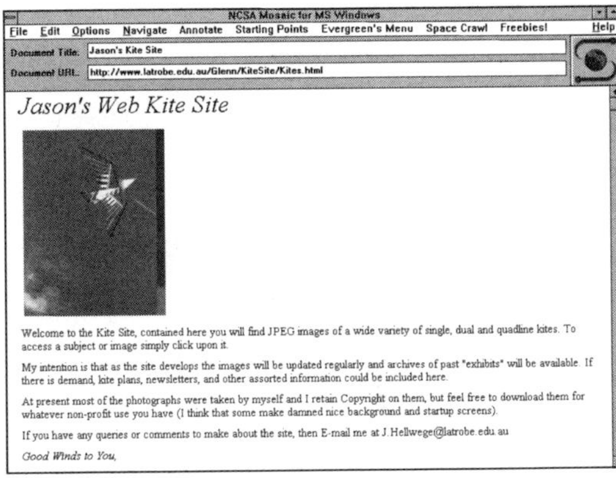

Jason's Web Kite Site home page

Tarot, Anyone?

What do the cards hold in store for you? In my case, I hope it's a straight flush. In any event, here's a popular site that's hard to resist. Access it to get three random cards from the Tarot's 78-card deck and find out what's coming in your future. Sure you don't believe in that stuff, but I'll bet you read your horoscope in the morning paper. So c'mon, give it a try and have fun. Who knows, maybe the cards will tell you not to get out of bed this morning. And if you should happen to win the lottery, remember who pointed you to this site.

Getting There

http://cad.ucla.edu:8001/tarot

Hot Links

No links, unless you count the ones to your past and future

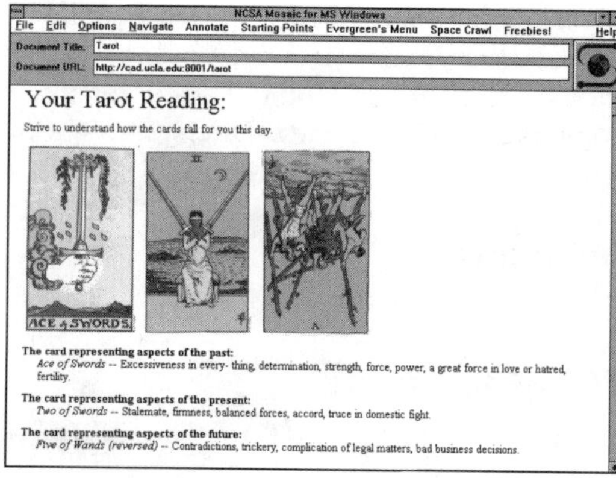

Web Tarot server

NHL Hockey Goes Hawaiian

Perhaps it was serious ice envy that led the University of Hawaii to put together their dazzling collection of NHL photos, movies, and statistics about the NHL. Tune in here and you'll find an answer to virtually any hockey question you can think of. You'll find the latest NHL scores, present league standings, 1994 Stanley Cup Playoffs matchups, links to home pages belonging to NHL teams, and more.

Getting There

`http://maxwell.uhh.hawaii.edu/hockey/hockey.html`

Hot Links

- Stanley Cup Playoffs
- 1994-1995 Regular Season
- Award and Trophy Recipients
- Other NHL Statistics

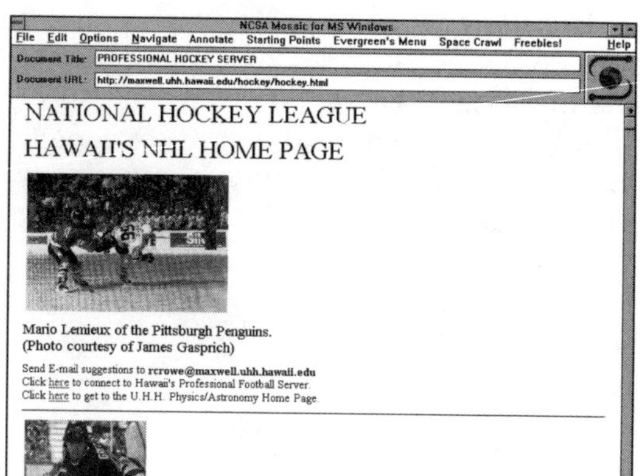

University of Hawaii (yes, Hawaii) NHL Hockey home page

Grand Central Station for Railophiles

This home page is a sort of "virtual magazine" for railroad buffs, including (to some extent) model railroaders. It is an eclectic compendium of links to many places storing information pertaining to rail travel, rail hardware, and rail modeling.

Among many other things, the page has links to a database of all known surviving steam locomotives in the U.S. and Canada, rosters of diesel locomotives in use at American railroads, pointers to non-Internet rail-related BBSs, lists of newsgroups that have a spin on railroads, and a database of folk songs, many of which are about trains and rail travel. There's even a selection of railroad maps available for downloading, though a few of the maps are disappointingly available only to educational institutions. One of the most unique items here is a discussion of how to use stepper motor technology in model railroads. Definitely the online resource for researchers interested in rail topics.

Getting There

http://www-cse.ucsd.edu/users/bowdidge/railroad/rail-home.html

Hot Links

- A Collection of Railroad Maps
- Train Schedules
- Other Railroad-Related Hypertext Documents

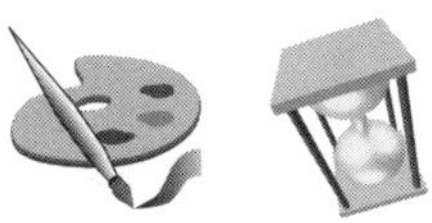

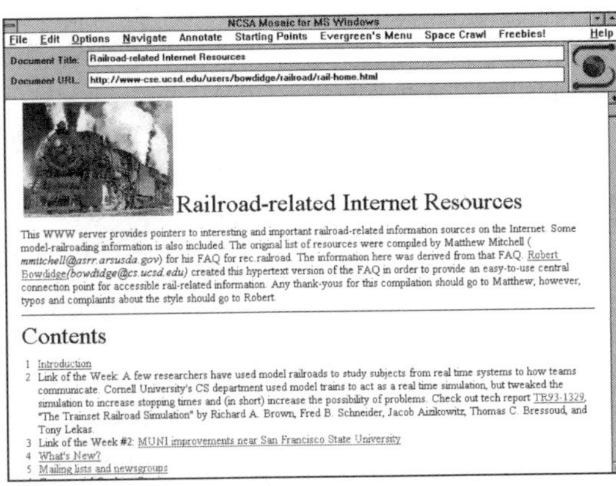

Information on anything that rides on tracks

Television

57 Channels and Nothing On

If you think dishes are for more than eating on, don't miss this terrific site for satellite TV and radio information. You'll find schedules for most of the popular services, reviews of recent satellite events and equipment, a KU-band FAQ, and much more, including some technical stuff so arcane that I wasn't sure what the heck it was for (but it sure looked important), like an Inclined Orbit Satellite Visual Prediction Appendix. Whew, I gotta get me one of those!

There are also some interesting articles by Gary Borgois on satellite TV for scroungers, as well as alternative satellite programming.

Getting There

`http://itre.uncecs.edu/misc/sat.html`

Hot Links

- Sci-Fi Channel
- Satellite TV Images
- Radio Free Berkeley

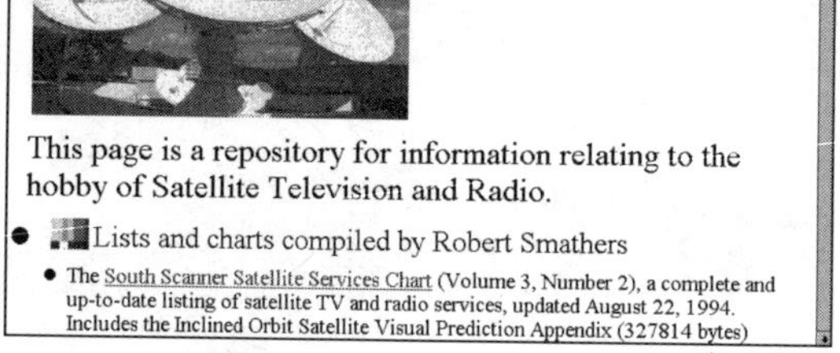

Satellite TV home page

Get Thee to a TV

Here's a television page with links to more TV-related sites than you could shake your clicker at. There are pointers to information on shows as diverse as *Mystery Science Theater 3000, Melrose Place, The Prisoner, The Late Show with David Letterman, Fawlty Towers, Max Headroom, Monty Python's Flying Circus, Babylon 5, Red Dwarf, The Simpsons, Seinfeld,* and that's just scratching the surface. Science fiction seems to predominate, but this *is* cyberspace, right? I mean, hey, is the world really ready for a *Roseanne* page?

Getting There

`http://www.cs.cmu.edu:8001/afs/cs.cmu.edu/user/clamen/misc/tv/README.html`

Hot Links

- Library of Monty Python Sketches
- The Simpsons Archive
- Television Lyrics

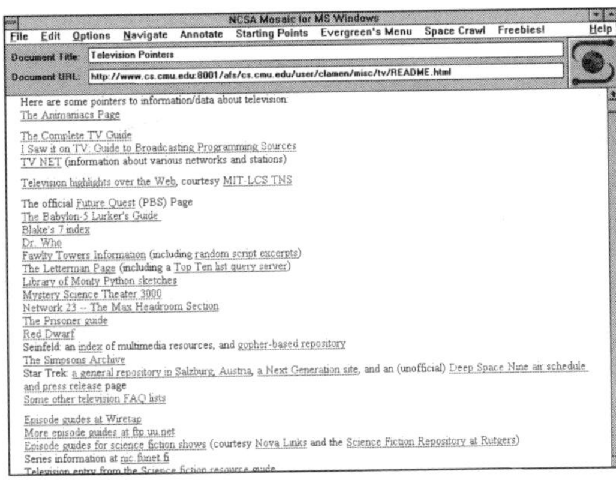

NCSA Mosaic for MS Windows
File Edit Options Navigate Annotate Starting Points Evergreen's Menu Space Crawl Freebies! Help
Document Title: Television Pointers
Document URL: http://www.cs.cmu.edu:8001/afs/cs.cmu.edu/user/clamen/misc/tv/README.html

Here are some pointers to information/data about television:
The Animaniacs Page

The Complete TV Guide
I Saw it on TV: Guide to Broadcasting Programming Sources
TV NET (information about various networks and stations)

Television highlights over the Web, courtesy MIT-LCS TNS

The official Future Quest (PBS) Page
The Babylon-5 Lurker's Guide
Blake's 7 index
Dr. Who
Fawlty Towers Information (including random script excerpts)
The Letterman Page (including a Top Ten list query server)
Library of Monty Python sketches
Mystery Science Theater 3000
Network 23 -- The Max Headroom Section
The Prisoner guide
Red Dwarf
Seinfeld: an index of multimedia resources, and gopher-based repository
The Simpsons Archive
Star Trek: a general repository in Salzburg, Austria, a Next Generation site, and an (unofficial) Deep Space Nine air schedule and press release page
Some other television FAQ lists

Episode guides at Wiretap
More episode guides at ftp.uu.net
Episode guides for science fiction shows (courtesy Nova Links and the Science Fiction Repository at Rutgers)
Series information at nic.funet.fi

If it's on TV, it's on the Web

With Gilligaaaan, the Skipper toooo . . .

Just sit right back and you'll hear a tale, a tale of one of TV's corniest comedies. Personally, I think I've seen every episode of *Gilligan's Island* at least a dozen times, which isn't exactly something I put on my resume. I even heard a bar band do a reggae version of the theme song once—living proof that classics never die. And just when you thought you may never hear the theme song again, along comes this cyber blast from the past.

Here's a site full of sounds, pictures, and trivia from the castaways on Gilligan's little South Pacific paradise. What was the Skipper's first name? What about the Professor? Just how *did* Ginger and Mrs. Howell manage to stash half the clothes from Tiffany's onto that little boat? These and other pressing Gilligan questions are sure to be answered here.

Getting There

`http://www.oac.uci.edu/indiv/dkrause/fun/television/gilligan/`

Hot Links

- Opening Theme
- Cast Photo
- Episode Guide

What do these seven stranded castaways have to smile about?

Browsing the Boob Tube

Billing itself as "The Complete TV Guide," this page is a well-organized collection of links to TV-related Web sites. Most useful are schedules for *The Discovery Channel*, *The Learning Channel*, and other cable services.

The most fun you'll have with this site is probably with the pointer to an interactive poll you're invited to take part in. At press time readers were asked to vote on topics they would like to see on daytime talk shows. Some of the winners:

- Geeks who vote on Internet polls and the people who hate them
- Men who hate Barney and the women who love them

- Talk show hosts discussing the unrestricted proliferation of talk show hosts
- People who think WWW is a real place

You get the idea.

Getting There

http://www.galcit.caltech.edu/~ta/tv

Hot Links

- Major Television Links
- The Hot List
- The TV Poll

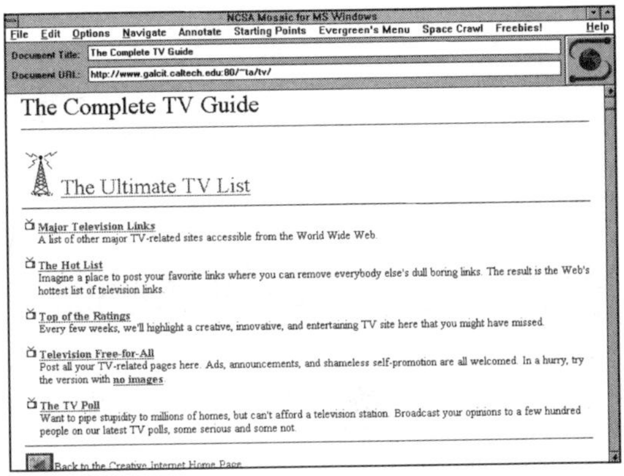

Television guide for tube boobs

The Late Show in Cyberspace

The dust has settled in the late-night TV wars, and the bodies of Arsenio, Chevy, and Dana, among others, are strewn on the battlefield. Jay is still breathing, though gasping for breath, and Dave is still on top.

Here's a great Web site to find info on the king of late-night television, Daaavid Letterrrmannn! You'll get the latest Top Ten lists, photos and sound bites, sneak previews of upcoming guests, and access to online fan clubs. Take *that*, NBC.

Getting There

http://bingen.cs.csbsju.edu/letterman.html

Hot Links

- Upcoming Guests
- Top Ten Lists
- Late Show News

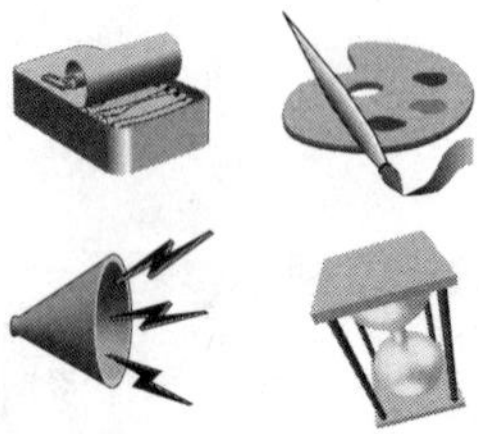

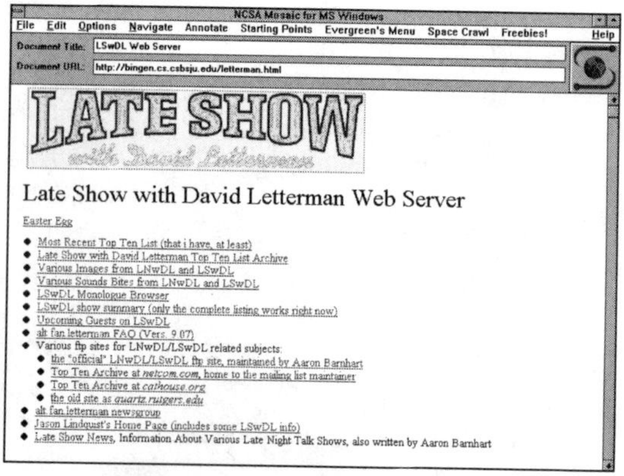

One of many Letterman Web sites

Now for Something Completely Different

Cyberspace is whacky enough without the Monty Python troupe adding to the mix, but what's whackiness to a bunch of guys who sing passionately of the merits of Spam? As John Cleese, the Minister of Funny Walks himself, would say, this Web page offers you something completely different.

1994 marked the 25th anniversary of Monty Python's Flying Circus. If you've never watched it, check out this site to find out about the show that laid the groundwork for on-the-edge television shows like *Saturday Night Live*, *SCTV*, and *In Living Color*. You can download all the Python movie scripts and many of the sketches, including The Argument, The Dead Parrot, The Cheese Shop, and lots of others guaranteed to make your brain hurt.

Getting There

`http://alfred.u.washington.edu:8080/~uffda/python.html`

Hot Links

- Pictures
- Movie Scripts

- Songs
- Sketches

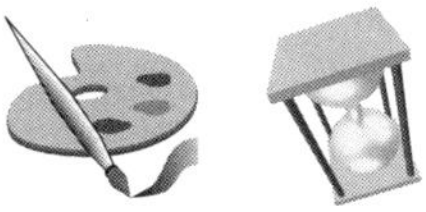

The Python cast while filming The Holy Grail

Travel

Online Hotels Welcome Weary Web Travelers

Cybertravelers will soon be able to make hotel reservations online as hotels begin plugging into the Internet. TravelWeb, the hotel industry's first interactive color catalog, showcases the Hyatt Hotels Corporation's 16 resorts and 87 other hotels in the U.S. and Caribbean. TravelWeb provides detailed room, recreation, special services, and destination info for each hotel, complete with color photographs.

Other hotels are also venturing into cyberspace, including Embassy Suites, Hampton Inns, and Homewood Suites. Check out this site and stay tuned for more links.

Getting There

`http://www.travelweb.com/travel.html`

Hot Links

- Hyatt Resorts Search Page

- Embassy Suites Home Page
- Hampton Inns Home Page
- Homewood Suites Home Page

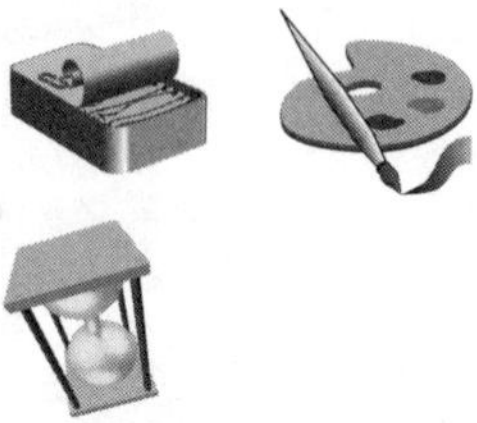

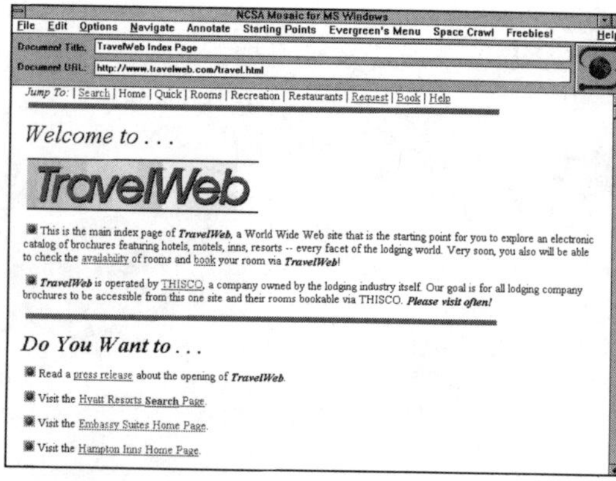

TravelWeb home page

When in Rome . . .

Or any other European city for that matter, you'll want to be prepared. This site will give you maps of Europe and links to many of its cities and countries, like London, Paris, Slovenija, and Rome.

Click on one of the links and get priceless information about the places you should see, the people you should meet, the dishes you should taste, the words and simple expressions you should know, and so much more. Don't forget to send me a postcard.

Getting There

`http://s700.uminho.pt/cult-europ.html`

Hot Links

- WWW Paris
- UK Guide

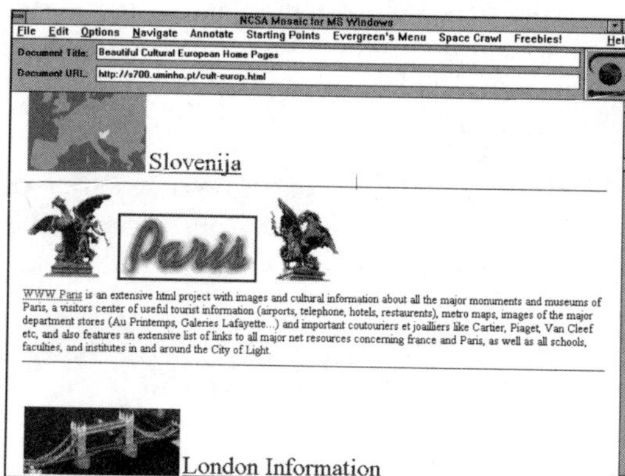

Culture comes to the Web at this site

Keep a Light on for Me

Living in Arizona, I'm about as likely to see a lighthouse as I am to suffer from frostbite. That's why it's nice to have people like Bill Britten creating Web pages. Bill has a love for lighthouses and it shows. While not the savior of ships that they once were (radar and satellite tracking have taken care of that, however unromantic), many lighthouses around the shores of the U.S. have been restored and are open to tourists.

Bill has made his impressive personal collection of photos available to Net users, along with facts, trivia, and tour schedules of historic lighthouses scattered from New England to California, and all coastal points in between.

Getting There

`http://gopher.lib.utk.edu:70/0/Other-Internet-Resources/pictures/lights/lights.html`

Hot Links

- New England Lights
- Outer Bank Lights
- California Lights
- Southeastern U.S. Lights

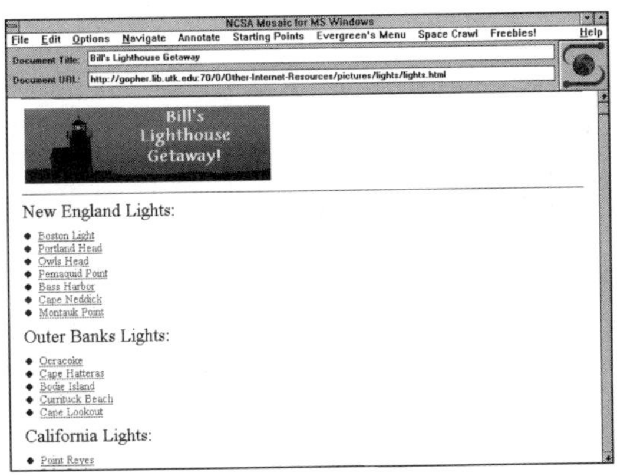

Lighthouses on the Web

The REAL Northern Exposure

Button up, it's colder than a polar bear's schnoz up here! Arctic Adventours, Inc. out of Oslo, Norway knows what cold *really* means, and they'll take you to the top of the world just to prove it. Put on your snow shoes, then tramp on over to this site for information on arctic tours, photos of past expeditions, and more.

Getting There

`http://www.oslonett.no/data/adv/AA/AA.html`

Hot Links

- Arctic Explorer
- GIF Images
- Virtual Tourist

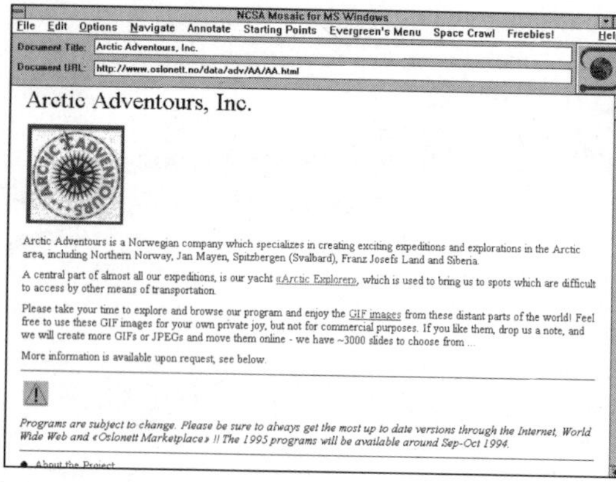

The Arctic Adventours, Inc. home page

Weather Is Here, Wish You Were Beautiful

It's no doubt happened to you: You're in the midst of making detailed travel plans, feeling woefully unprepared, and then suddenly you say to yourself, "Hey, if only I had up-to-the-minute, full color weather maps of the U.S. from the National Climatic Data Center! Then I'd be the travel sophisticate I always knew I could be!"

Okay, you want the latest maps? Well, we've got maps, or at least the NCDC does. Here's where to go to get full-color weather maps so you can regain a little control over your travel and weather destiny.

Getting There

`http://www.ncdc.noaa.gov/interesting/us-se-wxmap.html`

Hot Links

- Weather Symbol Legend

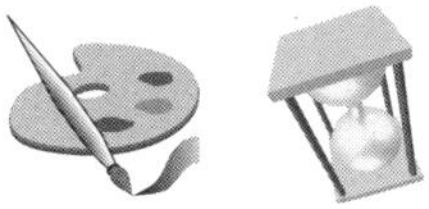

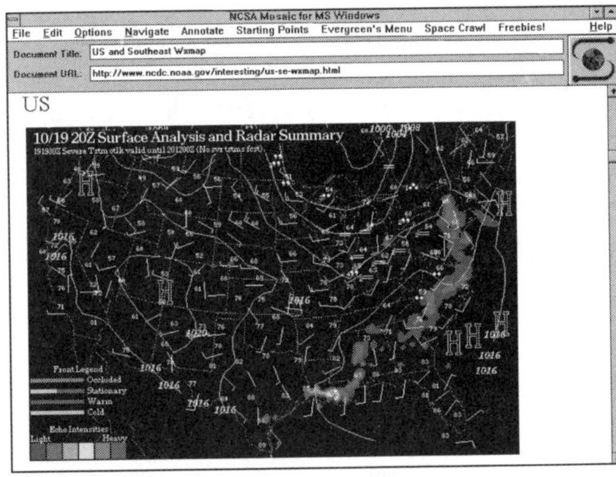

Weather map from the National Climatic Data Center

Have Cloak Will Travel

The World Factbook, loaded with information about scores of countries around the globe, is required reading for itinerant government employees to keep abreast of the political and social climates of the countries they visit.

Published annually by the CIA, the World Factbook provides valuable economic, political, and social information about each country, as well as monetary conversions and U.S. Embassy locations and phone numbers. Plus, there are travel warnings for those traveling to some of the more hostile corners of the globe. Great stuff for globetrotters.

Getting There

`http://www.ic.gov/94fact/fb94toc/fb94toc.html`

Hot Links

- Reference Maps
- Weights and Measures

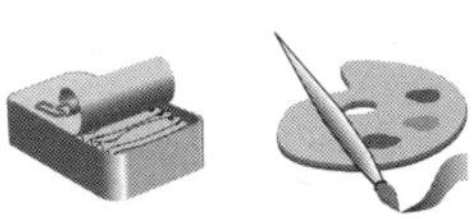

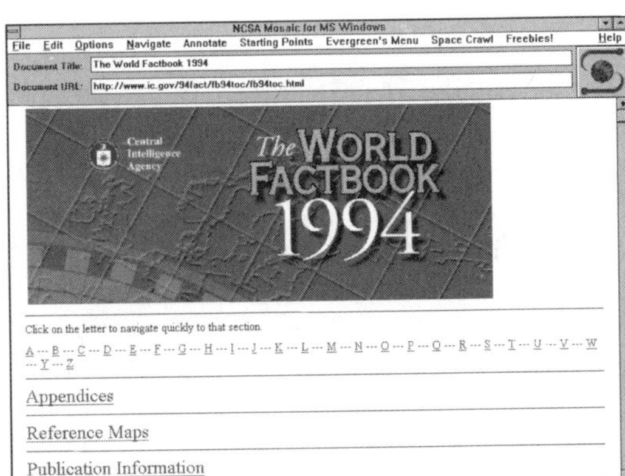

The place to go for world travelers to learn the facts of life

You're Speaking My Language

Se habla Español? Sprechen sie Deutsch? Like, what's happenin', duuude? If you just don't understand, try the Web's Human-Languages page. It offers foreign language dictionaries (like English-German), tutorials (like *Let's Learn Arabic* and *Travelers' Japanese Tutorial*), foreign literature, and other references and resources in French, Italian, Latin, Klingon (really), and many more.

Getting There

`http://www.willamette.edu/~tjones/Language-Page.html`

Hot Links

- Online Books Page
- Foreign Language and Culture
- Foreign Languages for Travellers

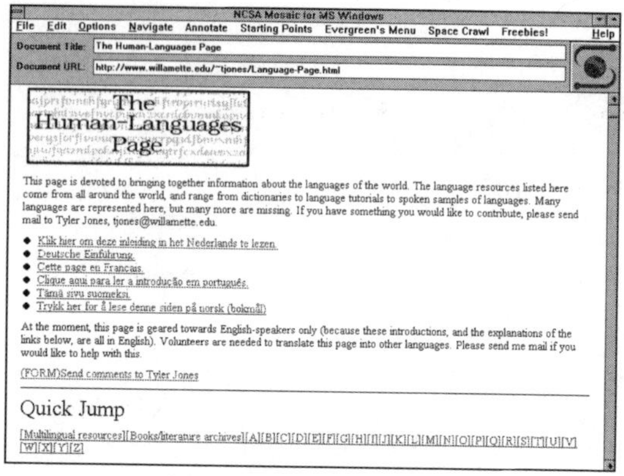

Human Languages home page

Do Birds Fly Upside Down, Down Under?

Ever wonder what a laughing kookaburra looks like? Neither did I, but somebody must have, because they put a picture of one at this site. If you're still trying to figure out what it is, maybe this place isn't for you, but if you're entranced by the beauty and sounds of exotic birds, as well as other flora and fauna, you'll appreciate what the Australian National Botanic Gardens has to offer.

If you're ever in Australia, be sure to visit this site in person. While fascinating to see through the eyes of modern technology, one can only imagine how beautiful it would be in real life. This site has a wealth of information about the Gardens, and many of the brochures you would receive there are available online.

Getting There

`http://155.187.10.12:80/anbg/birds.html`

Hot Links

- Australian National Botanic Gardens
- List of Birds

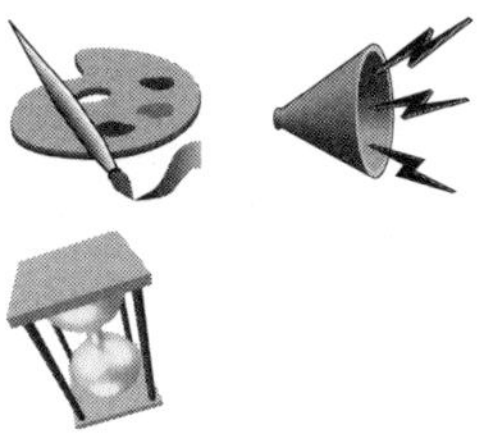

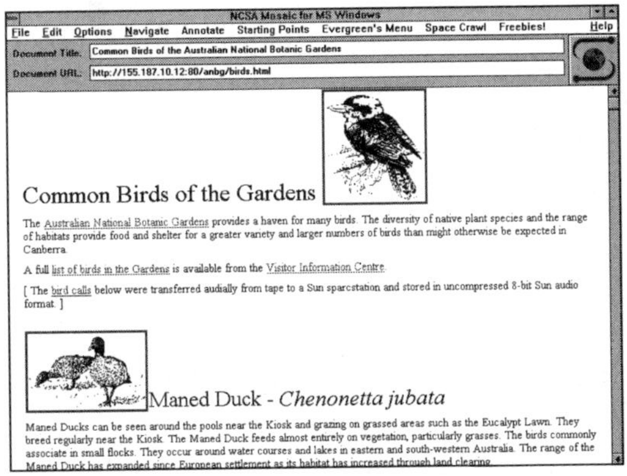

Australian National Botanic Gardens home page

And You Thought Net Traffic Was Bad

Access this site and you'll remember why you bought that quiet house in the country—or are planning to. You can access up-to-the-minute traffic reports in many cities in Southern California, with other major cities in the U.S. soon to follow. Get current areas of congestion, freeway maps, tables of current speeds by freeway, road closure information, and lots more. By clicking on a freeway sign found on one of the maps you can display, you'll get information about speed limits, accidents, and any other info you should know about before attempting to put the pedal to the metal.

L.A., San Diego, and Orange County are currently online, with plans to have Boston, Washington D.C., New York, the I-95 corridor, Atlanta, and Dallas/Ft. Worth online "soon."

Getting There

`http://www.scubed.com:8001/caltrans/transnet.html`

Hot Links

- CHP Road Reports
- California Weather
- Virtual Tourist - California

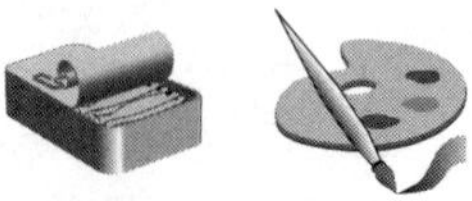

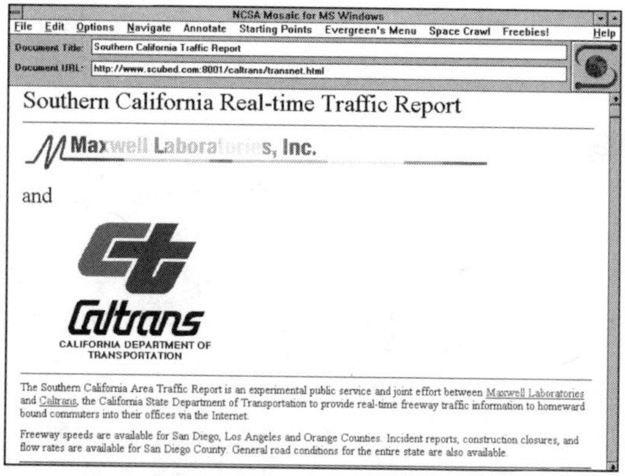

Traffic Reports on the Web

Hey, Isn't That George and Betty?

You just never know who you're going run into at the beach. And nude beaches are no exception. Want to know where the good ones are? Keep your shirt on and I'll tell you. This site will point you to a beach near you. (No, there aren't any pictures.)

Get information about nude beaches located around the country and around the world, including such hot spots as Black's Beach in California, Metro Beach in France, Tunel Boca Beach in Spain, and the list goes on. You'll also get answers to many of your frequently asked questions.

Getting There

http://pegasus.cc.ucf.edu/~kr4ah/naturist/beaches/index.html

Hot Links

- United Kingdom
- Site Reports

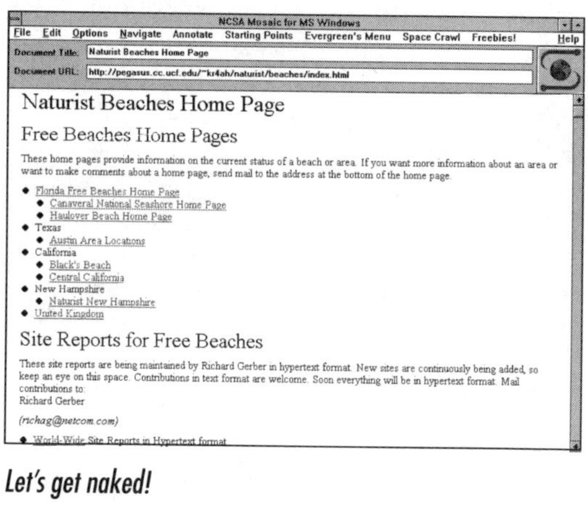

Let's get naked!

PART 4

A Dozen Whacky, Fun, and Useless Things You Can Do on the Web

Surfing the Web doesn't have to be all work and no play. To prove it, I've compiled a list of the whackiest ways to kill a few hours in cyberspace. Educational? No. Inspirational? Hardly. But that's what they said about *Hogan's Heroes* reruns.

One trend I noticed throughout these sites was the need for each page's Webmaster to try to justify his or her creation. "This site shows the future of the interactive potential for networking in cyberspace," or "We wanted to test the implications of . . . ." Right. At least a few were honest enough to admit their pages were written during times of extreme boredom. Here they are in no particular order (they're all weird).

Go Fish

Who needs a screen saver with electronic fish swimming by when you can have the real thing? This Web site gives you a fish-eye view of a freshwater aquarium, with the GIF updated every few minutes.

Watch closely and you might even see something lurking in the back. The Loch Ness Monster? No, just a co-worker known throughout Netdom as "the guy behind the fish tank."

Getting There

`http://www.mcom.com/fishcam/fishcam.html`

Maybe you'll get to see the food chain in action through this fish cam

Is That an Iguana in Your Pocket?

On the Web, even iguanas can become famous. This site shows the day-to-day happenings in one iguana's cage, updated every five minutes. One picture looks pretty much like the others, though (iguanas aren't known for doing much more than lying around). Still, a fun site for the herpetelogical crowd or for anyone who needs to get a life.

Getting There

http://iguana.images.com/dupecam.html

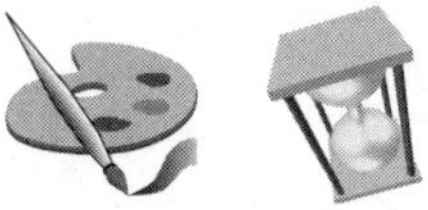

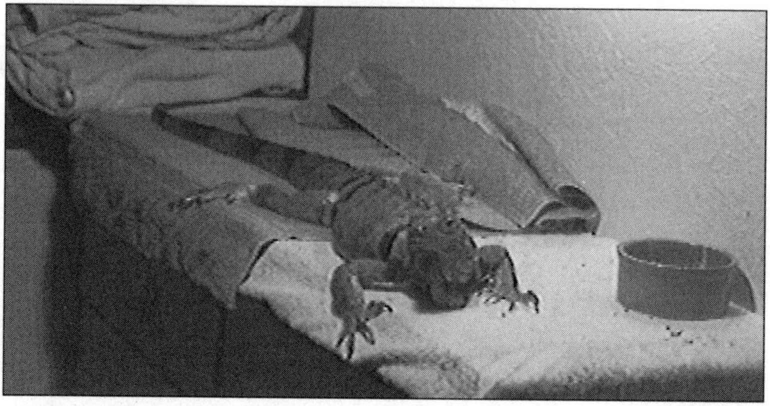

Is that an iguana in your pocket, or are you just glad to see me?

Surfing on the Net—Literally

What's up on the Web? The *surf's* up, doods! And this time I mean it. SurfNet is online, bringing you the latest conditions from Southern California, the South Pacific, and Hawaii. You also get surf predictions, satellite photos, and weather information.

But never mind the surf reports: Check out Surf Windows for a short video that actually *shows* you current conditions in San Diego. Every 10 minutes, a camera automatically takes a short video of the surf conditions and uploads the file to SurfNet. Never has surfing been so technical, or maybe technology has never been so fun.

Getting There

`http://sailfish.peregrine.com/surf/surf.html`

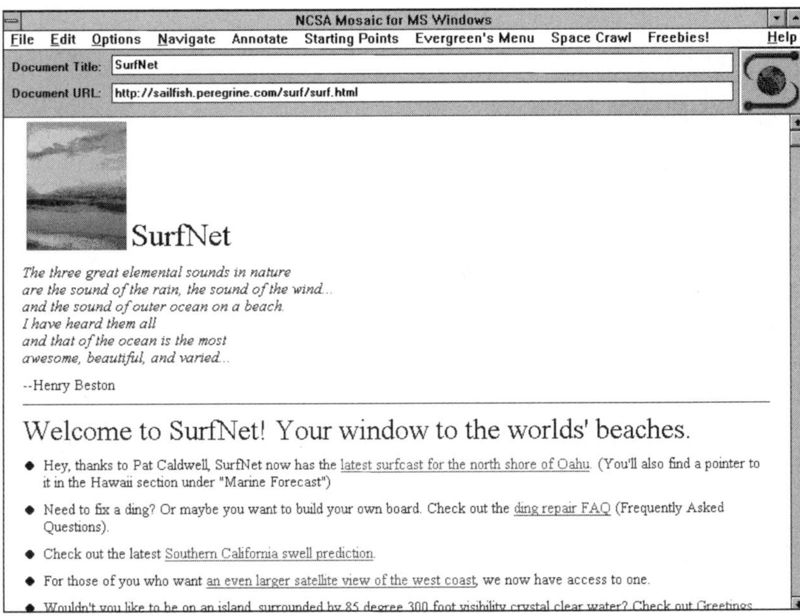

Ride the cyberwaves when the SurfNet's up

And the Sign Says . . .

Everyone deserves their 15 minutes in the spotlight. You won't get it here, but you might get a few seconds. Follow the instructions on this Web page and send E-mail to an electronic scrolling sign at the University of Illinois that will then display your profound (or is that profane?) electronic graffitti. Think of the fortune you'll save in spray paint.

Getting There

`http://www.acm.uiuc.edu:80/sigarch/projects.html`

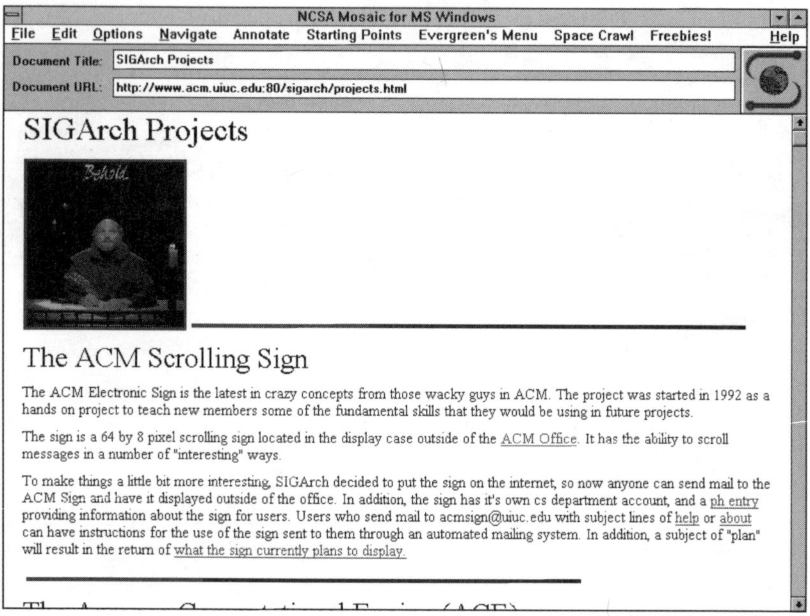

Is anybody reading this?

Owww! Hot Tub!

Okay, so you've heard of Coke machines wired to the Internet, and there's even a vending machine or two. But someone recognized a void and, by God, he filled it! Alert Web surfer Paul Haas determined that what the Internet *really* needs is a hot tub. At great personal time and expense, Paul has now corrected that shortcoming.

Paul's hot tub is online and working fine. Anyone can find out the current temperature (104 last I checked), as well as other vital information like the ozone generator's condition and the status of the backup battery. It's sort of like being fed up-to-the-minute reports on a party you weren't invited to. Maybe in the future he'll offer real-time photos.

Getting There

`http://hamjudo.com/cgi-bin/hottub`

TEXT

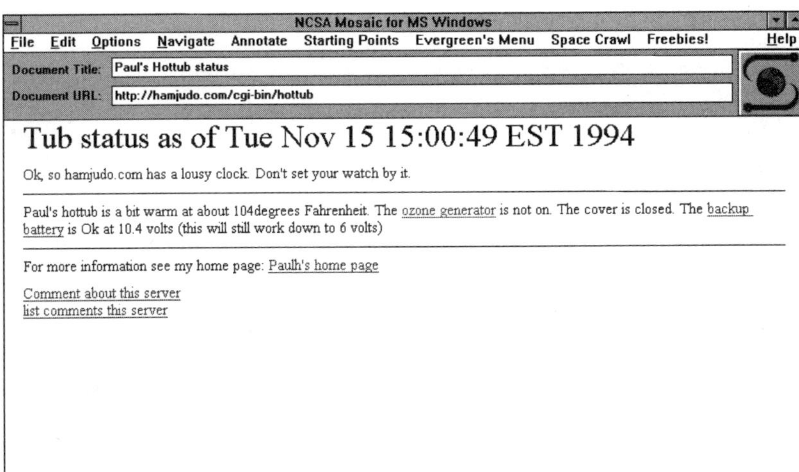

C'mon in, the water's fine

Put Another Dime in the Jukebox, Baby

Erik Nygren likes his music so much he wants to share it with the world. Or, more accurately, he was so bored one day he decided to share his music with the world. So Eric hooked up his computer's CD player to the Internet and now anyone can find out what he's playing. You can even download an audio clip of the current song.

I haven't been able to determine what kind of tastes Eric has in music. The few times I've checked, nothing's been playing. I can only say that someone who would think to plug a CD into the Web and would have the time and resources to do it does not strike me as a listener of Tiffany's Greatest Hits. This feat required a lot of rock and roll and heavy doses of caffeine.

Getting There

`http://foundation.mit.edu/cgi-bin/what-cd`

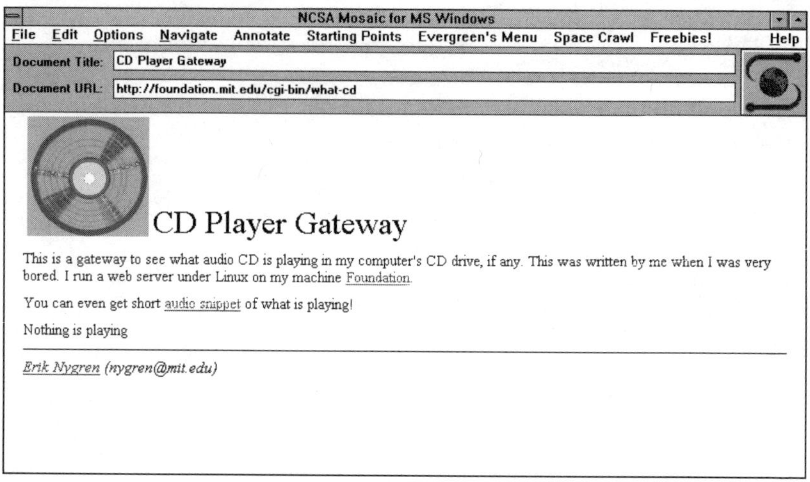

Any requests?

Chris and Larry's Excellent Geiger Counter

I'm not exactly sure what's gone wrong at the University of Texas, Austin, that Chris and Larry found it necessary to build a Geiger counter. But the rest of us can now monitor the campus for nuclear emanations from a safe distance.

Some of the charts are interesting, and you'll find information on how these two went about building their Geiger counter—good to know if you ever need to build one yourself. Maybe next they'll publish some plans for a do-it-yourself bomb shelter.

Getting There

http://gargravarr.cc.utexas.edu/geiger-server-ii/geiger.html

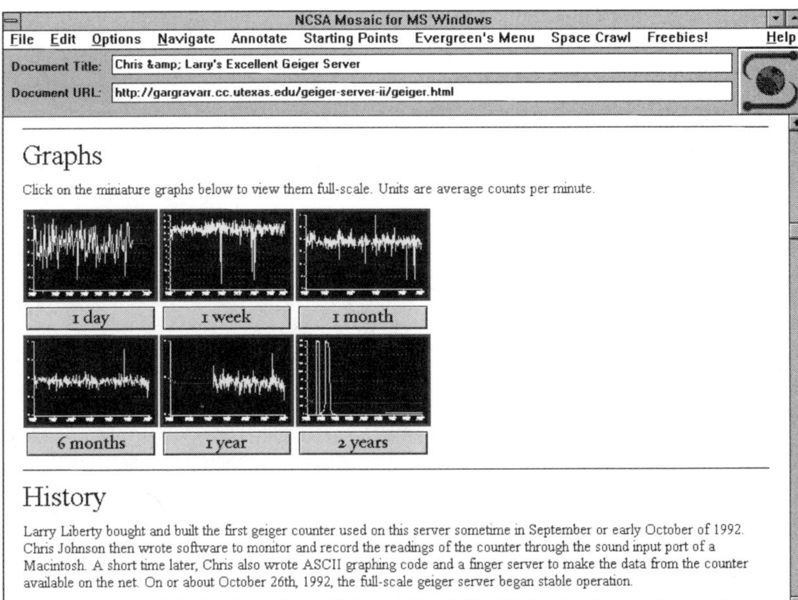

Don't forget to check the Geiger counter to see if it's safe to go outside

Guaranteed Delivery in 5 Minutes or Less

Get a hot, tasty, virtual pizza delivered right to your E-mail address in five minutes or less or you don't have to pay. All right, so you don't have to pay anyway, but still—what a bargain. This Web site tells you all you need to know to order your own GIF version of America's most popular fast food.

These guys have declared war on "analog pizzas," promising that digital pies are the wave of the future. Follow the instructions at this site to find out how to order, and be sure to order lots, since these pies aren't very filling (but then, they also aren't fattening). Your pizza will arrive in minutes on a checkered tablecloth. How's that for service? Still hungry? Beej promises more to come, including drinks and more toppings.

Getting There

`http://www2.ecst.csuchico.edu/~pizza/`

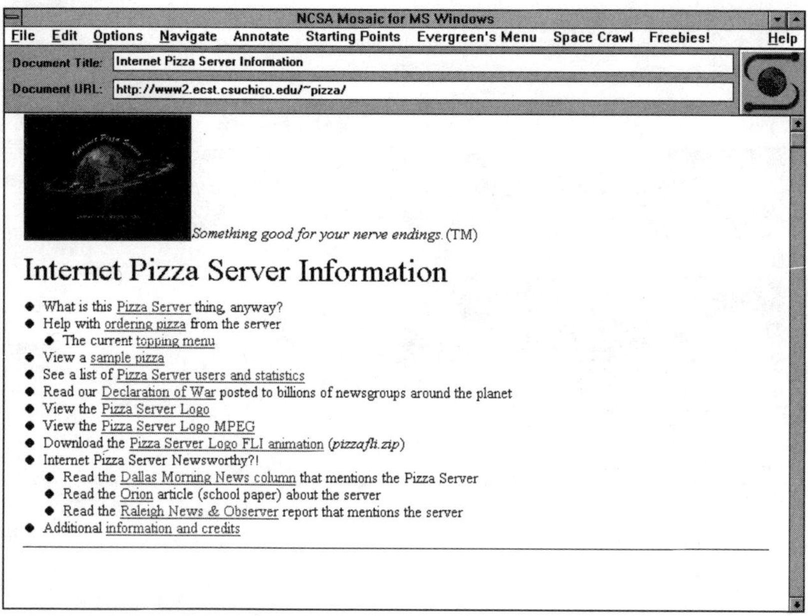

Digital pizza, fast food of the future

Have a Cup of Joe

When you think of Cambridge, don't you immediately think of coffee? I know I do. Now you can do more than think about it: You can actually see it—the coffee, that is. Though I'll probably get hundreds of mail messages telling me otherwise, as far as I know this is the only coffee pot on the Internet.

No word on how the java tastes, but then you probably won't be asked if you'd like a cup anyway.

Getting There

`http://www.cl.cam.ac.uk/coffee/coffee.html`

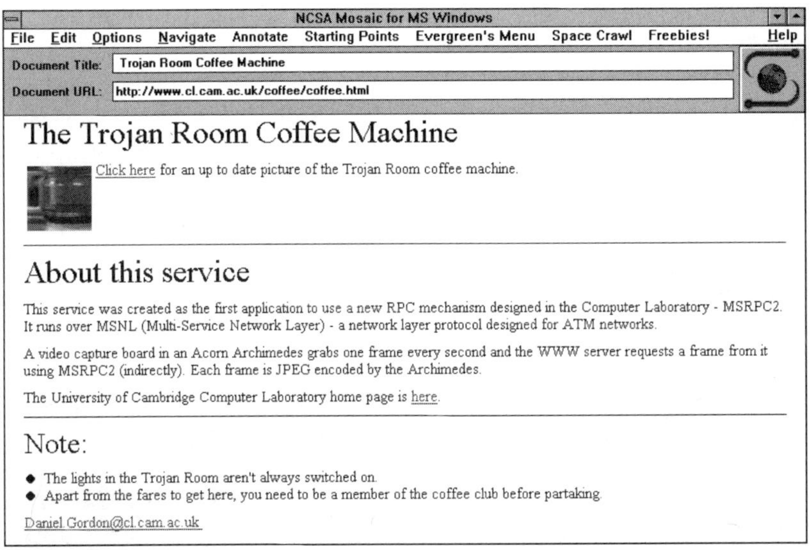

The Trojan Room Coffee Machine

Click here for an up to date picture of the Trojan Room coffee machine.

About this service

This service was created as the first application to use a new RPC mechanism designed in the Computer Laboratory - MSRPC2. It runs over MSNL (Multi-Service Network Layer) - a network layer protocol designed for ATM networks.

A video capture board in an Acorn Archimedes grabs one frame every second and the WWW server requests a frame from it using MSRPC2 (indirectly). Each frame is JPEG encoded by the Archimedes.

The University of Cambridge Computer Laboratory home page is here.

Note:

- The lights in the Trojan Room aren't always switched on.
- Apart from the fares to get here, you need to be a member of the coffee club before partaking.

Daniel.Gordon@cl.cam.ac.uk

I'll take mine black

Bay Watch

Get a Web's-eye view of San Diego Bay. Every half hour, a new picture of the current happenings on the bay is uploaded to the Internet for your viewing pleasure. Time it right and you can see some great shots of the boats docking. Time it wrong and you get a relaxing image of the water being, well, watery.

If the peace and tranquility are too much for you, jump to the San Diego Freeway's JamCam for a shot of the current rush hour woes on Interstate 5.

Getting There

`http://www.cts.com/~jtara/baycam.html`

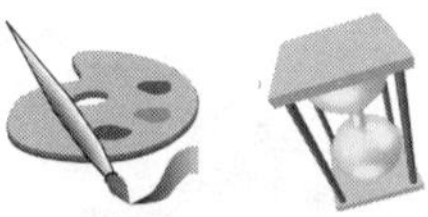

Watch the boats off San Diego Harbor through the BayCam

Brown Baggin' It

Are you eating another P.B.&J. for lunch and washing it down with a Twinkee? Yum, but how does that stack up against the lunches of other Web surfers? Out of some misguided compassion for mankind, or more likely out of boredom, some people have begun posting their daily lunch menus on the Internet. Now, to go even one step further, here's a Web site you can access to find out what Sho Kuwamoto brought to eat today. Just click on the bag to get a complete menu of Sho's lunch.

When I checked last, it was leftover mostaccioli and a veggie burrito. Sounds better than anything I've packed lately.

Getting There

`http://physics.purdue.edu/~sho/lunch_main.html`

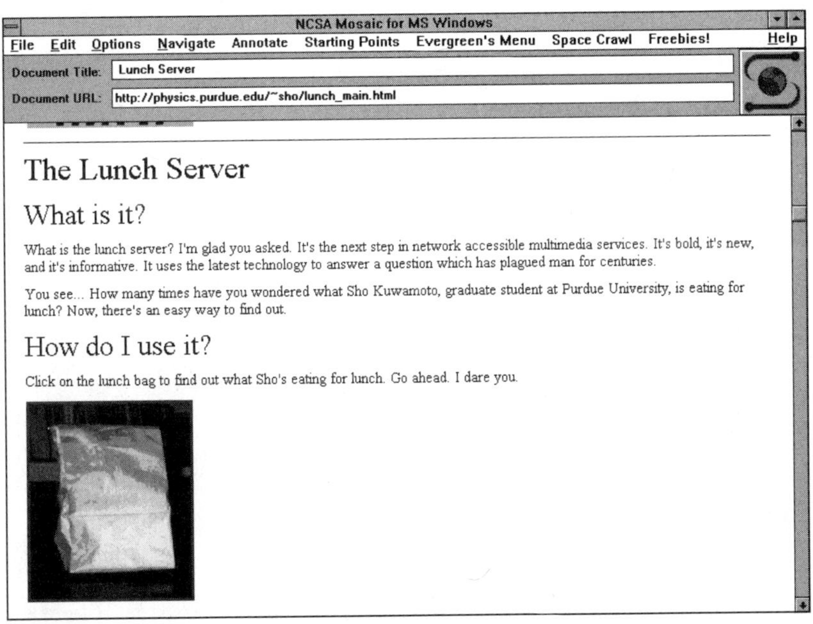

Don't worry, Mom; Sho's eating right

Chat with a Cat

Either Michael Witbrock loves cats or he hates them so much he was motivated to create this site. You decide. Through the magic of speech synthesis, you can post messages that are then broadcast through a voice synthesizer to Michael's cat, which he keeps chained up next to his modem (okay, it's not chained).

This feline's fur is no doubt falling out in clumps from not having a moment's peace as messages ranging from sweet ("Hello little kitty") to psychotic ("Kitty want a ride in the microwave?") flood this server. Send your own message and see if you get a response. Cat got your tongue? Browse the list of messages posted by others who also have too much time on their hands.

Getting There

http://queer.slip.cs.cmu.edu/cgi-bin/talktocat

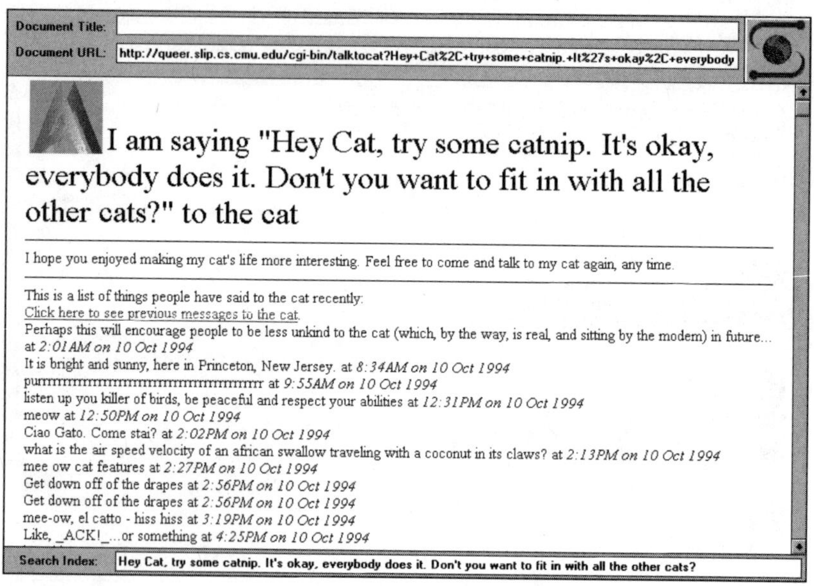

Document Title:

Document URL: http://queer.slip.cs.cmu.edu/cgi-bin/talktocat?Hey+Cat%2C+try+some+catnip.+It%27s+okay%2C+everybody

I am saying "Hey Cat, try some catnip. It's okay, everybody does it. Don't you want to fit in with all the other cats?" to the cat

I hope you enjoyed making my cat's life more interesting. Feel free to come and talk to my cat again, any time.

This is a list of things people have said to the cat recently:
Click here to see previous messages to the cat.
Perhaps this will encourage people to be less unkind to the cat (which, by the way, is real, and sitting by the modem) in future... at *2:01AM on 10 Oct 1994*
It is bright and sunny, here in Princeton, New Jersey. at *8:34AM on 10 Oct 1994*
purrrrrrrrrrrrrrrrrrrrrrrrrrrrrrrrrrrrrrrrr at *9:55AM on 10 Oct 1994*
listen up you killer of birds, be peaceful and respect your abilities at *12:31PM on 10 Oct 1994*
meow at *12:50PM on 10 Oct 1994*
Ciao Gato. Come stai? at *2:02PM on 10 Oct 1994*
what is the air speed velocity of an african swallow traveling with a coconut in its claws? at *2:13PM on 10 Oct 1994*
mee ow cat features at *2:27PM on 10 Oct 1994*
Get down off of the drapes at *2:56PM on 10 Oct 1994*
Get down off of the drapes at *2:56PM on 10 Oct 1994*
mee-ow, el catto - hiss hiss at *3:19PM on 10 Oct 1994*
Like, _ACK!_...or something at *4:25PM on 10 Oct 1994*

Search Index: Hey Cat, try some catnip. It's okay, everybody does it. Don't you want to fit in with all the other cats?

At last, voice mail for fur balls

If You Still Haven't Had Enough . . .

You're whackier than I thought! While I mentioned this site earlier on page 82, it bears repeating in this section: Check out the URouLette, "the world's first random URL generator" on the Web. Spin the wheel and there's no telling where in cyberspace you'll land. See if you can find a few whacky and worthless sites of your own. There are definitely enough to go around.

Getting There

`http://kuhttp.cc.ukans.edu/cwis/organizations/kucia/uroulette/uroulette.html`

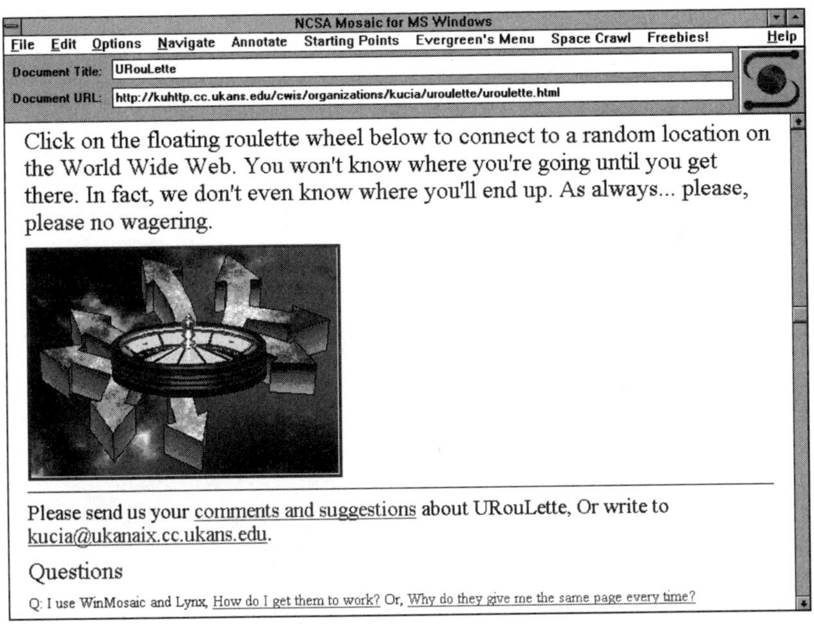

The URouLette home page's encore performance

5

All the HTML You Really Need . . .

How to Put Up Your Home Page in a Helluva Hurry!

HTML—you can pronounce it "hate mail," "hot meal," "hot metal" or just H-T-M-L. But any way you slice up the acronym, it still sounds like something you wouldn't want to tackle without some serious blood pressure medication (aka beer).

It's a fact that you need to learn HTML (Hyper Text Markup Language) if you want to create your own home page. What isn't so widely publicized is that a little HTML goes a very long way. We wrote this chapter to prove just that. Sit back, smile, read on, and do a little painless learning.

Avoiding HTML Overkill

Egad. Your Internet provider just told you that you now have World Wide Web page space "free" (ha!) with your account. All your friends have their own home pages and now *you* have to have one. Or . . . (worse yet) your boss tells you that in keeping with your miracle-maker status of being able to do things that no one else in the company knows how to do, you are now assigned the task of creating a home page for the company. And . . . um . . . can you have it done and ready to demo at the corporation board meeting Friday morning? (Just the tonic for a fine Wednesday afternoon, eh?)

Not to sweat. Web pages are made up of the mysterious-sounding HTML, but like a lot of things in this life (and supposedly the next) there's less to HTML than meets the eye. Consider a cocktail party I went to many years ago, at the home of a New Rich Guy who lucked into a company that went public at just the right time so that he actually got something for his stock options. He built a custom house with this audio/video room that had an entire wall of completely inexplicable black-and-chrome rack-mounted electronics and two speakers the size of refrigerators.

One of his long-haired friends, who was now utterly plastered and speaking the veritas proceeding from vino abundanto, stood before the jungle of blinking LEDs and yelled over his shoulder, "Cripes, Frank, how much of this crap do you really need just to listen to Def Leppard?"

How much indeed?

You could ask the same question of HTML—and Def Leppard has (mercifully) nothing at all to do with it.

Duntemann's Law for HTML

A suspicion I've had for years about computer languages in general holds especially true for HTML—true enough, in fact, for me to hang my name on it:

10 percent of the HTML language in fact does 90 percent of the work.

If you know that all-important 10 percent, you can create perfectly stunning Web pages. I'll teach you that here. It won't take long. The rest of it you can pick up later on. If you need to. And have time. And don't get interrupted. Or put on another project . . . .

Furthermore, although we're not supposed to be bitchy about this sort of thing, many of the Web browsers you can get today don't do a very good job with the flipside 90 percent of HTML that does 10 percent of the work. So if you get too fancy, what the user sees may *not* be what you are trying to give.

Right. Stick with that comfy, reliable 10 percent.

Tags Come in Pairs

HTML documents are simple 7-bit ASCII text files. There's no binary component at all, and you can edit them on any kind of brain-dead text editor you want. You pass commands to Web browsers like Mosaic through *tags*—simple commands enclosed between < and > symbols.

Many tags come in pairs, so that you can enclose some text between the two tags and thus control the text somehow. The first tag in a pair contains the name of the command. This *starts* the sense of the command. The second tag in a pair contains the name of the tag preceded by a forward slash. This *ends* the sense of the command.

For example, **<B>** and **</B>** enclose text that you want the browser to display in bold:

```
<B>This Page Contains All Human Knowledge</B>
```

The sense here is Start Bold, Text, End Bold. A few tags aren't like this. Most are.

The Shape of an HTML Document

There's not much to the structure of an HTML document. The part that you want the browser to interpret is enclosed between the **<HTML>** and **</HTML>** tag pair. Anything outside these two will be ignored by the browser.

Within the HTML portion of the file you need to define a header and a body. There are tag pairs for both of these, and their names are about as mysterious as a clop on the head with a brick: **<HEAD>** and **</HEAD>,** along with **<BODY>** and **</BODY>.**

The body contains, pretty obviously, the stuff you want the browser to display to the user. The header exists mostly to feed a title to the browser for display at the top of the browser's window on the user's screen. The header has to come before the body (for some browsers at least) but beyond that there aren't a lot of rules.

So from a height, an HTML document has this structure:

```
<HTML>
<HEAD>

Your title stuff here

</HEAD>

<BODY>

Your stuff to display to the user here

</BODY>
</HTML>
```

In fact, the **<HTML>** and **</HTML>** tag pair is optional. If you omit them, however, *everything* in the file will be examined and interpreted by the browser. I use them to give me the option of writing notes and comments above and below the HTML data proper.

Creating a Title

We can dispose of the title in one paragraph. Your title is defined between **<TITLE>** and **</TITLE>**. A title can only contain text. Don't bother with formatting. I don't know of any browsers that can format a title. Also, the title must fall within the **<HEAD>** and **</HEAD>** pair. Here's an example of a title:

```
<HEAD>
<TITLE>The Coriolis Vortex</TITLE>
</HEAD>
```

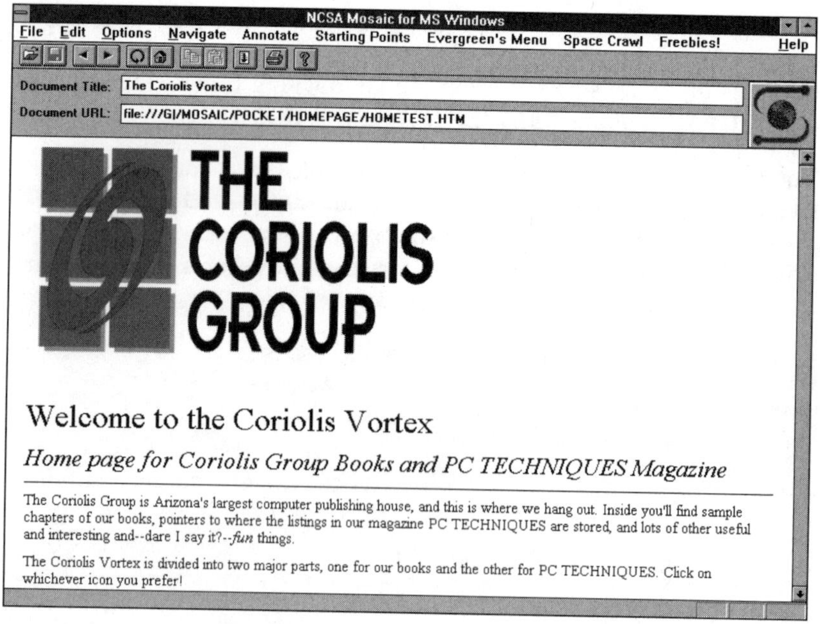

The Title of the Coriolis Home Page

Under Windows Mosaic, the title is displayed in the title bar of Mosaic's window, as shown in Figure 1. No big deal, huh?

Body Building

Now for the fun part. Anything between **<BODY>** and **</BODY>** will be displayed by the browser. Mostly that means text, but it can also include images and even sound files, which are "displayed" by the browser by playing them on the system speaker. Now, this is something you have to think about right here: *How many people will want to read your Web page but won't have Mosaic or multimedia hardware?*

Maybe it doesn't matter. But if you're putting something on the Web on behalf of your employer, it's something to consider. The vast majority of Internet people still don't have SLIP or PPP accounts or direct connections. That great graphically unwashed crowd can still read Web pages with browsers like Lynx—but all your pretty graphics and funny noises will be lost on them.

So keep this in mind: If the idea is to get maximal zillions of people to read your page, *don't go berserk with graphics and sound!*

Text and Paragraphs

Here's an HTML newbie-zinger First Class: Browsers don't necessarily display text the way you format it within the HTML file. The length of a line that the Mosaic user sees is the width of the screen they're currently using. Mosaic (and all the other browsers, too) reformat incoming text on the fly to wrap in accordance with the user's display.

If you simply place text in the HTML file, the browser will display it as one Godzillan paragraph. To be displayed as a separate paragraph, a block of text must *begin* with **<P>**. There is a **</P>** tag, and you can use it to indicate the end of a paragraph, but it doesn't really do much and most people don't use it. Also note that the details of exactly how a paragraph is formatted vary slightly from browser to browser. There's nothing you can do about that. Standards haven't really shaken out thoroughly yet. In another few years, this will almost certainly change.

Headings

HTML defines six different sizes of headings. They're used by enclosing heading text in tag pairs like **<H1> </H1>, <H2> </H2>** and so on up to **<H6> </H6>.** The **<H1>** heading format is the largest, and they get smaller from there. The **<H1>** heading is a pretty good size, and should generally be used only at the start of your pages. The following line produced the main heading shown on page 190.

```
<H1>Welcome to the Coriolis Vortex </H1>
```

You can format text inside a heading by using text formatting tags. I'll explain that next.

Formatting Text

Most browsers can display text in a number of formats, including bold, underlined, italic, and combinations thereof. The worm in the apple is that not all versions of all browsers can do all formats or (especially) all combinations of formats, so be careful what you try to accomplish. A lot of people are still running around with marginal early versions of Mosaic and think they're in hawg heaven. If something looks funny, do you think they'll blame their browser?

I mentioned **<B> </B>** earlier for bolding. In the same way, enclosing text in **<I> </I>** displays italics, and **<U> </U>** displays underlined text. You can combine formatting for a single string of text by enclosing that text in both sets of tags. There's no precedence or necessary nesting order, in that underlining doesn't have to be on the outside, and so forth. But some orders have been known to confuse some browsers. You can't always tell what the user will see once you get too fancy.

Here are some examples:

```
<B>I'm bold.</B>
<I>I'm emphatic!</I>
<U>I'm overworked and underscored.</U>
<I><U>I'm totally confusing.</U></I>
```

When a browser interprets these lines, you'll see something like this:

I'm bold.
I'm emphatic!
I'm overworked and underscored...
I'm totally confusing.

You can put formatting on headings by placing the formatting tags inside the heading tags:

```
<H3><I>Important Note!</I></H3>
```

Although it shouldn't happen, some browsers are known to be confused by placing formatting tags *outside* header definitions. Don't do it.

Preventing Lines from Wrapping

Most of the time, browsers ignore the format of text as it exists in the HTML file. It feels free to wrap text according to the width of the screen the user sees. This is convenient in most cases, but now and then it really gets in the way.

There are a couple of easy ways to force copy not to wrap. One is the **<ADDRESS>** tag pair. Text between **<ADDRESS>** and **</ADDRESS>** will appear exactly as it appears in the HTML file, with line breaks and line feeds as you typed them. As a bonus (if you consider it that) it forces the text into italics.

Another tag pair worth knowing about is **<PRE>**, for "preformatted." Text bracketed between **<PRE>** and **</PRE>** will keep its formatting as you entered it into the HTML file, and it will also force the text to a monospace font. This is handy for displaying computer source code and funny Bart Simpson pictures made of ASCII characters that depend on adjacent lines "lining up" just so.

Displaying Images

Hey, bitmapped images are what Mosaic and the Web are for, right? So this one is important. It's also a little subtler than what we've discussed so far. Worse, it can be done in a couple of different ways.

The simplest way is to use the **<IMG>** tag. The **<IMG>** tag specifies a filename, and when the browser encounters the tag, it will load and display the image cited in the filename. The name of the file is specified as a parameter through the "**SRC=**" subtag. The whole thing looks like this:

```
<IMG SRC="coriolis.gif">
```

You don't have to enclose the filename in quotes, but I've heard that doing so can prevent certain kinds of trouble with certain browsers when your filenames contain certain characters not certain to be either letters or numbers. Certainty is a scarce enough quantity. Why tempt fate to save four little tick marks?

Mosaic's "native" image file format is GIF. Export your image files in GIF format. GIF files are heavily compressed, and this is enormously helpful when your readers will be downloading your page through a bottom-feeder 9600-baud modem.

Line Breaks

Here's something else to keep in mind: Placing two **<IMG>** tags one after the other will *not* cause the images to display one atop the other. They will be shown side-by-side instead, unless you insert the line break tag **
** after the first, like so:

```
<IMG SRC="meat.gif"><BR>
<IMG SRC="potatoes.gif">
```

The **
** tag can also be used to force line breaks within text as well, though **<P>** is used most of the time. The snag is that **
** does not give you any "linefeed" space beneath it—it's more like a carriage return standing alone, without a linefeed. **<P>** will give you a half-space worth of line feed as well as a carriage return.

Blank Bitmaps as Spacers

You will probably want to add space between images, either horizontally or vertically, so that they're not smack up against one another on your page. The easiest way to do this (remarkably enough!) is to create little "blank" GIF bitmaps as spacers. Most image editors can do this. One trick we use at Coriolis is to load an image with some white in it somewhere and then copy a rectangular patch of white into a separate mini-image, which you then export as a GIF. Export a few that are of different sizes and shapes. If you have the time to do a little toolbuilding, export each one in two forms: one in "transparent" color (which will be invisible when displayed) and another in some other "real" color (which includes white), so that you can see how big it is on the browser display.

Although the transparent color is supported by the GIF bitmap standard, many graphics editors don't provide you any way to draw or fill in the transparent color. There is a freeware utility kicking around the Net called GIFTRANS that allows you to convert a GIF bitmap from some named color (say, white) to the transparent color, such that all white areas become transparent. This is a good item to have, although I don't have the room to explain its use fully here. You can obtain it from various places. I got it from:

```
http://melmac.corp.harris.com/files/giftrans.exe
```

Be sure you select **File | Load to Disk** on Mosaic (or the equivalent on the other browsers) before retrieving this URL! There is a good essay on using GIFTRANS for creating transparent colors at the following URL:

```
http://melmac.corp.harris.com/transparent_images.html
```

There's nothing special about loading spacer bitmaps. They're displayed the same way any other images are displayed:

```
<IMG SRC="whitespc.gif">
```

Hotlinks

What HTML is really about, of course, is hotlinks. Creating hotlinks is fairly easy, and can be done several different ways. The two most common ways (and the only ones we'll discuss here) are to define text hotlinks and image hotlinks.

Text first. In general terms, a hotlink has two parts: An *anchor*, which is the hotlink as the user sees it, and a URL associated with the anchor, which is where Mosaic goes to fetch the next item when the user clicks on the hotlink. For text hotlinks, the anchor and the URL may be the same thing but are usually different. For example, the text anchor could be the string "J. Random Hacker" but the address would in fact be the URL of J. Random's home page.

In any case, the anchor text is the text falling *between* the two anchor tags: **<A>** and **</A>.** The URL, on the other hand (note this well!) is placed *within* the <A> tag as a parameter, using the subtag **HREF=** to specify the URL. An entire text hotlink would look something like this:

```
<A HREF="http://gobble.wobble.foobity/shazam/flarf.html">FLARFNet</A>
```

Here, what the user would see is the simple (if inexplicable) text "FLARFNet" in blue. Upon clicking on the hotlink, Mosaic would fetch the item at the URL specified by **HREF=**. Keep in mind that the URL can be a local filename as well as an address somewhere way out on the Net somewhere. That is, you can hotlink to another HTML file on your hard disk as easily as you can to a Web site in Siberia. The syntax is the same.

Mosaic takes care of placing hotlinks in blue. Other browsers take care of marking hotlinks distinctively in their own way. You don't have to do anything.

Using an Image as a Hotlink

Image hotlinks are done very much the same way, through a pair of anchor tags. The sense here is that the **<IMG>** tag for the image to be used as the anchor takes the place of the anchor text, and, like the anchor text in a text hotlink, falls between the **<A>** and **</A>** tags. The **<IMG>** tag looks the same as it would look if you were simply displaying the image by itself.

The easiest way to clarify this is just to give you an example:

```
<A HREF="http://gobble.foo/blarg.html"><IMG SRC="blarg.gif"></A>
```

Note well that the **<IMG>** tag falls between the **<A>** and **</A>** tags. When it encounters this line, the browser will display the GIF file BLARG.GIF, outlined in blue (for Mosaic at least; other browsers may highlight differently) and associate the URL shown with the highlighted image. If the user clicks on the image, the stated URL will be fetched by the browser.

Aligning Images

If you're going to display images side-by-side on a page, it's sometimes handy to be able to align all of them somehow so that they look less random. There are three alignment specifiers you can use when displaying images: **ALIGN=top**, **ALIGN=middle**, and **ALIGN=bottom**. The **ALIGN** subtag must go inside the **<IMG>** tag. Here's an example:

```
<A HREF="pctechml.htm"><IMG ALIGN=TOP SRC="pctech75.gif"></A>
<IMG ALIGN=TOP SRC="whitespc.gif">
<A HREF="corbooks.htm"><IMG ALIGN=TOP SRC="corbooks.gif"></A>
```

These three **<IMG>** tags displayed the images shown at the center of the screen shot in the next screen. The background was set to grey so that you can better see the "invisible" spacer bitmap between the two other bitmaps. Notice that all three bitmaps are aligned from the top.

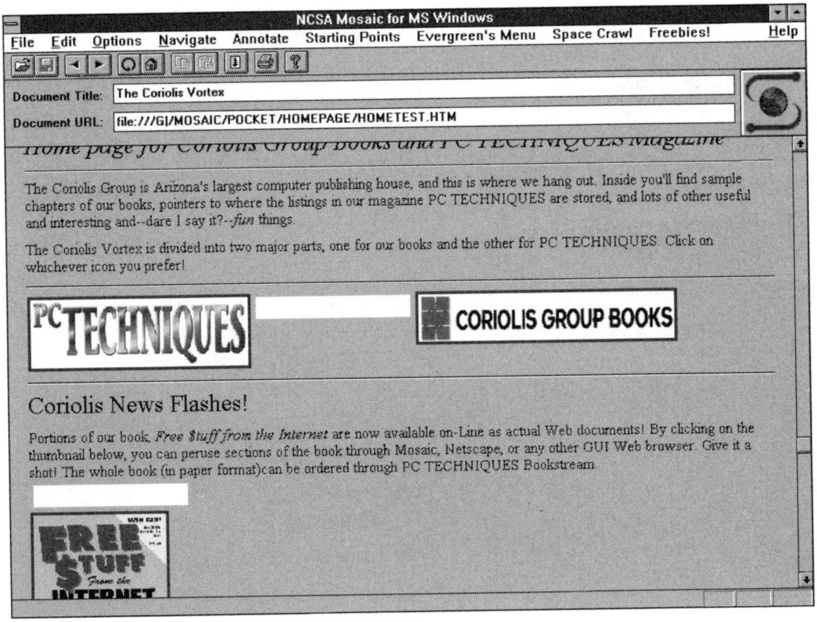

Aligning Bitmaps with the ALIGN Subtag

Substituting Text for Images for Text-Browser Users

As I mentioned earlier, more people surf the Net in text mode than use a GUI browser like Mosaic. If you don't want to completely blow them off, there are some things you can do. The most important is to define a text string that will be displayed on their screens in place of all your snazzy graphics. This is easily done anywhere you define an image to be displayed, using the **ALT=** subtag. **ALT=** defines a text string to be displayed whenever the graphics image cannot be displayed. Here's an example that should make this all clear:

```
<IMG ALT="Jeff Duntemann, author/editor" SRC="jeffd.gif">
```

When a text mode browser encounters this line, it will display the string "Jeff Duntemann, author/editor" instead of the image file JEFFD.GIF.

You can do this for images used as hotlinks as well. In fact, it's even more important to provide an **ALT=** reference within a graphics hotlink, because the **ALT=** text will be the only thing a text-mode browser user will see when encountering that (possibly important!) hotlink.

Testing Your Web Page

Mosaic's best kept secret is that it can load and interpret an HTML file stored right there on your hard disk. You don't have to have your HTML file up on your provider's server for you to "run" it from Mosaic. This is a godsend—you don't have to waste *any* of your valuable connect time testing a new page. You can check it out from your own machine, testing it as you build it, in fact. There's no "compile" step. You change the page's HTML file, then load it into Mosaic (or whatever browser you use) and look at it. If it doesn't look right, you load it into your text editor, tweak it, and then bounce back to Mosaic to test it.

Loading a file from your hard disk into Mosaic is done through the **File|Open Local File** menu option. When you select this option, you'll get the standard Windows file open dialog. Select a file. Click on OK. Mosaic will then do its best to load and interpret the file. Needless to say, if the file you load isn't an HTML file, almost anything can happen, but you can bet it won't be anything especially good.

The trick in loading local files is that your TCP/IP stack has to be active in memory so that WinSock API calls can be made by the browser. The stack doesn't have to be logged into anything; it just has to be down there patiently waiting at the bottom of your desktop. You run the stack and minimize it. If your stack isn't anywhere in memory, most browsers will simply refuse to run. Mosaic's error message will indicate that it can't find WINSOCK.DLL.

At some point, you will have to connect to your provider for testing. If your page contains hotlinks to other pages elsewhere on the Web, you'll have to connect your TCP/IP stack to test every hotlink. (Don't just *assume* that a 96-character URL is correct in every last detail!) The nice part is that you can test all the parts of a page that are local to your hard disk from your hard disk, and then once you connect you can still keep your page-in-progress on your hard disk and test hotlinks to other Web sites. There's nothing special or debilitating about running from your hard disk. Click on a hotlink and Mosaic will go out and get it, wherever it might happen to be.

Other HTML Tips

The best way, bar none, to get better at HTML is to look at other people's files and imitate them flagrantly. This is easy, because you can save any Web page to disk simply by selecting **Options | Load to Disk** before you load the page you want. You'll get the raw HTML code, which you can then print out and stare at until you learn something.

The NetScape browser (which is in many ways cleaner and more complete than the Alpha 2 version of Mosaic) has an option that allows you to open a "source window" displaying the HTML tags and text for the page that you're currently viewing. This is really *really* neat, and one reason I've been using NetScape much more than Mosaic in recent months. To do this under NetScape, select **View | Source**.

Here's a list of small things to keep in mind as you assemble your first pages:

- Keep the sizes of your images small. Many users are using bottom-feeder modems, and sizeable graphics take forever and a half to come over the line.
- Again, resist the temptation to get too fancy. The Web is still an evolving technology, and the browsers do not agree with one another (or with the HTML standard setters) about what every last detail of the HTML spec will look like on-screen.
- Especially, keep in mind that the width of the browser window will vary from user to user depending on how they prefer to set things up. The browser wraps text and images when a horizontal line exceeds the width of the displayed field, so if you design your lines too fancy and too wide, the line-wrap feature will turn your fancy page into a thorough mess.
- Not every user has a viewer for every data format. You can assume GIF support (which is built into Mosaic and all other viewers we've tested here) but little else.

Go for It!

That's the bulk of what you'll need to make simple Web pages—and simple Web pages are the only ones that will work for all (or even most) Web surfers. There's a lot of HTML that I haven't covered for that reason alone. Eventually the browser market will mature and things will shake out some, but for the next year or so it's going to be a real wild-west time in Web-land.

But hey, would you rather be bored?

Right. I knew I could count on you.

PART 6

Webs of the World

The Web is truly an international affair. We're writing this from the U.S., but we certainly acknowledge that a majority of Internet and Web users are outside of the U.S. So, toward this end, we've included a selected list of Web sites around the world. If you're looking for something local, and if local means something that most people think of as foreign, then you'll want to look here. We've included sites in virtually every "corner" of the globe.

Africa

Cape Town

http://www.cs.uct.ac.za/UCT.html
University of Cape Town Computer Science Department

Johannesburg

http://www.is.co.za/
Johannesburg

Witwatersrand

http://www.cs.wits.ac.za/
University of the Witwatersrand, Computer Science Department

http://www.rau.ac.za/
Rand Afrikaans University

Asia and Oceania

Australia

http://www.agsm.unsw.edu.au/Welcome.html
Australian Graduate School of Management

http://werple.apana.org.au/apanahome.html
Australian Public Access Network Association

http://www.cs.su.oz.au/
Basser Department of Computer Science, University of Sydney

Beijing

http://ihep.html
China Institute of High Energy Physics

Hong Kong

http://www.air.org/
The Association for Internet Resources

http://www.cuhk.hk/
The Chinese University of Hong Kong

India

http://iucaa.iucaa.ernet.in/welcome.html
Inter-University Centre for Astronomy and Astrophysics

Japan

http://www.huie.hokudai.ac.jp/
Hokkaido University

http://www.hirosaki-u.ac.jp/index.html
Hirosaki University

http://www.sendai-ct.ac.jp/welcome.html
Sendai National College of Technology

http://www.tia.ad.jp/welcome.html
Tohoku internet Association

http://www.u-aizu.ac.jp/
The University of Aizu

http://ks001.kj.utsunomiya-u.ac.jp
Utsunomiya University

http://www.atom.co.jp/
Minato-ku

Korea

http://silla.dongguk.ac.kr
Dongguk University

http://www.cs.usm.my/
Universiti Sains Malaysia, Penang

New Zealand

http://icair.iac.org.nz/
International Centre for Antarctic Information and Research

http://hmu1.cs.auckland.ac.nz/
The University of Auckland

Singapore

http://biomed.nus.sg:80/
National University of Singapore

Taiwan

http://peacock.tnjc.edu.tw/NEW/WELCOME.HTML
Tung Nan Junior College of Technology

Thailand

http://emailhost.ait.ac.th:80
Asian Institute of Technology

Europe

Austria

http://info.uibk.ac.at:80/
Innsbruck

http://www.ifs.uni-linz.ac.at/home.html
Johannes-Kepler-University, Linz

http://www.tcs.co.at/
TechConsult, Fremdenverkehrs informations system

Belgium

http://www.bekaert.com/
ÜjÜŒBekaert

http://www.belnet.be/
Belgian National Research Network

http://info1.vub.ac.be:8080/index.html
Free University of Brussels

http://pespmc1.vub.ac.be/
Free University of Brussels

Croatia

http://tjev.tel.etf.hr/zzt/zzt.html
University of Zagreb

http://wwws.irb.hr/
Rudjer Boskovich Institute

http://animafest.hr/
World Festival of Animated Films, Zagreb

Czech Republic

http://www.cuni.cz/
Charles University

Denmark

http://www.dd.dk/
Damgaard International

http://gopher.ku.dk/
University of Copenhagen

Estonia

http://www.eenet.ee/english.html
Estonian Research and Education Network

Finland

http://honeybee.helsinki.fi/index.html
Faculty of Agriculture and Forestry

http://www.hut.fi/English/www.english.html
Helsinki University of Technology, Espoo

http://www.tky.hut.fi/
Helsinki University of Technology, Espoo, Student Union

http://www.tky.hut.fi/.publish/tf/
Teknologföreningen, the Swedish Student Union

http://www.uwasa.fi/
University of Vaasa

http://www.freenet.hut.fi/
Freenet Finland

http://www.pcuf.fi/
PC-Users of Finland

http://www.fuug.fi/
Finnish Unix User's Group

http://www.jyu.fi/~otto/42.html
Jyväskylä Science Fiction Club 42

http://www.funet.fi/pub/doc/telecom/phonecard/afpc/
Association of Finnish Phonecard Collectors

France

http://www.calvacom.fr/
Paris

http://www.cert.fr/
Toulouse

http://www.ciril.fr/CIRIL/
Lorraine

http://cirm.univ-mrs.fr
Marseille

http://www.ipl.fr/
Lyon

http://www.fdn.fr
Paris

http://www.sct.fr
World-Net

Germany

http://www.augusta.de/
INGA, Internet-Gruppe des ACF e.V

http://www.chemie.fu-berlin.de/adressen/berlin.html
Berlin

http://www.artcom.de/
ART+COM

http://www.cnb.compunet.de/
CompuNet

http://www.contrib.de/
Contributed Software

http://www.dfn.de/home.html
Deutsches Forschungsnetz

http://www.dhzb.de/OpeningPage.html
Deutsches Herzzentrum

http://www.zblmath.fiz-karlsruhe.de/
Fachinformationszentrum Karlsruhe

http://www.fta-berlin.de/HOME-PAGE.html
Forschungs- und Technologiepark Berlin-Adlershof

http://www.chemie.fu-berlin.de/index.html
Fachbereich Chemie

http://www.chemie.fu-berlin.de/index_e.html
Fachbereich Kommunikationswissenschaften

http://www.inf.fu-berlin.de:80/~weisshuh/infwiss/
Arbeitsbereich Informationswissenschaft

http://www.math.fu-berlin.de/
Fachbereich Mathematik und Informatik

http://www.chemie.fu-berlin.de/tmp/phil/philos.html
Fachbereich Philosophie und Sozialwissenschaften

http://www.rz-berlin.mpg.de/
Fritz-Haber-Institut der Max-Planck-Gesellschaft

http://www.rz.hu-berlin.de/inside/rz/
Rechenzentrum

http://www.netcs.com/
netCS

http://sun24.tfh-berlin.de:8000/
Technische Fachhochschule

http://www.cs.tu-berlin.de/
Fachbereich Informatik

http://www.math.tu-berlin.de/
Fachbereich Mathematik

http://keynes.fb12.tu-berlin.de/
Fachbereich Verkehrswesen und phys. Ingenieurwissenschaften

http://www.prz.tu-berlin.de/
Prozessrechnerverbund-Zentrale

http://www.tu-berlin.de/zrz/index.html
Zentraleinrichtung Rechenzentrum

http://duplox.wz-berlin.de/
Technik - Arbeit - Umwelt/Organisation und Technikgenese

http://www.nordwest.germany.eu.net/
POP NordWest

http://www.techfak.uni-bielefeld.de/blfd/blfd.html
Bielefeld

http://peel.lili.uni-bielefeld.de/foebud/foebudHome.html
FoeBud e.V

http://www.hrz.uni-bielefeld.de/
hochschulrechenzentrum

http://www.ep1.ruhr-uni-bochum.de/
Experimentalphysik 1

http://wti.tp4.ruhr-uni-bochum
.de/www/html/homepage.html
Physik / Education Server WTI2000

http://speckled.mpifr-bonn.mpg
.de:8001i/home/spckle/ms/html/bonn.html
Bonn

http://orade.ora.com/home.html
O'Reilly International Thomson Verlag

http://www.rhein.de/
Regionalnetz Bonn/Rhein.DE

http://opalr2.physik.uni-bonn.de/
OPAL Group

http://www.rhrz.uni-bonn.de/index.html
Regionales Hochschulrechenzentrum

http://sfb350.ipb.uni-bonn.de/
Sonderforschungsbereich 350

http://www.cs.tu-bs.de/
Fachgebiet Informatik

http://ramz.ing.tu-bs.de/
Rechenanlage des Mechanikzentrums

http://asterix.ipmi.uni-bremen.de/
fb7home.html
Fachbereich Wirtschaftswissenschaft

http://www.ins.de/
Inter Networking Systems

http://www.tu-chemnitz.de/home/ins/
chemnitz.html
Chemnitz-Zwickau

http://www.rz.tu-clausthal.de/
Rechenzentrum

http://www.heim2.tu-clausthal.de/
Wohnheime I und II

http://www.th-darmstadt.de/darmstadt.html
Darmstadt

http://www.igd.fhg.de/
haus der Graphischen Datenverarbeitung

http://zgdv.igd.fhg.de/
Computer Graphics Center

http://www.th-darmstadt.de:/
Technische Hochschule

http://tutor.oc.chemie.th-darmstadt.de/
Tutorenzentrum Chemie

http://www.dvs1.informatik.th-darmstadt
.de/
Datenverwaltungssysteme 1

Fachbereich Maschinenbau

http://www.dik.maschinenbau.th-darmstadt
.de/
Datenverarbeitung in der Konstruktion

http://venus.muk.maschinenbau
.th-darmstadt.de/
Maschinenelemente und
Konstruktionslehre

http://www.physik.th-darmstadt
.de/
Fachbereich Physik

http://www.fibronics.de/
Fibronics GmbH

http://www.germany.eu.net/
EUnet Deutschland GmbH

http://www.informatik.uni-dortmund.de/
EXUG/EXUG.html
European X User Group

http://jwd.ping.de/
Windows Programmer's Group

http://www.chemie.uni-dortmund
.de/index.html
Fachbereich Chemie

http://www.informatik.uni-dortmund.de/
Fachbereich Informatik

http://www.venture.net/
VentureNET

http://www.nacamar.de/rheinmain.html
Dreieich

http://www.nacamar.de/
Nacamar

http://www.tu-dresden.de/dresden/
dresden.html
Dresden

http://radon.uni-duisburg.de/
Fachbereich Chemie

http://ateg.uni-duisburg.de/
Fachgebiet Allgemeine und Theoretische Elektrotechnik

http://sent5.uni-duisburg.de/Welcome.html
Fachgebiet Nachrichtentechnik

http://www.fb9-ti.uni-duisburg.de:8080/
Fachgebiet Technische Informatik

http://hlt3.uni-duisburg.de/
Halbleitertechnologie

http://WWW.thp.Uni-Duisburg.DE/
Theoretische Physik

http://www.novell.de/
Novell European Support Center

http://www.fho-emden.de/
Fachhochschule Ostfriesland

http://www.rrze.uni-erlangen.de/docs/Erlangen/
Erlangen

http://pctc.chemie.uni-erlangen.de/fakultaet/chemie.html
Fachbereich Chemie

http://www.lte.e-technik.uni-erlangen.de/
Lehrstuhl Technische Elektronik

http://www.rrze.uni-erlangen.de/
Regionales Rechenzentrum

http://www_win.rrze.uni-erlangen.de/
WiN-Labor

http://www.franken.de/
Kommunikationsnetz Franken e.V.

http://callisto.fsag.rhein-main.de/
Free Software Association of Germany

http://www.omnilink.net/
Omnilink GbR

http://hpfrs6.physik.uni-freiburg.de/
Physik

http://www.psychologie.uni-freiburg.de/
Psychologisches Institut

Fraunhofer-Gesellschaft

http://www.freinet.de/
Freinet

http://http.hq.eso.org/eso-homepage.html
ESO, European Southern Observatory

http://www.ipp-garching.mpg.de/rzg.html
Plasmaphysik

http://www.physik.tu-muenchen.de/tumphy/d/einrichtungen/wsi/
Walter Schottky Institut

http://www.gkss.de/Geesthacht.html
Geesthacht

http://www.gkss.de/
GKSS Forschungszentrum

http://www.med-stat.gwdg.de/
Abteilung Medizinische Statistik

http://risc350b.mdv.gwdg.de/jura/welcome.html
Fachbereich Rechtswissenschaften

http://www.uni-geochem.gwdg.de/docs/home.htm
Geochemisches Institut

http://www.physik.uni-greifswald.de/general/greifswald.html
Greifswald

http://www.physik.uni-greifswald.de/
Fachbereich Physik

http://www-kommsys.fernuni-hagen.de/welcome.html
Fachgebiet Kommunikationssysteme

http://www.uni-halle.de/HALLE/HAL-Home.html
halle

http://www.mathematik.uni-halle.de/
Fachbereich Mathematik und Informatik

http://www.uni-hamburg.de/Hamburg/HH_homepage.html
hamburg

http://info.desy.de:80/
Deutsches Elektronen-Synchrotron

http://dxhral.desy.de:80/hERMES-Experiment

http://www.dkrz.de/
Deutsches Klimarechenzentrum

http://nda.net/nda/
Norddeutsche Datenautobahn

http://idom-www.informatik.uni-hamburg.de/external-entry.html
Arbeitsbereich Datenbanken und Informationsysteme

http://www.math.uni-hamburg.de/math/
Fachbereich Mathematik

http://www.econ.uni-hamburg.de/
Fachbereich Wirtschaftswissenschaften

http://energie1.en.tu-harburg.de/AB_Energietechnik.html
Arbeitsbereich Energietechnik

http://abnt2.et2.tu-harburg.de/Welcome.html
Arbeitsbereich Nachrichtentechnik

http://www.tu-harburg.de:80/sde/
Fachschaftsrat Elektrotechnik

http://bashir.ti1.tu-harburg.de/home.html
Technische Informatik I

http://www.ix.de/
iX-Redaktion, Heise-Verlag

http://www.urz.uni-heidelberg.de/city-info/index.html
Heidelberg

http://www.dante.de/
DANTE, Deutschsprachige Anwendervereinigung TeX e.V

http://www.dkfz-heidelberg.de/index.html
DKFZ, Deutsches Krebsforschungszentrum

http://iris02a.inet.dkfz-heidelberg.de/
Abteilung Histodiagnostik und Pathomorphologische Dokumentation

http://mbi.dkfz-heidelberg.de/
Abteilung Medizinische und Biologische Informatik/Bildverarbeitungsgruppe

http://www.embl-heidelberg.de/
EMBL, European Molecular Biology Laboratory

http://www.oci.uni-heidelberg.de/index.html
Axels Experimenteller Server

http://www.astro.uni-jena.de/
Staub in Sternentstehungsgebieten

http://www.uni-kl.de/Stadt/
Kaiserslautern

http://klinfo.unix-ag.uni-kl.de/de/kl_server
Unix-AG

http://uklirb.informatik.uni-kl.de/
Fachbereich Informatik

http://www.uni-kl.de/
Regionales Hochschulrechenzentrum

http://klinfo.unix-ag.uni-kl.de/
UNIX-AG

http://www.ba-karlsruhe.de/KA/KA.html
Karlsruhe

http://www.ba-karlsruhe.de/
Berufsakademie

http://www.zblmath.fiz-karlsruhe.de/
Fachinformationszentrum Karlsruhe, Abt. Mathematik und Informatik

http://www.fzi.de/
Forschungszentrum Informatik

http://www.xlink.net/
NTG/Xlink

http://www.ask.uni-karlsruhe.de/welcome.html
Akademische Software Kooperation

http://www.nic.de/
DEutsches Network Information Center

http://www.cls.de/
Commercial Link Systems

http://www.fh-kiel.de/
Fachhochschule

http://www.netuse.de/
NetUSE GmbH

http://rhodesit.min.uni-kiel.de/Welcome.html
Mineralogisch-Petrographisches Institut und Museum

http://www.uni-koblenz.de/local/CityGuide/index.html
Koblenz

http://sunny.metaworks.de/
MetaWorks GmbH

http://www.fh-konstanz.de/
Fachhochschule, Rechenzentrum

http://imperia.fh-konstanz.de/
Imperia

http://www.lake.de/
Lake.de

http://www.roka.net/
roka EDV und Datenkommunikationsberatung GmbH

http://hiris.anorg.chemie.tu-muenchen.de/AAL/
Astronomische Arbeitsgruppe Laufen e.V

http://www.uni-leipzig.de/leipzig/
Leipzig

http://rzws01.grz.fh-lueneburg.de/
Fachhochschule Nordostniedersachsen

http://www.tu-magdeburg.de/~schroede/mdstadt.html
Magdeburg

http://www.nacamar.de/city/mainz/g_mainz.html
Mainz

http://radbruch.jura.uni-mainz.de/
Fachbereich Rechtswissenschaft

http://www.ba-mannheim.de/
Berufsakademie

http://www.uni-mannheim.de/users/ddz/index.html
Dokumentations- und Datenbankzentrum

http://WWW.Informatik.Uni-Mannheim.DE/
Fachbereich Mathematik und Informatik

http://www.mathematik.uni-marburg.de/
Fachbereich Mathematik/Informatik

http://www.physik.uni-marburg.de/
Fachbereich Physik

http://www.wiwi.uni-marburg.de/
Fachbereich Wirtschaftswissenschaften

http://i53s.ifi.th-merseburg.de/menu/Merseburg1.html
Merseburg

http://www.nonlin.tu-muenchen.de/chaos/chaos.html
Chaosgruppe e.V.

http://www.cycom.de/
CyberWebCommunications

http://www.ecrc.de/
European Computer-Industry Research Center GmbH

http://www.isar.de/
I.S.A.R Netzwerke GbRmbH

http://www.lrz-muenchen.de/Lrz/homepage_ge.html
Leibniz-Rechenzentrum

http://www.bl.physik.tu-muenchen.de/
Beschleunigerlaboratorium

http://www.mch.sni.de/welcome.html
Siemens Nixdorf Informationssysteme AG

http://www.physik.tu-muenchen.de/tumphy/d/einrichtungen/wsi/
Walter Schottky Institut

http://www.uni-muenster.de/math/
Fachbereich Mathematik

http://aquila.uni-muenster.de/
Astronomisches Institut

http://www.uni-muenster.de/WiWi/
Fachbereich Wirtschaftswissenschaften

http://smurf.noris.de/
Noris Network GbR

http://pid.da.op.dlr.de/
DFD - Deutsches Fernerkundungsdatenzentrum

http://www.informatik.uni-oldenburg.de/~xray/Oldenburg_index.html
Oldenburg

http://www.hrz.uni-oldenburg.de/fb9.html
Fachbereich Chemie

http://www.informatik.uni-oldenburg.de/index.html
Fachbereich Informatik

http://www.physik.uni-oldenburg.de/welcome.html
Fachbereich Physik

http://www.hrz.uni-oldenburg.de/hrzhome.html
hochschulrechenzentrum

http://www.north.de/
OLIS - Oldenburger Informationssysteme

http://esther.mathematik.uni-osnabrueck.de/
Fachbereich Mathematik / Informatik

http://godard.oec.uni-osnabrueck.de/
Fachbereich Wirtschaftswissenschaften

http://www.uni-paderborn.de/paderborn.html
Paderborn

http://www.uni-paderborn.de/pcpc/pcpc.html
Paderborn Center for Parallel Computing

http://www.sni.de/
Siemens Nixdorf Informationssysteme AG

http://pooh.uni-paderborn.de/
heinz Nixdorf Institut

http://www.uni-paderborn.de/
Informatik

http://math-www.uni-paderborn.de/
Mathematik

http://www.fmi.uni-passau.de/passau/uebersicht.html
Passau

http://www.gfz-potsdam.de/
GeoForschungsZentrum

http://www.pik-potsdam.de/
Institute for Climate Impact Research

http://excalibur.rz.uni-potsdam.de/homepage.htm
Geisteswissenschaften

http://www.ba-ravensburg.de/
Berufsakademie

http://www.fh-reutlingen.de/index.html
Fachhochschule

Rheinstetten
Rheinstetten

http://jil.informatik.uni-rostock.de:8000/index.html
Fachbereich Informatik

http://www-dbis.informatik.uni-rostock.de/
Lehrstuhl Datenbank- und Informationssysteme

http://hp710.math.uni-rostock.de:8001/home.html
Fachbereich Mathematik

http://www.saar.de/index.html
Internet Privat e.V

http://ps-www.dfki.uni-sb.de/
Forschungsbereich Programmiersysteme

http://www.jura.uni-sb.de/
Server der Rechtsinformatik

http://www.gmd.de/
GMD German National Research Center for Computer Science

http://www.uni-stuttgart.de/Ist/Ist.html
Stuttgart

http://www.belwue.de/belwue.html
BelWue

http://www.mpi-stuttgart.mpg.de/
Max-Planck-Institute

http://192.253.114.31/
Patch American High School

http://www.pem.com/
PEM GmbH

http://www.uni-stuttgart.de/Cis/cis.html
Campus Informationssystem

http://www.uni-stuttgart.de/
Regionales Rechenzentrum

http://www.uni-trier.de/trier/trier.html
Trier

http://www.trier.fh-rpl.de/
Fachhochschule Rheinland-Pfalz, Rechenzentrum

http://fsai.trier.fh-rpl.de/
Fachschaft Angewandte Informatik

http://www.informatik.uni-trier.de/
Informatik / Computer Science

http://www.uni-trier.de/urt/urt.html
Rechenzentrum

http://greco.gris.informatik.uni-tuebingen.de/
Arbeitsbereich Computer-Graphik

http://sunwww.informatik.uni-tuebingen.de:8080/
Arbeitsbereich Datenbanken und Informationssysteme

http://www-pu.informatik.uni-tuebingen.de/
Arbeitsbereich Programmierung

http://aorta.tat.physik.uni-tuebingen.de/
Theoretische Astrophysik und Computational Physics

http://www.mathematik.uni-ulm.de/stadtulm/ulm.html
Ulm

http://www.nacamar.de/city/wiesbaden/g_wiesbaden.html
Wiesbaden

http://www.ploenzke.de/
Ploenzke AG

http://www.fh-wolfenbuettel.de/rz/
Rechenzentrum

http://w3.worms.fh-rpl.de/
Rechenzentrum

http://tkz-220.tkz.fh-rpl.de/
Telekommunikations-Zentrum

http://www.uni-wuppertal.de/misc/wuppertal/welcome.html
Wuppertal

http://wmwapl.math.uni-wuppertal.de/pub/Mosaic/Mathematics_WWW.html
Fachbereich Mathematik

http://www.uni-wuppertal.de/fachbereiche/FB8/welcome.html
Fachbereich Physik

http://www.uni-wuppertal.de/welcome.englisch.html
Rechenzentrum

http://www.ifh.de/
DESY-IfH

Greece

http://www.ics.forth.gr/
Foundation for Research and Technology Hellas - Institute of Computer Science

http://www.cc.uch.gr/
University Of Crete Computer Center

http://www.duth.gr/
Demokritos University of Thrace

http://iris.di.uoa.ariadne-t.gr/
Department of Informatics, University of Athens

Hungary

http://www.fsz.bme.hu/hungary/budapest/budapest.html
Budapest

http://www.fsz.bme.hu/bme/bme.html
Technical University of Budapest

http://www.univet.hu/
University of Veterinary Science

http://www.lib.klte.hu/
Kossuth Lajos University of Sciences

http://www.abc.hu/
Agricultural Biotechnology Center

http://gold.uni-miskolc.hu/
University of Miskolc

http://woland.iit.uni-miskolc.hu/
Multimedia Archive of the Maniacs

Iceland

http://www.isnet.is/
ISnet

http://www.isnet.is/iceuug/
The Icelandic Unix Systems User Group

http://www.hafro.is/welcome.e.html
Marine Research Inst./Directorate of Fisheries

http://www.rhi.hi.is/
University of Iceland

Ireland

http://star.arm.ac.uk/planet/planet.html
Armagh Observatory

http://www.cis.ie/
Cork Internet Services

http://curia.ucc.ie/
CURIA Irish Literature archive

http://147.252.133.152/
Dublin Institute of Technology

http://granuaile.ieunet.ie:80/
IEunet Networking Information regarding Ireland, and Links to the rest of Europe

http://www.iol.ie/IOL-HOME.html
Ireland Online

http://www.regiodesk.ie/
Regiodesk Ireland

http://www.hq2.telecom.ie/
Museum of Communications

http://www.tcd.ie/
Trinity College Dublin

http://www.ucc.ie/webentry.html
University College Cork

http://www.ucd.ie
University College Dublin

http://www.webnet.ie/
WebNet

Italy

http://cstv12.to.cnr.it/
Centro di Studio per la Televisione

http://sun01.iigb.na.cnr.it/
Istituto Internazionale di Genetica e Biofisica

http://www.iasi.rm.cnr.it/../WelcomeIASI.html
Istituto di Analisi dei Sistemi ed Informatica

http://www.esrin.esa.it/htdocs/esrin/esrin.html
ESRIN - European Space Research Institute

http://www.ist.unige.it/Welcome.html
Istituto Nazionale per la Ricerca sul Cancro - CBA Centro Biotecnologie Avanzate

http://rea.ei.jrc.it/
Environment Institute

http://www.saclantc.nato.int/
Undersea Research Center

Latvia

http://www.vernet.lv/ Latvia OnLine
The Latvia Home Page

http://www.riga.lv/ LVNet-Teleport
Beautiful Riga Map

http://www.latnet.lv/LU/lu.html
University of Latvia

http://www.latnet.lv/LATNET/head.html
LATNET

Lithunia

http://neris.mii.lt
Lithuania WWW

Luxembourg

http://www.echo.lu/
I'M-EUROPE

http://www.restena.lu/
RESTENA, the National Network for Education and Research

Netherlands

http://www.caos.kun.nl/
CAOS/CAMM Center, the Dutch National Expertise Center for Computer Aided Chemistry and BioInformatics

http://colibri.let.ruu.nl
Colibri language, speech, logic and information

http://www.cwi.nl/index.html
Center for Mathematics and Computer Science, Amsterdam

http://www.icce.rug.nl
ICCE, State University of Groningen

http://kviexp.kvi.nl/
Kernfysisch Versneller Instituut

http://www.ripe.net/ripe/default.html
European IP group

http://www_trese.cs.utwente.nl/
The TRESE Project at the SETI

http://www.twi.tudelft.nl/welcome.html
Delft University of Technology

http://www.cca.vu.nl
Vrije Universiteit Amsterdam

Norway

http://www.service.uit.no/homepage-no
Norway

http://ananse.irv.uit.no/trade_law/nav/trade.html
Ananse International Trade Law

http://www.bibsys.no/bibsys.html
BIBSYS

http://www.ii.uib.no/
Department of Informatics, University of Bergen

http://www.uio.no/
University of Oslo

http://www.uib.no/
University of Bergen

http://www.idt.unit.no/
University of Trondheim

http://www.dhhalden.no/
Ostfold Distriktshogskole

http://www.odh.no/
Oppland Distriktshogskole

http://www.aid.no/homepage-aid.html
Agder Ingenior- og Distriktshogskole

http://harpe.tdh.no/tdh.html
Telemark Distriktshogskole

http://www.hsr.no/
Hogskolen i Stavanger

http://www.ludvigsen.dhhalden.no/
The Ludvigsen Residence

http://www.oslonett.no/
Oslonett, Inc.

http://www.service.uit.no/homepage-uit.no
University of Tromsoe

http://www.odh.no/
Oppland College

http://www.unik.no
Center for Technology at Kjeller

http://www.mogul.no/
Mogul Media

http://www.datametrix.no/
DAXNET

http://info.cern.ch/hypertext/WWW/People/howcome/NorskeLover.html
Norwegian Laws

http://www.bbb.no/ Bergen By Byte A/S
BBS / Commercial Internet provider

http://www.eunet.no/nuug/nuug.html
Norwegian Unix systems User Group

http://www.uit.no/npt/homepage-npt.en.html
The Northern Lights Planetarium

Poland

http://info.fuw.edu.pl/pl/poland.html
Poland

http://www.if.uj.edu.pl/
Physics Department, Jagiellonian University

http://www.pg.gda.pl/pg.html
Computer Centre, Gdansk Technical University

http://www.gliwice.edu.pl/
Silesian Technical University, Gliwice

http://zsku.p.lodz.pl/
Technical University, Lodz

http://www.umcs.lublin.pl/
Maria Curie-Sklodowska University, Lublin

http://www.amu.edu.pl/welcome.html
Adam Mickiewicz University, Poznan

http://www.ncac.torun.pl
Nicolaus Copernicus University, Torun

http://www.cc.uni.torun.pl/
Torun home page

http://info.ippt.gov.pl/Welcome.html
Warsaw

http://www.astrouw.edu.pl/
Astronomical Observatory, Warsaw University

Portugal

http://s700.uminho.pt/homepage-pt
Portugal Home Page

http://www.uminho.pt
Universidade do Minho

Russia

http://www.mnts.msk.su
Russian House for International and Technological Cooperation

http://www.jinr.dubna.su/JINR Welcome
Joint Institute for Nuclear Research, Physics

http://top.rector.msu.su/
Moscow State University

http://www.kiae.su/www/wtr/
Window-to-Russia

Slovakia

http://www.tuzvo.sk/
Slovakia Home Page

http://turing.upjs.sk/
University of Pavol Jozef Safarik

Slovenia

http://www.ijs.si/slo.html
Slovenia Home Page

Spain

http://www.uji.es/
Department of Education, Universitat Jaume

http://dftuz.unizar.es/
University of Zaragoza

http://www.uniovi.es/
Universidad de Oviedo

Sweden

http://www.abc.se/
ABC Computer Club

http://www.jmk.su.se/Aftonbladet.kultur/home.html
Aftonbladet Kultur

http://www.algonet.se/
AlgoNet

http://www.pi.se/as-sayf/
As-Sayf

http://www.astrakan.hgs.se/
NuclearWar Mud and Astrakan Computer Club

http://www.cd.chalmers.se/
Computer Society at Chalmers University, Gothenburg

http://europen.swip.net/europen
Swedish Unix Users Group

http://www.gu.se/
Göteborg University

http://www.svt-falun.sr.se/
Gold of Gaia

http://www.nordic.ibm.com/
IBM Nordic Information Network

http://www.ideon.lth.se/
IDEON Research Park in Lund

http://www.island.lysator.liu.se/
Industrial Engineering and Management, LiTH

http://www.ids.se/
Information Dimensions Scandinavia

http://www.sb.gov.se/
Information Rosenbad

http://www.wblab.lu.se/itl/
Informationsteknologi i Lund

http://www.mm.se/interakt/home.html
Interakt, Interactive art and media magazine

http://www.pi.se/ivo.html
Internet Venture Organization

http://www.lu.se/
Lund University

http://www.forv.mh.se/
Mid Sweden University

http://www.kth.se/
Royal Institute of Technology

http://www.su.se/
Stockholm University

http://www.sunet.se/ SUNET
Swedish University Network

http://www.uu.se/
Uppsala University

http://www.bmc.uu.se
Biomedical Centre of Uppsala

http://www.csd.uu.se/
Computing Science Department

http://www.cmd.uu.se/
Center for Human-Computer studies

http://xray.uu.se/
X-Ray Server

http://www.surfchem.kth.se/
YKI - Institute for Surface Chemistry

Switzerland

http://info.hasler.ascom.ch/Web/mosaic-home.html
Ascom Tech WWW Server

http://www.cern.ch/
CERN

http://delinfo.cern.ch/Delphi/
DELPHI Experiment

http://info.cern.ch/
The server for the World-Wide Web initiative

http://www.cim.ch/
CIM Action Programme Switzerland

http://www.ethz.ch/
ETHZ Main WWW Server

http://rock0.ethz.ch/
Institute of Geotechnics at the Swiss Federal Institute ofTechnology

http://www.math.ethz.ch/
International Congress of Mathematicians

http://www.math.ethz.ch/~zari/
European Aviation Server

http://www.unige.ch/crystal/crystal_index.html
European Crystallography Committee

http://www.eunet.ch/top.html
Official WWW server for EUnet Switzerland

http://beta.embnet.unibas.ch/embnet/info.html
European Molecular Biology Network information

http://www.eunet.ch/GenevaGuide
The Geneva International Guide

http://www.zurich.ibm.com/
IBM Zurich Research Laboratory

http://heiwww.unige.ch/
Graduate Institute of International Studies

http://www.ifh.ee.ethz.ch
Lab. for Electromagnetic Fields Theory and Microwaves Electronics

http://www.ntb.ch
Neu-Technikum Buchs

http://www.osilab.ch/
OSILAB

http://www.psi.ch/
Paul Scherrer Institut

http://www.ping.ch/
Ping Switzerland

http://www.policom.ch/Customers/POLICOM
POLICOM WWW Server

http://www.rs.ch/
RadioSuisse Services

http://www.isbe.ch
School of Engineering Bern HTL

http://zoo4.isburg.ch
School of Engineering of Burgdorf

http://www.switch.ch/
Swiss Academic and Research Network

http://www.ubilab.ubs.ch/
UBS Information Technology Laboratory

http://iamwww.unibe.ch/index.html
Institute for Informatics and Applied Mathematics

http://www.unil.ch/
University of Lausanne

http://www-imt.unine.ch
Institute of Microtechnology, Research activities at IMT,Neuchatel

http://www-iwi.unisg.ch
Institute for Information Management

http://www.unizh.ch/
University of Zurich

http://www.who.ch/
World Health Organization

Turkey

http://www.bilkent.edu.tr/
Bilkent Main Web Server

http://www.ege.edu.tr
Ege University Unix Web Server

http://www.itu.edu.tr
Istanbul Technical University Web Server

http://www.tubitak.gov.tr
Tubitak Main Web Server

http://www.tcmb.gov.tr
Central Bank Web Server

http://gopher.bilkent.edu.tr:7001/1s/inet-hotel/tmd/
Turkish Mathematical Society

http://gopher.bilkent.edu.tr:7001/1s/inet-hotel/yad/
Operational Research Society of Turkey

http://gopher.bilkent.edu.tr:7001/1s/inet-hotel/tuba/
Turkish Academy of Sciences - TUBA

http://www.ee.bilkent.edu.tr/~ieee/ieee.html
IEEE Turkey Section Web Server

http://dec002.cmpe.boun.edu.tr/
Boun CS Web server

United Kingdom

http://www.abdn.ac.uk/
University of Aberdeen

http://www.dct.ac.uk/
The University of Abertay Dundee

http://www.dct.ac.uk/www/steps.html
The Steps Theatre Cinema Programme

http://www.dcs.aber.ac.uk/
Aberystwyth, University of Wales

http://www.ihi.aber.ac.uk/index.html
Institute for Health Informatics

http://star.arm.ac.uk/
Armagh Observatory

http://www.aston.ac.uk/home.html
Aston University

http://www.bubl.bath.ac.uk/BUBL/home.html
Bulletin Board for Libraries Information Service

http://www.bath.ac.uk/home.html
University of Bath

http://www.bbk.ac.uk/
Birkbeck College, University of London

http://web.dcs.bbk.ac.uk/ukuug/home.html
UKUUG-UK Unix User Group

http://www.bham.ac.uk/
The University of Birmingham

http://sun1.bham.ac.uk/acs/home_page.html
Academic Computing Service

http://sun1.bham.ac.uk/ctimath/home_page.html
CTI Centre for Mathematics and Statistics

http://ugsun1a.ph.bham.ac.uk:3006/
Cloud 9 at Birmingham University

http://wcl-rs.bham.ac.uk/GamesDomain
Games Domain

http://www.brad.ac.uk/
University of Bradford

http://www.bton.ac.uk/
University of Brighton

http://www.bris.ac.uk/
University of Bristol

http://www.icbl.hw.ac.uk/bcs/bcsmain.html
The British Computer Society

http://ub.nmh.ac.uk/
British Geological Survey

http://httpl.brunel.ac.uk/
Brunel University

http://www.cam.ac.uk/
University of Cambridge

http://www.cup.cam.ac.uk/
Cambridge University Press

http://www.cl.cam.ac.uk/coffee/coffee.html
Coffee Machine

http://svr-www.eng.cam.ac.uk/
Speech, Vision & Robotics Group

http://web.city.ac.uk/
The City University, London

http://www.ucl.ac.uk/home.html
University College, University of London

http://www.cs.ucl.ac.uk/misc/uk/intro.html
Guide to the UK

http://info.cf.ac.uk/
College of Cardiff, University of Wales

http://www.cm.cf.ac.uk/Movies
Cardiff's Movie Database Browser

http://www.cm.cf.ac.uk:80/CLE/
The Eiffel Page

http://www.cranfield.ac.uk/
Cranfield University

http://www.dl.ac.uk/
Daresbury Laboratory

http://www.dmu.ac.uk/0h/www/home.html
De Montfort University

http://gotwo.dundee.ac.uk/
University of Dundee

http://forteana.mic.dundee.ac.uk/ft/
Fortean Times, The Journal of Strange Phenomena

http://www.dur.ac.uk/
Durham University

http://cpca3.uea.ac.uk/welcome.html
University of East Anglia

http://www.cru.uea.ac.uk/ukdiving/index.htm
UK Diving

http://www.sys.uea.ac.uk/MacSupporters.html
Mac-Supporters

http://www.uel.ac.uk/
University Of East London

http://www.ed.ac.uk/
Edinburgh University

http://www.chemeng.ed.ac.uk:80/ecosse/
The Ecosse Group

http://www.dcs.ed.ac.uk/staff/jhb/whisky/
The Scotch Malt Whisky Society

http://www.vet.ed.ac.uk/
The Royal School of Veterinary Studies

http://tardis.ed.ac.uk/
Tardis Public-Access Service

http://www.ucs.ed.ac.uk/Unixhelp/TOP_.html
Hypertext of helpful information for new users of the UNIX operating system

http://www.essex.ac.uk/
University of Essex.

http://www.essex.ac.uk/law/human-rights/
On line human-rights information

http://www.dcs.exeter.ac.uk/
Department of Computer Science, University of Exeter

http://www.gla.ac.uk
University of Glasgow

http://www.stats.gla.ac.uk/home.html
Department of Statistics

http://www.gold.ac.uk/
Goldsmiths College, University of London

http://www.gre.ac.uk/
University of Greenwich

http://www.cee.hw.ac.uk/index.html
Department of Computing & Electrical Engineering, Heriot-Watt University

http://www.efr.hw.ac.uk/EDC/Edinburgh.html
Tourist Guide to Edinburgh

http://micros.hensa.ac.uk/
Higher Educational National Software Archives

http://www.hull.ac.uk/homepage.html
University of Hull

http://gea.lif.icnet.uk/
Imperial Cancer Research Fund, Reference Library DataBase

http://www.ic.ac.uk/
Imperial College, University of London

http://euclid.tp.ph.ic.ac.uk/
Theoretical Physics Group

http://src.doc.ic.ac.uk/
SunSITE Northern Europe

http://src.doc.ic.ac.uk/bySubject/Computing/Overview.html
The World-Wide Web Virtual Library: Computing

http://src.doc.ic.ac.uk/gnn/GNNhome.html
Global Network Navigator

http://src.doc.ic.ac.uk/req-eng/index.html
Requirements Engineering Newsletter Index

http://src.doc.ic.ac.uk/all-uk.html
United Kingdom Based WWW Servers.

httpp://cen.ex.ac.uk/economics/ICAEW/accweblib.html
Institute of Chartered Accountants of England and Wales, Accounting Information Service.

http://www.ioppublishing.com
The Institute of Physics

http://sunrae.uel.ac.uk/palaeo/index.html
International Organisation of Palaeobotany

http://www.keele.ac.uk/
Keele University

http://www.ukc.ac.uk/
University of Kent at Canterbury

http://ee016.eee.kcl.ac.uk/vrlhome.htm
Department of Electronic and Electrical Engineering, Kings College, University of London

http://www.kingston.ac.uk/
Kingston Universtity

http://www.lancs.ac.uk/
Lancaster University

http://www.leeds.ac.uk/
The University of Leeds

http://www.le.ac.uk/
University of Leicester

http://www.linux.org.uk/
Information about Linux, the Unix-like operating system for PCs

http://www.liv.ac.uk/
The University of Liverpool

http://www.lbs.lon.ac.uk/
London Business School

http://www.lpac.ac.uk/SEL-HPC/
London & South East High Performance Computing Centre

http://info.lut.ac.uk/
Loughborough University of Technology

http://info.mcc.ac.uk/UofM.html
The University of Manchester

http://www.mdx.ac.uk/
Middlesex University

http://server.nrs.ac.uk/NRS/
NRS Central Database

http://ncet.csv.warwick.ac.uk/
National Council for Educational Technology

http://www.ncl.ac.uk/
University of Newcastle

http://www.unl.ac.uk/
University of North London

http://www.nott.ac.uk/
University of Nottingham

http://www.doc.ntu.ac.uk/index.html
Department of Computing, Nottingham Trent University

http://hcrl.open.ac.uk/ou/ouhome.html
The Open University

http://www.ox.ac.uk/
University of Oxford

http://linux1.balliol.ox.ac.uk/fax/faxsend.html
The Oxford Internet Fax Server

http://www.brookes.ac.uk/
Oxford Brookes University

http://dan.see.plym.ac.uk/
The Network Research Group

http://www.port.ac.uk/
The University of Portsmouth

http://www.qub.ac.uk/
Queen's University of Belfast

http://www.dcs.qmw.ac.uk/
Department of Computer Science, Queen Mary and Westfield College, University of London

http://www.rdg.ac.uk/
University of Reading

http://www.rfhsm.ac.uk/
The Royal Free Hospital School of Medicine

http://www.rhbnc.ac.uk/
Royal Holloway, University of London

http://www.roe.ac.uk/
Royal Observatory, Edinburgh.

http://www.salford.ac.uk/
University of Salford

http://www.salford.ac.uk/os2power/os2power.html
Page for OS/2 users

http://www2.shef.ac.uk/
The University of Sheffield

http://www2.shef.ac.uk/chemistry/collegiate/collegiate-home.html
Sheffield Collegiate Cricket Club

http://pine.shu.ac.uk/
Sheffield Hallam University

http://www.sbu.ac.uk/
South Bank University

http://www.sbu.ac.uk/
Department of Architecture & Civil Engineering

http://avebury.arch.soton.ac.uk/
Department of Archaeology, University of Southampton

http://warp.dcs.st-and.ac.uk
Warp: systems group, University of St. Andrews

http://www.stir.ac.uk/
University of Stirling

http://www.strath.ac.uk/
University of Strathclyde

http://orac.sunderland.ac.uk/
University of Sunderland

http://www.surrey.ac.uk/
University of Surrey

http://www.ee.surrey.ac.uk/Personal/sf.html
Science Fiction TV series Guides

http://www.surrart.ac.uk/
Surrey Institute of Art and Design

http://www.swan.ac.uk/
Swansea University

http://www.ulst.ac.uk/
University of Ulster.

http://www.bangor.ac.uk/
University of Wales, Bangor.

http://www.csv.warwick.ac.uk/default.html
Warwick University

http://www.csv.warwick.ac.uk/WWW/law/default.html
CTI Law Technology Centre.

http://www.maths.warwick.ac.uk/
Mathematics Institute.

http://www.csv.warwick.ac.uk:8000/default.html
WWW Service for Nurses

http://www.csv.warwick.ac.uk:8000/midwifery.html
Midwifery page.

http://www.westminster.ac.uk/
University of Westminster.

http://www.wlv.ac.uk/
University of Wolverhampton.

http://www.york.ac.uk/
University of York

Central America

Costa Rica

http://ns.cr/
Costa Rica's Research Network

North America

Alberta

http://www.arc.ab.ca/
Alberta Research Council

http://www.nofc.forestry.ca/
Canadian Forest Service

http://www.tcel.com/index.html
Telnet Canada Enterprises

http://web.cs.ualberta.ca/UAlberta.html
University of Alberta

http://inuit.phys.ualberta.ca/
Center for Subatomic Research

http://www.ucalgary.ca/Welcome.html
University of Calgary

British Columbia

http://www.aurora.net/
auroraNET

http://www.camosun.bc.ca/camosun.html
Camosun College

http://www.cdnair.ca/
Canadian Airlines International

http://www.col.org/
Commonwealth of Learning

http://www.env.gov.bc.ca/
Ministry of Environment Lands &Parks

http://hrbwww.env.gov.bc.ca/
Human Resources Branch

http://www.cg94.freenet.victoria.bc.ca/
Ministry of Small Business, Tourism and Culture

http://kh.botany.ubc.ca/welcome.htm
Haughn/Kunst Laboratory

http://www.island.net/
Island Internet

http://bbs.sd68.nanaimo.bc.ca:8001/welcome.html
Nanaimo School District

http://cadc.dao.nrc.ca/CADC-homepage.html
Canadian Astrophysical Data Center

http://spanky.triumf.ca/
Spanky Fractal Database

http://pine.pfc.forestry.ca/
Advanced Forest Technologies Program

http://sol.uvic.ca/nami
North American Institute - Canada

http://freenet.unbc.edu/
Prince George Free-Net Association

http://www.seawest.seachange.com/
Sea Change Corporation

http://www.sfu.ca/
Simon Fraser University

http://view.ubc.ca/
University of British Columbia

http://www.uvic.ca/
University of Victoria

http://www.wimsey.com/~bmiddlet/vampyre/vampyre.html
Vampyres Only

http://freenet.vancouver.bc.ca/
Vancouver Regional FreeNet Association

http://freenet.victoria.bc.ca/vifa.html
Victoria Free-Net

http://interchange.idc.uvic.ca/
Westcoast Interchange

http://www.eitc.mb.ca/eitc.html
Economic Innovation and Technology Council

http://www.umanitoba.ca/
University of Manitoba

New Brunswick

http://www.gov.nb.ca/
Government of New Brunswick

http://www.mta.ca/
Mount Allison University

http://degaulle.hil.unb.ca/UNB.html
University of New Brunswick

Nova Scotia

http://www.acadiau.ca/
Acadia University

http://www.cfn.cs.dal.ca/
Chebucto FreeNet

http://ac.dal.ca/
Dalhousie University

http://www.stmarys.ca/
Saint Mary's University

http://www.tuns.ca/index.html
Technical University of Nova Scotia

Ontario

http://tourism.807-city.on.ca/
807-CITY

http://www.canadorec.on.ca/index.htm
Canadore College of Applied Arts and Technology

http://www.canadorec.on.ca/northbay.htm
City of North Bay

http://www.lakeheadu.ca/menu.html
Lakehead University

http://www.carleton.ca/
Carleton University

http://debra.dgbt.doc.ca/cbc/cbc.html
Canadian Broadcasting Corporation

http://www.chin.doc.ca/
Canadian Heritage Information Network

http://www.magi.com/
MAGI Data Consulting Inc.

http://ai.iit.nrc.ca/home_page.html
Knowledge Systems Laboratory

http://www.emr.ca/
Natural Resources Canada

http://ccm-10.ccm.emr.ca/
Canada Centre for Mapping

http://info.queensu.ca/index.html
Queen's University

http://mango.genie.uottawa.ca/Welcome.html
Multimedia Communications Research Laboratory, University of Ottawa

http://www.physics.brocku.ca/
Department of Physics, Brock University

http://www.netpart.com/che/brochure.html
Canadian Himalayan Expeditions

http://www.ists.ca/Welcome.html
Institute for Space and Terrestrial Science

http://www.eol.ists.ca/Welcome.html
Earth Observations Laboratory

http://www.sal.ists.ca/Welcome.html
Space Astrophysics Laboratory

http://www.lambton.on.ca/index.html
Lambton College

http://www.physics.mcmaster.ca/
Department of Physics and Astronomy, McMaster University

http://www.utoronto.ca/uoft.html
University of Toronto

http://www.scar.toronto.edu/
Scarborough College

http://csclub.uwaterloo.ca/
Computer Science Club, University of Waterloo

http://phobos.astro.uwo.ca/
Department of Astronomy, University of Western Ontario

http://turner.lamf.uwindsor.ca/
Science OnLine, University of Windsor

http://www.yorku.ca/
York University

http://www.crafts-council.pe.ca/vg/index.html
Prince Edward Island Tourism

http://www.upei.ca/index.html
University of Prince Edward Island

http://www.meteo.mcgill.ca/welcome.html
Centre for Climate and Global Change Research, Montreal

http://www-vlsi.concordia.ca/HomePage.html
VLSI Design Laboratory, Concordia University

http://www.ee.mcgill.ca/efc/efc.html
Electronic Frontier Canada/ Frontiere Electronique Canada

http://www.mcgill.ca/
McGill University

http://www.usask.ca/
University of Saskatchewan

http://www.cfht.hawaii.edu/
Canada-France-Hawaii Telescope

Mexico

http://info.pue.udlap.mx/
Universidad de las Americas

http://www.udg.mx/
Universidad de Guadalajara

http://www.mty.itesm.mx/
ITESM Campus Monterrey

http://www.dsi.uanl.mx/
Universidad Autonoma de Nuevo Leon

http://infux.mxl.cetys.mx/
Centro de Ensenanza Tecnica y Superior

http://bufa.reduaz.mx/
Universidad Autonoma de Zacatecas

http://info.main.conacyt.mx/
Consejo Nacional de Ciencia y Tecnologia

http://sparc.ciateq.conacyt.mx/homeciateq.html
CIATEQ, AC

http://kin.cieamer.conacyt.mx/
CINVESTAV-IPN Unidad Merida

http://www.ccu.umich.mx/
Universidad Michoacana

http://www.labvis.unam.mx/
Laboratorio de Visualizacion, UNAM

http://sunulsa.ulsa.mx/home-page.html
Universidad La Salle A.C.

http://www.astroscu.unam.mx/
Instituto de Astronomia, UNAM

http://tonatiuh.uam.mx/
Universidad Autonoma Metropolitana

http://www.ucol.mx/
Universidad de Colima

http://www.cicese.mx/DOCUMENTOS_CICESE/CICESE.html
Centro de Investigacion Cientifica y de Educacion Superior deEnsenada

http://dch.mty.itesm.mx/
Tec de Monterrey

http://www.lania.mx/
Laboratorio Nacional de Informatica Avanzada, A.C.

http://axp1.iiecuer.unam.mx/
Instituto de Investigaciones Electricas

http://cronos.sgia.imp.mx/General.html
Instituto Mexicano del Petroleo

http://www.ugto.mx/
Universidad de Guanajuato

http://www.ibt.unam.mx/
Instituto de Biotecnologia. UNAM

Puerto Rico

http://www.naic.edu/
National Astronomy and Ionosphere Center

http://hpprdk01.prd.hp.com/
Puerto Rico WWW

United States of America

http://sgisrvr.asc.edu/index.html ASN
Alabama Supercomputer Network

http://www.auburn.edu/
Auburn University

http://138.26.184.4/stumedia.htm
The StuMedia WWW Server

http://info.uah.edu
The University of Alabama in Huntsville

http://tdcems.tdc.redstone.army.mil/micom/home.html
U.S. Army Missile Command, Technology Development Laboratory

http://www.af.mil/
USAF Web Server

http://www.arsc.edu
Arctic Region Supercomputing Center

http://www.amug.org/index.html
Arizona Macintosh Users Group WWW Server

http://www.asu.edu/Welcome.html
Arizona State University

http://info.ccit.arizona.edu/
University of Arizona information

http://www.tucson.ihs.gov/
Indian Health Service

http://www.indirect.com/
Internet Direct

http://www.sibylline.com/
Sibylline, Inc.

http://161.31.2.29/
College of Business,
University of Central Arkansas

http://emerson.netmedia.com/IMS/rest/ba_rest_guide.html
Bay Area Restaurant Guide, Palo Alto

http://www.election.ca.gov
California Election Results, Sacramento

http://smaug.ucr.edu/Quakes/quake_page.html
Earthquake Information, Riverside

http://www.hotelres.com
Hotel Information and Reservations, San Francisco

http://www.northcoast.com/unlimited/unlimited.html
Redwood Country Unlimited, Eureka

http://www.cccd.edu/ski.html
Southland Ski Server, Costa Mesa

http://sailfish.peregrine.com/surf/surf.html
Surfing reports, Carlsbad

http://www.cts.com/~health
Center for Anxiety and Stress Treatment, San Diego

http://www.clarinet.com/
ClariNet Communications, San Jose

http://www.dvts.com/
daVinci Time & Space, Los Angeles

http://www.northcoast.com/
Evergreen Technologies, Eureka

http://www.lp.org/lp/ca/lpsc.html
Libertarian Party, San Jose

http://www.mojones.com/motherjones.html
Mother Jones, San Francisco

Glossary

Over the years, Internet users have adopted and adapted their own language and subculture—sometimes, it seems, solely to keep the Internet a closed club. If you're new to the Internet, learning the language can be a lot like learning Morse code or CB lingo. But you've got to do it in order to travel freely and confidently in cyberspace. We can't provide an exhaustive list of terms that you'll hear and read on the Internet and the Web, but we can give you a sampling of some of the terms you'll encounter frequently—especially those terms that relate specifically to the Web. Incidentally, italicized terms have their own definitions within the glossary.

:-) Probably one of the most overused sets of characters on the Internet, this signifies a smile, or that you meant the text that you just wrote to be humorous. Here's our Grinch-like opinion on that: If what you wrote was humorous, then readers will know; otherwise, maybe you should hone your writing skills. Yes, we get crabby about this, because it's basically the online version of an applause sign. In other words, :-(.

<G> Stands for Grin. See also :-).

Anonymous FTP A simple technique for downloading files from an *FTP* site of which you do not have a logon ID (in other words, a privileged account). Many (but by no means all) FTP servers make their file archives accessible to all Internet users, which means you can access the site by logging in using the ID "anonymous." When you access an FTP site via Mosaic, you're automatically logged in anonymously, so you probably didn't even need to bother reading this glossary definition. Sorry we wasted your time.

Browser In connection with the World Wide Web, any graphical interface that uses *HTML* to display and find information on the Internet. Mosaic is a browser, and is still the most popular one, although WinWeb, MacWeb, Cello, and others also do a respectable job of bringing order to the *Web*.

Direct Connection An Internet connection (way expensive!) in which you have your own IP address and connect physically and directly to the Internet via a dedicated line leased to you by your phone company.

DNS Stands for Domain Name Server, which is the UNIX software required by a service provider to keep track of Internet host systems and domain addresses. Beyond that, you don't wanna know, trust us.

Domain A portion of a *URL* address that identifies a *host* system or a part of the system dedicated to a specific user group. In the URL "oak.oakland.edu", "oakland.edu" is the domain for the "oak" system. The domain description provides a human-language technique for specifying a host system's *IP* address. Essentially, it's just a friendlier, easier-to-remember (seemingly) way of identifying a system than using the numbers that make up its IP address (such as 141.130.188.2).

Eudora A freeware Windows-based E-mail utility that can be used to send and receive mail across the Internet via a *SLIP* or *PPP* account.

FAQ Probably one of the most Frequently Asked Questions on the Internet is "What in hell does FAQ stand for?"—hint. See also RTFM.

File menu The first drop-down menu in the Mosaic menu bar. You'll use **File | Open URL** most frequently, because this set of menu commands displays the *Open URL* dialog box in which you can type URL addresses.

Finger A command that displays a brief file of information about an Internet user. The finger command is actually a search utility available on the Internet; it is not part of Mosaic or *HTML*. However, you can typically access the finger utility within Mosaic by selecting Finger in your *Starting Points* menu if your copy of Mosaic was configured with this menu.

Flame What other Internet users will do to you if you ask (in their opinion) a dumb question online, or if you become an annoying Internaut. Flames usually come in the form of grumpy, irritated, sometimes downright angry responses to questions or to inflammatory statements you make. Sometimes, you'll be gang-flamed, in which case many (sometimes many, many, many) users will seek revenge on you (for whatever reason) by dumping your E-mail address with thousands upon thousands of worthless messages. Avoid flames. Be nice.

FTP Stands for File Transfer Protocol, which defines the communications standards used to upload and download files to and from an *FTP* server.

GIF Stands for Graphic Interchange Format, a highly compressed format for storing and transferring graphic images. The GIF format was created by CompuServe to speed the time required to download graphics, but has since been absconded by Internet users and is easily the most widely used graphic format on the Internet and the Web.

Gopher A text search and retrieval system named after the mascot of the University of Minnesota, where Gopher was created. A Gopher server treats the hierarchy of Internet databases, directories, and files as a series of menus, which you can browse through to find specific information. You can access Gopher either by selecting Gopher Sites from the *Starting Points* menu or by typing a Gopher *URL* in the *Open URL* dialog box.

Home Page The starting point (first screen) in a *Web page*.

Host A computer—usually one with a fast processor or multiple processors and some whopping big hard disk space—that can provide a physical link to the Internet. A host computer is identified via its system and domain names. The system name is just that: It's simply what the computer's users have labeled the system for purposes of network identification. The domain provides information about the location or function of the computer within an organization (such as a university or research facility). In the *URL* "oak.oakland.edu", "oak" is the system name and ".oakland.edu" is the domain. The terms *host*, *site*, and *server* all essentially are the same.

Hotlink An underlined word, phrase, or address that you can click on to jump to other information about the linked phrase or to jump to a related Web page.

Hotlist A list of frequently accessed Web sites, which you can create using the Mosaic Add to Current Hotlist function.

HTML Stands for Hyper Text Markup Language, which is a standardized method for defining formatting, links, and other special handling of text, images, and objects within a *Web page*. You need to learn HTML only if you plan on creating your own Web page.

http Stands for hyper text transfer protocol, and is a bona fide *resource type* used to locate a Web server directly from within Mosaic.

Hypertext See *HTML.*

Hyper Text Markup Language See *HTML.*

IMHO Stands for In My Humble Opinion. You'll see this one a lot in newsgroups, and usually the writer is being anything but humble, IMHO.

Inline Image A graphic that is part of a *Web page,* and can optionally be viewed whenever the page is loaded or when you click on the inline image's icon (the preferred time-saving method).

Internet Protocol See *TCP/IP.*

IP See *TCP/IP.*

JPEG Stands for Joint Photographic Experts Group, which defined a standard compression format for high-resolution color images.

Leased-Line Connection See *Direct Connection.*

MPEG Stands for Motion Pictures Expert Group, which defined a standard compression format for video and sound used to display and hear online movies.

Open URL The dialog box you use to type the complete URL address for a *Web page* or other Internet server.

Page See *Web Page.*

POP Stands for Point of Presence, and is really something you don't need to know about unless you plan on becoming a *service provider* or if you want your own *direct connection* to the Internet. However, you'll see and hear this term occasionally during your cyberspace travels, so here's the lowdown: A POP is the collection of communications hardware (modems, routers, etc.) that a service provider implements to physically connect its users to the Internet. Aren't you glad you asked?

PPP Stands for Point to Point Protocol, an alternative dialup protocol connection to *SLIP.* Like SLIP, PPP establishes the intial connection between your computer and your service provider's host system, but includes a far more robust set of protocols than SLIP. For this reason, PPP is more efficient than SLIP, especially when you're using a high-speed modem (read that as 14.4 kbps or higher). For this reason, too, PPP can be more difficult to configure than SLIP. See also *SLIP*, *Service Provider*, and *TCP/IP*.

Provider See *Service Provider*.

Resource Type Defines the type of transfer protocol, server, or database to be used in making a connection to a host. The resource type is always the first portion of a *URL* and is followed by a colon and two slashes, as in http://, ftp://, gopher://, telnet://, and file://.

RTFM Stands for Read the Flippin' Manual (or some such similar thing). This is a standard response to a user's question when the answer is immediately available in a README, STD, FAQ, or FYI file. Read first, ask questions later.

Server Essentially means the same as *host*; however, in cyberspace the term "server" has come to take on a separate connotation, in which "server" is preceded by an adjective that identifies the type of Internet service it provides—for instance, you can connect to a Web server, an FTP server, a Gopher server, or a host (pun intended) of other server types.

Service Provider The place that takes all your money. Unless you're set up with direct access to the Internet (which generally requires the help of a rocket scientist and the budget of Wayne Newton), you need to pay startup and monthly fees to a service provider, which provides you with the initial host connection to the rest of the Internet. Having paid your money, yell at your provider loud and long whenever you need to have a network-related problem solved, because that's the job you're paying them to do, whether they like it or not—and they probably don't like it.

Site See *Host*.

SLIP Stands for Serial Line Internet Protocol, and is a standard method for connecting to a service provider via telephone lines. Since your computer (most likely) does not have its own *IP* address, your modem needs some way of making itself known to the *TCP/IP* world. SLIP software provides this connection so that the Internet treats your computer as though it were your service provider's host system. Not all service providers use SLIP as their dialup protocol, though. See also *TCP/IP*, *PPP*, and *Service Provider*.

Starting Points Menu A Mosaic menu that lists common Internet starting points by name (such as Gopher Servers or FTP Sites). The content of your Starting Points menu will depend on what your Mosaic (or Mosaic clone) provider placed there. You can customize your Starting Points menu by adding your own names of frequently used sites and services.

Tag Any of a number of intimidating-looking formatting codes (such as <B> or <A NAME="My Page">) used in *HTML* to indicate special handling of text, images, or other objects within a *Web page* displayed by Mosaic or some other Web *browser*. HTML tags are placed within angle brackets and are usually paired, which means there is a starting tag, followed by the object being coded, and then an ending tag. Tags are used to specify font characteristics, hypertext links, image handling, and many other format characteristics.

TCP/IP Stands for Transmission Control Protocol/Internet Protocol, which defines the communications standards for passing information back and forth across the Internet. TCP/IP is actually a collection of more than 100 transmission protocols and can seem complex (only because it is) to new and even experienced network users. Think of TCP/IP as the common language that controls all communications hardware linked to the Internet, thereby helping to avoid communications conflicts and "misunderstandings" when data is shuttled among computers linked to the Internet. On your humble PC, Mac, or UNIX workstation, your TCP/IP stack is a set of commands that collectively serve as the modem software used in connecting to and transferring information across the Internet. If you want to connect to the Internet via *SLIP* or *PPP* and you don't have a TCP/'IP stack, you're dead in the water.

TIFF Stands for Tagged Interchange File Format, a graphics format mutually established by Adobe and Microsoft for use in importing graphics into different applications. TIFF is a common graphics standard among PC applications, but can't be used with some GIF/JPEG *viewers*.

Trumpet Winsock Widely used utility for TCP/IP stack implementation for windows.

URL Stands for Uniform Resource Locator (also called Universal Resource Locator, depending on whom you ask). A URL is essentially the address and path that Mosaic uses to find a Web site. A URL contains the *resource type*, followed by the system and *domain* names, and optionally, the name of a database or file stored on a Web server.

USENET A massive (really massive) networked collection of newsgroups, which in turn refers to special-interest forums where Internet users gather to discuss, well, their special interests. To access USENET newsgroups from Mosaic, simply begin the URL with news:// followed by the domain of the newsgroup (such as alt.barney.die.die.die, one of our personal favorites).

Telnet A powerful networking tool that could use a serious overhaul. Essentially, Telnet is a utility that allows your computer to emulate a terminal connected to a particular network. Unlike FTP, which only allows you to access files from a remote computer, Telnet actually allows you to log into a network and run programs and other services available on the network. Telnet is text-based, which is why we say it's in sore need of a graphical facelift.

Transfer Protocol In a *URL*, this identifies the set of standard transfer procedures that will be used to access and exchange information on the Internet and the *Web*. Examples of transfer protocols are *http* and *ftp*. A transfer protocol is an example of a *resource type*.

Veronica Internet gossip has it that this actually stands for Very Easy Rodent-Oriented Network Index to Computerized Archives, but that's beside the point. More simply put, Veronica is an index of all Gopher menu items. Since a Veronica search is based on the name of a menu rather than keywords within databases, these searches tend to be less reliable than other methods.

Viewer A software utility that allows you to open and view GIF and JPEG images online. If you don't already have one of these, you need one.

WAIS Stands for Wide Area Information Server, which is an Internet text search and retrieval system that works much like *Gopher* in that you use keywords to locate items within an online database. Unlike Gopher, WAIS searches are limited to keyword searches; you can't navigate databases through a series of menus. You shouldn't assume, though, that this lack of friendliness means that WAIS is more limited than Gopher. On the contrary, a Gopher server actually uses WAIS to conduct a search.

Web See *World Wide Web.*

Web Page Typically used to refer to a site on the Internet that uses *HTML* as its interface. Web pages can only be viewed with an HTML-based *browser* like Mosaic.

Winsock One of several Windows implementations of the Berkeley Sockets TCP/IP stack for UNIX. *Trumpet Winsock* is the most common of these.

World Wide Web A *hypertext*-based system for linking databases, servers, and pages of information available across the far-flung Internet. To access the Web, you need only a modem, a *SLIP* or *PPP* account, a *TCP/IP* stack (Hah! Easier said than done.), and an *HTML*-based browser like Mosaic.

Index

—F—

—I—

—J—

—S—

—T—

—U—

—V—

—W—